John Marsh has been making and helpir
fifty years. Here, in his usual clear and helpful teaching style he shares
his wisdom and encouragement. This is a key time for making disciples
and this is a key book to help us do it.

Robin Gamble
Leading Your Church into Growth team leader

—

This is a book rich in biblical wisdom, insights, deep encouragement, and
practical outworkings. John Marsh assembles so much of what he learnt
about making disciples in his long Christian ministry and offers it to us
in accessible and moving narrative. I love the way he grounds his teaching
utterly in the person of Jesus, and his relationships with the Father, his
followers and us. John's writing also taps strongly into the empowering
of the Holy Spirit and the holism of the Gospel; he gives us confidence
to reach out to our own needy generation, knowing that we can always
draw on God's strength in our weakness. I love the personal touches too.
One of John's former parishes, Christ Church, South Ossett, was my first
home church. It's so good to know that what John taught there and in
Huddersfield can now enrich others far beyond Yorkshire!

Elaine Storkey
Theologian

—

In this stimulating and rich book, John Marsh has poured a lifetime of
loving and distinguished service. This timely book should be widely read
and joyfully celebrated.

George Carey
Former Archbishop of Canterbury

Go . . . make disciples

— JOHN MARSH —

Sacristy
Press

Sacristy Press
PO Box 612, Durham, DH1 9HT

www.sacristy.co.uk

First published in 1988 by Monarch Books.
This revised edition published in 2024 by Sacristy Press, Durham.

Sacristy Limited, registered in England & Wales, number 7565667

British Library Cataloguing-in-Publication Data
A catalogue record for the book is available from the British Library

ISBN 978-1-78959-343-3

For the church family at Christ Church, South Ossett,
who have contributed themselves to this book

Contents

Foreword

Whilst exercising my ministry as a bishop, I quite often have the words from the concluding prayer of the ASB Communion service in my mind: I am "sent out in the power of the Spirit" as I have the privilege of travelling round my diocese—the mixture of towns, villages and country which make up a large part of West and South Yorkshire—to meet and talk to all sorts of people. One overriding impression I have is of the immense goodwill towards the Church of England in general, shown by all the people I meet (many with little or no "church" connection in their present lives). Continually I am helped to reflect that we as a church too easily acquire a "ghetto" mentality, that nobody loves us and nobody listens to us—that is not my experience.

We should never forget that we have been sent by God, just as he sent Jesus into the world because of his love for all creation. That should give us the energy and the direction to live out our Christian lives with confidence and with hope. This book by John Marsh will help each and every one of us in our understanding of what it means to be sent. Starting with an exposition of the close relationship that we must have with the Father, he then goes on to outline various "mission principles" and the consequences of living them out in our lives. Each one is fully worked out with great reference to the Bible, and also with personal anecdotes, so that a full picture is built up of the way we, as a Christian people and presence, ought to be working in the world.

I would agree with John that each Christian is fully equipped for mission. There is good news to tell despite, and sometimes as a result of, the very real problems and tragedies that we all encounter in our lives. Our thrust must be forward and future as a church, and to make sure we are going in the right direction we need constantly to be looking at our relationship with God—in prayer, in the reading and sharing of God's word, in worship together and in the fellowship of the Christian community. This book will help all of us to think through and act upon the various principles and consequences of mission, so that in the strength of him who died, rose again and now lives and reigns in the mighty power of his Holy Spirit, present with us and within us to the close of the age, each one of us must go forth and go out—sent, just as Jesus Christ was sent. "As the Father has sent me, I am sending you."

I feel sure that what John Marsh has to say will both encourage and help many folk in living the Christian life. I am very happy to commend the book to you all.

The Rt Revd David Hope
Bishop of Wakefield, 1985–1990[1]

---

[1] Bishop David subsequently moved on to be Bishop of London (1990–5) and then Archbishop of York (1995–2005). He is now living in West Yorkshire in retirement.

Thanks

Although mine is the name that appears as author of this book, there are others who have greatly influenced me and have therefore contributed to it. There are two, in particular, that I want to acknowledge.

Just before I went to York University, I was told: "If you're going to York, you want to find St Cuthbert's Church and David Watson." It was 1966 and I had never heard of David then, but over the next eight years I got to know him well. I was privileged to be taught by him, to be part of a fast-growing church, and to be involved in mission with him and others. I learned much under David's leadership, and it was marvellous training for future ministry.

Then, just a few years ago, one of my colleagues on the staff of St Thomas' Church, Crookes, in Sheffield, went to a meeting in London; he came back enthusing about an American pastor he had heard speaking, John Wimber. Again, I had never heard of him, but since then I have been to a number of his conferences, listened to his teaching tapes and read his books. What David began for me, John has expanded and extended: he has blown open the pages of scripture for me in new and exciting ways, helping me to see principles that I had missed. He has also launched me into a new style of ministry and a new way of doing mission, both for me and my church. We shall never be the same again—praise God!

I am grateful to God for the ministries of these two men in particular: they have both played a major part in forming me and shaping this book.

The principles I have written about in this book have been learned and tested out in the life and mission of local churches where I have served. I am grateful, therefore, for the enormous help those church families have given me over the years, often without realizing it—St Matthew's in Cambridge; Christ Church, Pitsmoor; St Thomas', Crookes in Sheffield; and Christ Church, South Ossett.

I have also appreciated the luxury of getting away from the telephone and the doorbell to write; so I am grateful to the brethren of the Community of the Resurrection at Mirfield for allowing me to use their facilities so freely: to pray in their church, to work in their library, to walk in their grounds.

I am grateful to John and Christine Bullimore of Thornhill, and Steve and Margaret Dye of my own church family, who have read the manuscript, survived the experience, and offered some helpful comments.

I have greatly appreciated the encouragement of my bishop, David (of Wakefield), in this venture and, even more, his willingness to find time in his busy schedule to write a Foreword.

Last, but not least, a big thank you to the two girls in my life: my wife Gill and my daughter Joanna, who have had to put up with me being "otherwise engaged" so often over the last two years and more that it has taken me to write this book. I hope they think it has been worth it!

John Marsh
Christ Church, South Ossett
April 1988

Here we go again!

As is clear from the preceding pages, I wrote this book originally back in the late 1980s when I was vicar of Christ Church, South Ossett—Ossett is a market town in West Yorkshire where Yorkshire's two great industries, coal and wool, were prominent. It was in the lively, growing community at Christ Church that I was able to develop and hone the principles I discuss here, and I am grateful to the members of that church for responding so willingly and being so supportive and encouraging—they feature in the book and some of them still worship and serve at Christ Church.

Unfortunately, nearly all copies of the book were lost about a year after publication as a result of a fire in the warehouse where they were being stored, along with numerous other Christian titles—today, second-hand copies occasionally appear going cheap on Amazon or eBay! However, Sacristy Press of Durham, who published my little book *Singing the Lord's Song in a Strange Land* in 2022, are committed to republishing books which are often long out of print. On that basis, they have agreed to republish *Go . . . Make Disciples*—and I am grateful to them for that.

This has given me an opportunity to revisit the text, tweaking it in places, updating it where necessary, and adding a few additional comments. I have also decided, with agreement, to change the title to *Go . . . Make Disciples*. There are two reasons for this change: first, since *So I Send You* was published, several other books have appeared with precisely the same title; second, the new title expresses exactly the same challenge as the original: John and Matthew, in their distinctive Gospels, both summarize Jesus' parting challenge to his followers, and thus to us (John 20:21; Matthew 28:19). As I have revisited the text, I have linked the two titles together wherever appropriate.

Since writing the book, I have continued to share these principles in parishes where I have served and also in teaching: for some 15 years I have been a member of the *Leading Your Church Into Growth* team and also involved in training Church of England Readers (Lay Ministers as we now call them).

I reckon the best books, on whatever subject, are written not just conveying facts or information but communicating a passion for the subject. I was certainly passionate about mission when I wrote originally and that passion remains with me—if anything it is stronger now than ever. What is more, there was a great need for the church to be effective in mission in a world which was becoming more secular and less spiritual, certainly turning its back on organized religion. In the 35 years since, that need has grown significantly and the challenge to the church is all the greater and more urgent. We need to be reminded constantly of the task that is ours, the privilege of bringing the good news of Jesus to our generation, not allowing other issues, however relevant or important, to undermine this primary task. What is more, we need to recognize and use the equipment that is available in order to respond effectively to our task—to make disciples. If this book helps at all in addressing this desperate situation, then I would simply say: "Praise God!"

John Marsh
Huddersfield
November 2023

Whom Shall I Send?

Mention the word "apostle" or "apostolic" to a group of Christians, and you will receive a variety of responses.

From some, there will be scarcely a flicker of response. Perhaps they are vaguely aware that it has something to do with Christianity, that it's in the Bible somewhere. Or maybe they are Anglicans and recognize that "apostolic" is one of the things they are supposed to believe about the church—they say it every Sunday in the Nicene Creed: "We believe in one, holy, catholic, and apostolic Church." But have they ever stopped to think what it means?

Some, probably of a "high-church" persuasion, may well add the word "succession": "apostolic succession" is concerned with the ordination of ministers by bishops, whose authority can be traced back in an unbroken line to the first apostles. It's an important principle for them.

Some, mostly from the "house church" stable, would link "apostle" to church structures and in particular to leadership. According to the blueprint for church leadership in Ephesians 4:11–12, every church, if it is properly (i.e. biblically) constituted, needs to have recognized apostles among its leaders. It's an important principle for them.

Others, often from a more traditional "evangelical" background, would challenge this view of apostles, stressing that the apostles were unique and, therefore, unrepeatable. On that basis, it is wrong to expect apostles today. It's an important principle for them. Unfortunately, ignorance on the one hand and strong convictions on the other have both tended to cloud the real issue: as far as the New Testament is concerned, all Christians are "apostles" and all churches should be "apostolic". For these English words are based on a Greek verb, *apostello*, which means "to send forth". So, an "apostle" is one who is sent (to say or do something)—a messenger, if you like; and an "apostolic" church is one which recognizes and demonstrates its "sent-ness".

Our God is a sending God: he sent messengers, prophets and leaders to his people throughout the Old Testament. Then, supremely, he sent his Son, Jesus, into the world. Jesus knew he had been sent: he kept saying so, time after time. What is more, he was quite clear about God's purpose in sending him: it was to save the world. That was his "mission"—and that's a word based on the Latin word for "send".

It's clear, too, that Jesus intended that mission to continue even after he had left this world. Just before he did so, he said to his disciples: "Go and make disciples of all nations" (Matthew 28:19). And just in case they wondered how on earth they were supposed to do that he also said: "As the Father sent me, so I send you" (John 20:21, GNB). I believe that these are very significant words, implying that our mission is the same as Jesus' mission. It is the purpose of this book to unpack these words of Jesus, to reflect on them, and to ask: "What is our mission?" and "What are our resources?"

About 700 years before the time of Jesus, Isaiah, a prophet of God, had a vision of God in glory—you can read it in Isaiah 6: 1–9. In that vision, God asked this question: "Whom shall I send? Who will go for us?" (v. 8). God still asks that today—and he's waiting for an answer! Yet for all kinds of reasons we chicken out and do what Moses did, which was, in effect, to say to God: "Here I am. Please send someone else!" (Exodus 4:10–13). But as the story of Moses shows us, God doesn't give up that easily and he doesn't take "No" for an answer.

God's question stands: "Whom shall I send?" It is my hope and prayer that this book will help us to respond positively, and go—as Isaiah did.

"As the Father has sent me, I am sending you."

1

Sent . . . As Children

I was in my study talking with Steve, a student who had not long been a Christian. We were talking about the privilege of knowing God as Father. The door opened and my daughter, Joanna (then about three years old), came in: she came straight to me, climbed up on my knee, sat down and put her arm round my neck.

What a perfectly timed visual aid! Steve was there having asked for an appointment, knocked on my door, and waited to be invited in. Joanna was there with no appointment, no knocking, no invitation—and she got closer to me than Steve did! The difference? To Steve I was pastor; to Joanna I am father.

Missing the heart

The longer I am a Christian the more I realize the crucial importance of knowing God as "Father"; in fact, I reckon that if you have missed that, you have missed the heart of Christianity. I did for quite a few years: I was brought up in a Christian home and involved in a local church from the cradle upwards. By the time I was a teenager, I was in every church activity I was eligible for and at 13 I became a member of the church. But it was not until I was 17 that I had my eyes opened to the heart of the gospel: the need for a personal commitment to Jesus as Saviour and Lord. That is when I began to know God as Father—and it made so much difference.

Having been a minister in various local churches over the years, I have often met church people who seem to have missed the heart of the gospel: they don't really know God as Father. They may acknowledge him as Lord to be served and obeyed, but they don't recognize him as Father to be known and loved.

But does it matter? Yes, because they are missing out on so much that God has to offer through Jesus: it is as if they are living in the Old Testament rather than the New. It matters, too, because knowing God as Father is the only secure foundation for all that we do as Christians: our worship, our fellowship, our service and, especially, our mission. Without the security of knowing God as Father, mission will always be a struggle.

What is God like?

The Old Testament tells the story of how God's people, the Jews, over many centuries, gradually found out what God was like. Through events in their history, they saw God in action, and through their prophets they heard God speaking. So, they were able to build up a picture of God: he is Creator God; Almighty God; God of peace, of justice, of mercy, of love; a holy God; an unchanging God. All this and more they learned about God.

But at the same time, they formed the impression that God was so great, so powerful, so holy, so far above and beyond people that there must be an unbridgeable gap between Creator and creature, between holy God and sinful people—and people should keep their distance! So, if people wanted to worship God, it could only be done with proper respect, reverence and awe; and the words used in worship must be carefully chosen too. So strong was this feeling that they even had a special name for God (Yahweh), which they dared not use, just in case they ended up breaking the third commandment: "You shall not misuse the name of the LORD your God . . . " (Exodus 20:7).

It was into this religious environment that Jesus came; and he came talking about God. There was nothing surprising about that—except for the way he talked about him. It was as if he cared nothing for that right respect and reverence for God; he insisted on calling him "Father". And that was a shock to the religious system! The religious leaders objected strongly and challenged Jesus about it time and again; he was making himself equal with God, and that was blasphemy—a serious charge, punishable by stoning. Yet to know God as Father was at the heart of the new thing Jesus had come to do—the Bible calls it the "New Covenant" (or agreement). The religious teachers of Jesus' day ought to have realized it if they really knew their scriptures (the Old Testament) as thoroughly as they claimed—it is all there!

Knowing God

About 500 years before Jesus came, the prophet Jeremiah, inspired by God, spoke these words:

> "The days are coming," declares the LORD, "when I will make a new covenant with the people of Israel and with the people of Judah . . . This is the covenant that I will make with the people of Israel after that time," declares the LORD. "I will put my law in their minds and write it on their hearts. I will be their God, and they will be my people. No longer will they teach their neighbour, or say to one another, 'Know the LORD,' because they will all know me, from the least of them to the greatest," declares the LORD. "For I will forgive their wickedness and will remember their sins no more." (Jeremiah 31:31,33–4).

There are three significant features of this New Covenant between God and his people.

First, it will be an internal job. Under the old covenant, given in the time of Moses, God's people were required to keep God's law, which was originally carved on lumps of stone (Deuteronomy 5:1–22). Under the New Covenant, God is going to write his law on the minds and hearts of his people—it will be inside them rather than outside!

Second, it will mean a new start. God promises to forgive the sins of his people, even to forget all the wicked things they have done.

Third, it offers a new relationship with God. At the heart of the New Covenant is his marvellous promise: "They will all know me." To emphasize that God really means "all", he adds: "from the least of them to the greatest"—everyone is included, no one is left out. What is more, the relationship offered is a special, intimate one: this is not knowing about God intellectually, but knowing God personally, intimately—"[it] will be an inward relationship, as when a friend knows another friend in the trust . . . of personal relationship."[1] Indeed, in Hebrew (the language in which the Old Testament was originally written), the same word is used here as is used when a man "knows" his wife in the intimacy of sexual intercourse. The relationship with God on offer is that intimate!

This is the promise of the New Covenant. The prophet Ezekiel, living just a few years after Jeremiah, and similarly inspired by God, spoke of the same things in slightly different words:

> I will sprinkle clean water on you, and you will be clean; I will cleanse you from all your impurities and from all your idols. I will give you a new heart and put a new spirit in you; I will remove from you your heart of stone and give you a heart of flesh. And I will put my Spirit in you and move you to follow my decrees and be careful to keep my laws . . . You will be my people, and I will be your God (Ezekiel 36:25–8).

Here is the same promise Jeremiah spoke about: a new start, an internal operation of the heart, forgiveness of sins and relationship with God, with the added involvement of God's Spirit.

The promise fulfilled

This is the background to Jesus' teaching about God. Particularly significant are his words at the Last Supper. As he ate with his disciples, he took a cup of wine and giving thanks to God said: "This is my blood of the (new) covenant, which is poured out for many for the forgiveness of sins" (Matthew 26:28). We still repeat those words today at our Communion services, often quoting 1 Corinthians 11:23–25, in one form or another. But how many communicants appreciate the full significance of them? The death of Jesus for us, which we remember and celebrate

---

[1]   Bernard W. Anderson, *The Living World of the Old Testament* (London: Longman, 1967), p. 352.

in Communion, has inaugurated the New Covenant spoken about by Jeremiah and Ezekiel: Jesus, through the cross, has made available to us all the blessings of that covenant. Through him we may receive forgiveness, experience that internal work of God in our hearts and, best of all, enter into a new and intimate relationship with God.

New language please!

With the coming of Jesus, the Old Testament understanding of God was blown apart. As a result, the Old Testament names for God, such as Almighty God, Sovereign Lord, Holy One, etc., are no longer adequate. They are still true, of course, but in no way do they express intimate relationship. New language is needed to describe the new relationship now on offer.

Jesus introduced that new language when he spoke about God as Father. Whenever he referred to God he spoke of "the Father" or "my Father", and when he prayed, rather than using the many titles available to him in the prayer language of the Jews, he addressed God as "Father". For example, in the Garden of Gethsemane: "*Abba*, Father," he said, "everything is possible for you. Take this cup from me. Yet not what I will, but what you will" (Mark 14:36). Even more remarkable is that in his own language, Aramaic, the word Jesus actually used was Abba. (It is preserved in most English translations of the Bible in Mark 14.36, quoted above.) As far as the religious leaders of Jesus' day were concerned, that made it worse. Why? Because a child called its father Abba—you can hear it the streets of some Middle Eastern towns today as children call after their fathers. (I have often been reminded that we can hear the same father–child conversation in the streets of West Yorkshire, where I live, and in other parts of the country too.) It speaks of affection and of intimacy:

> It would have seemed disrespectful, indeed, unthinkable, to the sensibilities of Jesus' contemporaries to address God with this familiar word. Jesus dared to use Abba as a form of address to

God . . . He spoke to God as a child to its father: confidently and securely, and yet at the same time reverently and obediently.[2]

This was new, shockingly new, for the Jews. This was relationship with God as it ought to be, but it was far too familiar for them; they couldn't cope with it. If they had but known, Jesus was simply expressing in words what he experienced of God in his inner being as he communicated with him—"the intimacy, trust and obedience of a child with his father".[3]

Jesus and his Father

. . . loving

A careful reading of the Gospel accounts of Jesus' life reveals something of what that intimacy with God meant for Jesus. At the heart of any close relationship is love: that's what makes the relationship tick! Jesus' relationship with God was no exception.

Teaching his disciples just before his death he spoke of that love: "As the Father has loved me, so have I loved you. Now remain in my love. If you keep my commands, you will remain in my love, just as I have obeyed my Father's commands and remain in his love" (John 15:9–10). Then in his great prayer recorded in John 17, he prays to his Father that "the love you have for me may be in them" (v. 26). Clearly, Jesus was very aware of his Father's love for him—it was the basis of their intimacy.

. . . trusting

Within a healthy relationship, love encourages trust. Certainly, Father God trusted Jesus: "The Father loves the Son and has placed everything in his hands" (John 3:35); "All things have been committed to me by my Father" (Matthew 11:27). Even the greatest of all responsibilities, to be judge of all people, the Father has entrusted to the Son: "the Father judges no one, but has entrusted all judgment to the Son" (John 5:22).

---

[2]   J. Jeremias, *New Testament Theology* (London: SCM Press, 1971), p. 67.

[3]   J. D. G. Dunn, *Jesus and the Spirit* (London: SCM Press, 1975), p. 24.

The trust was mutual too: Jesus showed perfect trust in his Father. He trusted him when he prayed at the grave of his friend, Lazarus: "Father, I thank you that you have heard me. I knew that you always hear me . . ." (John 11:41–2). He trusted him to provide all he needed: "Do not worry about it . . . your Father knows that you need them. But seek his kingdom, and these things will be given to you as well" (Luke 12:29–31)—at least, he taught others to trust the Father, so presumably he practised what he preached! And he trusted his Father at the moment of his death: "Father, into your hands I commit my spirit" (Luke 23:46).

. . . understanding

There was complete understanding between them, too. Jesus understood perfectly what his Father wanted to do:

> And this is the will of him who sent me, that I shall lose none of all those he has given me, but raise them up at the last day. For my Father's will is that everyone who looks to the Son and believes in him shall have eternal life, and I will raise them up at the last day (John 6:39–40).

And if ever there seemed to be any doubt in Jesus' mind about his Father's intentions, he would wait and pray for confirmation. Is that what Jesus was doing in the Garden of Gethsemane? The prospect before him was dreadful: at that crucial moment could it be that Jesus was pausing to check that he had rightly understood his Father's intentions? Certainly, Matthew records an interesting variation in Jesus' prayer in the garden. First, Jesus prays: "My Father, if it is possible, may this cup be taken from me. Yet not as I will, but as you will" (Matthew 26:39). Is Jesus, in effect, asking: "Have I understood the plan correctly? Is the plan fixed? Is there any room for negotiation? Have I got to go through with this?" When he prays the second time, he says: "My Father, if it is not possible for this cup to be taken away unless I drink it, may your will be done" (Matthew 26:42). If there was any doubt before, there is none now: he has clarified the Father's will.

So he rose from prayer ready for anything that will come to him, because he knew it was his Father's will and he trusted him: he was ready for Judas' betrayal, Peter's failure, scheming priests, fickle crowds, vacillating Pilate, mocking soldiers, scourge, cross, nails, pain—and death. Through it all Jesus demonstrated a quiet confidence, almost as if he were in control rather than the others present, as if he were judge rather than accused, as if he were simply watching things happen according to plan.

Even when Pilate tried to pull rank on him, Jesus quietly replied: "You would have no power over me if it were not given to you from above" (John 19:11). It must have been the most frustrating trial Pilate had ever tried to conduct! Reflecting on these events later, Peter wrote: "When they hurled their insults at him, he did not retaliate; when he suffered, he made no threats. Instead, he entrusted himself to him who judges justly" (1 Peter 2:23).

The key

But how did Jesus do it? How was he able to remain so calm in the face of such terrifying events? Answer: he knew the security of his Father's love. And that is the key to the whole of his life and ministry. That security provided the inner strength he needed: so he was able to be single-minded in his mission, despite the misunderstanding of family, the failure of friends, the opposition of religious leaders and the gross injustice of his trial. He was secure in his relationship with God, secure in his Father's love—and that's what mattered.

This relationship was fundamental to Jesus, the key to the success of his mission—and it needs to be for us too! If we are to be effective in mission, then we need to grasp this principle: the only starting point for effective mission for God is personal relationship with God.

When Jesus said to his disciples just before he left them: "As the Father has sent me, I am sending you" (John 20:21), he was offering them, among other things, the security of an intimate relationship with God from which to start. That is why Jesus took the trouble to explain how it is possible for us to know God in the same intimate way he did.

Knowing God as Father

In the opening chapter of John's Gospel we read: "Yet to all who did receive [Jesus], to those who believed in his name, he gave the right to become children of God—children born not of natural descent, nor of human decision or a husband's will, but born of God" (John 1:12–13). The offer is that we should become "children of God".

How does that happen? From our side, when we receive Jesus, believe in Jesus (v. 12); from God's side, when he causes us to be born, not physically, but spiritually (v. 13). Jesus unpacks this idea a little more in conversation with Nicodemus (John 3).

Born again

Nicodemus was a "nice-to-know-kind-of-a-guy". He was respected in the community, a leader of men and devoutly religious. Presumably he had heard about Jesus and was curious to find out more. Just in case his friends and colleagues disapproved, he came to Jesus at night. He had some questions he wanted to ask this fascinating religious teacher.

He began by speaking approvingly of Jesus' ministry (John 3:2). Jesus apparently ignored his flattery: he could see right through Nicodemus and was aware of his greatest need, and it was that which Jesus responded to: "Very truly I tell you, no one can see the kingdom of God unless they are born again" (v. 3). Nicodemus was surprised and puzzled: could a man climb back into his mother's womb and be born again? (v. 4). Jesus repeated his challenge, with slight amendments: "'Very truly I tell you, no one can enter the kingdom of God unless they are born of water and the Spirit" (v. 5).

Jesus was saying something of great seriousness and importance: the fact that he said it twice and prefaced it each time with "Very truly I tell you" confirms that seriousness. But what did he mean?

How can this be?

Jesus was talking about the way into God's kingdom. Translating that into our situation, he was really explaining what it means to be Christian. Being a good teacher, Jesus often used pictures to illustrate and clarify his message. Here he chose the picture of birth, which is illuminating in a number of ways.

First, birth is a radical thing. One moment you are not born, the next you are; one moment you are safe in mother's womb, the next you are thrust into the hubbub of life. That is a big change! Some people have the impression that to become Christian is little more than a determination to live better, in a more Christian way—to pull up one's moral socks! Jesus' picture of the new birth suggests it is something rather more radical.

Second, not one of us gave birth to ourselves—someone had to do it for us. What is true physically is also true spiritually: physically, it was our mother who did it; in the new birth, it is God who does it. (Remember John 1:13.)

That is important to grasp, because many seem to think that they are Christian on the basis of what they do: they go to church; they say their prayers; they live Christian lives, and so on. These are all good, Christian things to do but, of themselves, they make no one Christian; according to Jesus, that is something only God can do.

Paul certainly grasped this truth. Having reflected on his experience of God, he wrote towards the end of his life: "But when the kindness and love of God our Saviour appeared, he saved us, not because of righteous things we had done, but because of his mercy. He saved us through the washing of rebirth and renewal by the Holy Spirit" (Titus 3:4–5).

Jesus explains this further when he says: "Flesh gives birth to flesh, but the Spirit gives birth to spirit" (John 3:6). In other words, in order to enjoy physical life you need to be born physically; in order to enjoy spiritual life you need to be born spiritually.

Third, birth is something that has to happen to each of us personally, otherwise we are not alive. You cannot have an understudy or a substitute at your birth, you cannot be born by proxy—if you are not there you are not born! Again, what is true physically is true spiritually: each of us needs to be born personally. Sadly, many have failed to grasp this, too: they are second-generation Christians—their parents were Christian (or nominally so), they were brought up in a vaguely Christian environment. But, as someone has helpfully said: "God has no grandchildren, only children." That's true! I was a grandchild of God for 17 years. But God wants us to be born into his family as children and know him as Father.

Any births recently?

The late Canon David Watson, teaching on this theme, used to tell the story of the teenager who had to write an essay on human reproduction for his biology homework. In order to research the subject, he asked his mum: "Mum, how was I born?" Slightly embarrassed, she replied: "A stork flew over, and you were born—just like that!" Not entirely satisfied, he asked: "Well, how were you born, Mum?" Slightly more embarrassed, she replied: "The same way: a stork flew over, and I was born." He decided some further research was necessary, so he went to see his grandma. "Grandma, how were you born?" he asked. Even more embarrassed than his mum had been, grandma replied: "A stork flew over; that's how I was born." When he sat down to write his essay, he began: "There has not been a natural birth in our family for at least three generations."

David had a marvellous way of telling the story, with a twinkle in his eye. While the congregation was still enjoying the humour, laughing freely, he would add: "And there may not have been a spiritual birth in your family for even longer." The laughter would subside to be replaced with an uncomfortable silence. That story captures well the challenge of Jesus' teaching: you must be born again!

While I was working on this chapter, Shirley, a member of the church family where I was then vicar, came to see me. She was reflecting on her experience of God recently, in particular how she was "born again" some months previously. When I asked her what difference that had made, she replied: "I used to fear God: now I know my God." That is exactly what God promised through Jeremiah all those years ago: everyone will know him.

In discussing Jesus' conversation with Nicodemus, and wanting to be true to what I think the text of John's Gospel is saying, I may have given the impression that being born again, spiritual birth, is always a moment of crisis. However, I am keenly aware that for many this is a process rather than a crisis, a journey into personal faith. Bishop John Finney in his book *Emerging Evangelism* offers us this helpful imagery:

> Others have seen [the experience of conversion] as a *process* like
> the rising of the sun: the sky changes from black to grey, and then

come the first pink clouds until gradually the sun begins a new day. At what time during dawn do we actually experience sunrise? The important thing is that the sun has come.

John adds:

> My own research showed that 69 per cent of adults experienced their coming to faith as a gradual process while 31 per cent could give a date on which they experienced conversion.[4]

The important thing is that we know we are children of God: this is the basis for all our life and ministry as Christians, the place of security and resource as we engage in mission, the starting point if we are going to be involved in making disciples.

But more!
Not only does God long for us to be his children and know him as Father, not only does Jesus challenge us with the need for new birth, but we are given the Holy Spirit to reinforce the truth and to make it real for us.

Paul put it like this when he wrote to the Christians in Galatia:

> But when the set time had fully come, God sent his Son, born of a woman, born under the law, to redeem those under the law, that we might receive adoption to sonship. Because you are his sons, God sent the Spirit of his Son into our hearts, the Spirit who calls out, "*Abba*, Father" (Galatians 4:4–6).

Jesus came so that we could become children of God. The Spirit comes to reinforce it: by coming into our hearts and, from inside us, helping us to know we are God's children and moving us to call God "Father", or even "Dad" (Abba). Here is the internal operation of the heart spoken of by Jeremiah and Ezekiel.

4   John Finney, *Emerging Evangelism* (London: Darton, Longman & Todd, 2004), pp. 19–20.

Paul wrote of this again to the Christians in Rome: "The Spirit you received does not make you slaves, so that you live in fear again; rather, the Spirit you received brought about your adoption to sonship. And by him we cry, 'Abba, Father.' The Spirit himself testifies with our spirit that we are God's children" (Romans 8:15–16). We, who have become children of God, have been given the Spirit of sonship: he affirms within us that we are God's children and moves us to call God "Father".

John agreed with Paul. In his first epistle, he wrote: "See what great love the Father has lavished on us, that we should be called children of God!" (1 John 3:1). John was amazed at the depth of God's love for us: he loves us so much that he has made it possible for us to be his children. It is as if John was reflecting on that truth and the reality of it hit him afresh. So he added: "And that is what we are!" (1 John 3:1).

How can we be sure it is true? How does it become real for us? John explained: "And this is how we know that he lives in us: we know it by the Spirit he gave us" (1 John 3:24).

Review

"Knowing God" is a central, recurring theme of scripture. We have seen God, back in the time of Jeremiah and Ezekiel, promising to do a new thing, at the heart of which is the promise of a new relationship with him. We have seen Jesus enjoying an intimacy with God which was the underlying security for all he did. We have seen how he explained that others may enjoy relationship with God as children too. We have seen how the Holy Spirit makes the experience of intimacy with God a reality. We have seen both Paul and John testifying to their experience of that.

Intimacy with God, knowing God as Father, experiencing the reality of being a child of God, is the heart of being Christian. It is also the starting point of all Christian enterprise, because intimacy creates security—and we need to be secure before we can be effective.

Child psychologists tell us how crucial it is for children to have a secure home environment, to be sure of their parents' love. Given that security, young people can usually cope with the variety of pressures and challenges life throws at them. Take that basic security away and a young person is vulnerable, liable to struggle with life, if not come unstuck.

Again, what is true of human life is true of spiritual life. It is the assurance of the Father's love that provides the security for Christians to live, to love, to serve, to witness—to be involved in mission. That's the pattern we find in the life of Jesus; it needs to be the pattern for us too.

Of course, Jesus is the "only begotten" Son of God, and in that sense he is special. But we have been given the privilege of being adopted children. If that sounds like second best, remember that under Roman law (and much the same is true in Britain today), the adopted child was literally and absolutely the child of its new father: its old life was wiped out (even any outstanding debts!), and it enjoyed all the same rights and privileges of any natural child. Thus, Paul wrote: "Now if we are children, then we are heirs—heirs of God and co-heirs with Christ" (Romans 8:17).

That means that all the resources God shared with Jesus because he is his Son are available to us, too, because we are his children—all that God gave to his Son to equip him for life and mission in the world he offers to us too. It is when we begin to realize that this is our right as children of God, and to tap the potential of it, that we begin to be effective in mission.

All this potential is implied when Jesus said: "As the Father has sent me, I am sending you." Secure in this personal relationship with God we are resourced to go and invite others to be disciples.

2

Sent . . . To Do The Father's Will

We can all look back to times in our lives which have been particularly significant, those moments or experiences that have left their mark on us—after them we are never quite the same again! I have already mentioned my discovery of the heart of Christianity at the age of 17.

Some seven years later my eyes were opened again, this time to the person and work of the Holy Spirit; I began to discover what it meant to be filled with the Spirit and to experience gifts of the Spirit—a whole new world of the Spirit which had been virtually a closed book to me till then.

I remember, too, how God met with me through counselling, as a result of which I saw myself in a new light, with God's perspective. That revelation initiated a change in me (my wife noticed the difference!) which, I hope, is still going on. All these are spiritual milestones in my life, the fruit of which I am still enjoying.

A memorable experience

There were spiritual milestones in Jesus' life too. One of the most significant was when he was about to embark on his public ministry and went to the River Jordan to be baptized by John the Baptist. The fact that it is referred to in all four Gospels emphasizes its significance—there are relatively few incidents in the life of Jesus recorded in all four Gospels.

Commentators have written pages about it, often puzzling over its real meaning. What did Jesus mean when he said to John: "Let it be so now; it is proper for us to do this to fulfil all righteousness" (Matthew 3:15)? Was Jesus simply concerned to identify with the sinful people he had come to rescue and so felt he had to go through a baptism for repentance (which was what John's baptism was all about), although he had nothing to repent of (Matthew 3:11)?

It is, of course, impossible for us really to know what his baptism meant for Jesus; however, from the information we have in the Gospels, I believe there are at least two important things Jesus experienced at that time.

First, in the act of baptism Jesus submitted himself to his Father, acknowledging that God was his Father and that he was his Son. God responded to that act of submission by speaking to him: "You are my Son, whom I love; with you I am well pleased" (Mark 1:11)—words reminiscent of well-known Old Testament themes from Psalms (2:7) and Isaiah (42:1). Jesus would have been familiar with the words already, but they must have felt so encouraging just then: if ever he needed affirming in his relationship to God it was surely now as he moved out of the security and privacy of the family home into public ministry—and God knew that! We all need affirming from time to time; so did Jesus. In baptism, he was affirmed by God in his relationship with him.

Second, in the act of baptism Jesus committed himself to the mission his Father had given him. He knew he had come with a special mission, he knew that God's time had come for him to begin that mission in earnest, and now he willingly committed himself to it. Again, God responded: by resourcing him for that mission, giving him his Holy Spirit—the Gospels record the Spirit coming on Jesus like a dove (Mark 1:10). As he faced the demands of his God-given ministry, he was equipped for it by God. According to Mark's Gospel, the first words Jesus spoke publicly after his baptism were: "The time has come," he said. "The kingdom of God has come near. Repent and believe the good news" (Mark 1:15).

So, in the experience of baptism, Jesus was affirmed as God's Son and resourced for God's mission. He went out secure in his relationship with God and confident in his resources from God—related and resourced! This is the secret of successful mission: it was for Jesus; it must be for us.

Working it out . . .

We can see that principle worked out in Jesus' ministry, particularly as it is recorded in John's Gospel. If we look closely, we realize that the relating and the resourcing are inseparably connected: the resourcing comes out of the relating. It is as Jesus enjoys the intimacy of relationship with his Father that he receives the resources he needs for ministry. We first see this hinted at in John 3:35: "The Father loves the Son and has placed everything in his hands." God gives everything to Jesus because he loves him as a father loves his son—he trusts him!

This principle is further unpacked when Jesus responds to criticism from other religious leaders who didn't like what he said and did. Jesus replied: "Very truly I tell you, the Son can do nothing by himself; he can do only what he sees his Father doing, because whatever the Father does the Son also does. For the Father loves the Son and shows him all he does" (John 5:19–20a).

Have you ever observed a child avidly watching its father doing something and then eagerly saying: "Let me do it too, Dad!"? Children love to do what Dad does. Jesus apparently behaved in the same way: he watched what his Father did and did it too.

Those of us who are parents (or grandparents) know too that if we have something special to show our children, we don't throw it at them; we don't shout it down the garden. We wait till they are close, maybe sitting on our knee (if they are not too big!), and then we say: "Let me show you something." It is an intimate moment and, within the intimacy of the parent–child relationship, the parent shares the secret with the child. So it is with Jesus: the Father loves him and within the intimacy of that relationship shows him things—the Son is let in on all the Father's secrets, allowed to see all that the Father is doing (John 5:20a). Thus, Jesus is resourced out of his relationship.

As a result, all that Jesus said and did was what his Father said and did: he had come to do Father's will. "For I have come down from heaven not to do my will but to do the will of him who sent me" (John 6:38). And he knew what that will was "For my Father's will is that everyone who looks to the Son and believes in him shall have eternal life, and I will raise them up at the last day" (John 6:40).

When Jesus spoke, he said what his Father told him to say: "But he who sent me is trustworthy, and what I have heard from him I tell the world" (John 8:26). Jesus was "a man who has told you the truth that I heard from God" (John 8:40). When he taught others, he was passing on what he had already learned from his Father: "I do nothing on my own but speak just what the Father has taught me" (John 8:28). He shared with others what his Father had shown him: "I am telling you what I have seen in the Father's presence" (John 8:38). And the Father not only told him what to say but how to say it: "For I did not speak of my own, but the Father who sent me commanded me to say all that I have spoken . . . So whatever I say is just what the Father has told me to say" (John 12:49–50).

All the time, Jesus spoke only about what he really knew and had actually seen (John 3:11). Even when he passed judgement, he was passing on the judgement of his Father (John 5:30). And when he was alone with his disciples, he shared with them the things that the Father shared with him (John 15:15).

As well as sharing what the Father told him, Jesus also did what the Father showed him. He was doing the work the Father had given him (John 5:36), responding to the Father's command (John 15:10), so all that he did was pleasing to his Father (John 8:29). " . . . the world may learn," Jesus said, "that I love the Father and do exactly what my Father has commanded me!" (John 14:31).

In John's Gospel, then, we are offered this fascinating insight into the secret of the success of Jesus' ministry—all the time he was simply doing what his Father told him. This insight is both exciting and challenging, not least because it offers us a model for our mission. It also throws light on some incidents in the ministry of Jesus which are a little puzzling.

. . . at the pool of Bethesda

Take, for instance, Jesus' visit to the pool at Bethesda (John 5:1–9). The water in this pool was well known for its curative properties and naturally, therefore, attracted many sick people who sat around it hoping for healing. We have no reason to doubt that the usual crowd of hopefuls were there the day Jesus visited. But Jesus singled out one man and healed him. That's great! But wait a minute: what about the rest? Why heal just one and leave the rest to suffer? I don't know the answer to that. But what

I now understand, as a result of the "insight" we have just been thinking about, is this: as Jesus arrived at the pool, he listened to his Father, waiting for instructions. God said, "That one!", and Jesus did what his Father told him: he healed "that one". That is what he saw his Father doing at that particular moment. This suggestion still leaves me puzzling over the unhealed ones, but maybe we are being given a glimpse at the behind-the-scenes activity that was going on within the Father–Son relationship.

. . . at Jairus' house

Or what about the healing of Jairus' daughter (Mark 5:21–43)? Jesus was on an emergency mission, called to the home of a dying girl. Despite the urgency of the situation, he stopped on the way to talk to another woman who had touched his clothes and been healed. I can imagine some of his disciples, and others who were with him, getting anxious. "What's he doing?" "Why doesn't he get rid of that woman?" "If he doesn't hurry up, he'll be too late!" And he was: the message came from the girl's home that she had died. But Jesus didn't panic or rush, neither did he turn away and give up. He went quietly and confidently to the home, put out the crying mourners, and brought the girl back to life. He gives the impression that he knew exactly what he was doing the whole time—he did, because he knew what his Father was doing.

. . . at the Sea of Galilee

And consider the stilling of the storm as Mark tells it (4:35–41). It would appear that Jesus had been ministering to crowds of people, teaching them about the kingdom of God and presumably healing the sick—Mark does not specifically mention healing at this point, but it was the usual pattern for Jesus. At the end of the day, Jesus said to his disciples: "Let us go over to the other side [of the lake]" (v. 35). I wonder if his disciples responded with: "What on earth for, Lord? The crowds are here: why go over there? It's a crazy idea! In any case, don't you know how dangerous that lake can be, particularly at night? A violent storm could blow up without warning and then we'd be in trouble!"

Whether or not they complained, Jesus got his way and they took him across the lake, "leaving the crowd behind", as Mark records (v. 36). A storm did blow up and they were in trouble, until Jesus miraculously came to the rescue. He simply stood up in the boat and told the storm: "Stop it!" (or words to that effect!), and it stopped—just like that! (v. 39).

When they reached the other side, Jesus healed one man who was suffering from a mental health condition, climbed back in the boat and returned to the other side of the lake, where a crowd gathered round him again (Mark 5:1–21). That kind of itinerary makes no sense on the face of it: the "time and motion" people would be horrified! Leave a successful ministry, take a dangerous journey, help one man, make the return (equally dangerous) journey, and continue the ministry again! Why? Presumably, Jesus knew that was what he had to do: that was what his Father was doing.

. . . at the grave of Lazarus

Then there is the death of Lazarus, that poignant incident so graphically and honestly told in John's Gospel (11:1–44), in which we catch a glimpse of the human Jesus as he wept at the grave of his friend. (Incidentally, men, I reckon that means it's OK for us to cry—Jesus did it, why shouldn't we?) In the light of the close relationship between Father and Son which I have suggested Jesus modelled for us, I now see this incident in a new light. Let me explain. Have you ever watched a play or TV drama in which there are two separate "actions" happening simultaneously? The effect is achieved by constantly alternating between the two situations or, in the theatre, by having one at the side or front of curtain while the other is centre stage. I reckon there is something rather like that going on in the story of Jesus and Lazarus. The "main action" is the story as told in John 11. But there are a number of puzzling features which need explaining. For example, when Jesus was told of Lazarus' illness (v. 3), his immediate response is "This illness will not end in death. No, it is for God's glory so that God's Son may be glorified through it" (v. 4). How did he know that? How could he be so sure? Stranger still was Jesus' lack of action. If you heard that one of your best friends was seriously ill, you would want to do something, wouldn't you? I would—visit, write or phone. We are told that having heard about Lazarus' illness, Jesus "stayed where he was two more days" (v. 6). Why? Didn't he care?

When Jesus did eventually set off to Bethany with his disciples, he told them: "Our friend Lazarus has fallen asleep; but I am going there to wake him up" (v. 11). When it was apparent that his disciples had misunderstood him, he spelt it out more clearly: "Lazarus is dead . . . But let us go to him" (vv. 14–15). How did he know that Lazarus was now dead? There is no mention of any second message coming from Bethany. In any case, he said it wouldn't end in death: had it all gone horribly wrong?

When Jesus arrived in Bethany, he comforted Lazarus' two sisters, Mary and Martha, encouraging them to have faith. More than that, he said to Martha: "Your brother will rise again" (v. 23). He seemed certain of it, and he made it clear to Martha that he meant here and now and not just on the last day (vv. 24–6). He was taken to the tomb, where he wept—he did care after all; he loved Lazarus very much! When he was ready, he asked for the stone to be taken away from the mouth of the tomb.

It is then that the action suddenly changed—our eyes are taken to another part of the stage, as it were. Jesus, who has talked with his disciples and then with Mary and Martha, now talked to his Father: "Father, I thank you that you have heard me. I knew that you always hear me, but I said this for the benefit of the people standing here, that they may believe that you sent me" (vv. 41–2). Then, returning to the "main action", he called Lazarus out of the tomb, and Lazarus came.

What was happening? Could it be that this "subsidiary action" (i.e. Jesus talking to his Father) had actually been going on the whole time, simultaneously with the "main action" of the story? While we have been watching the action "centre stage", Jesus had been in constant touch with his Father. That would certainly go some way to explain the puzzling features we have noted. Jesus knew Lazarus' sickness would not end in death because his Father had showed him that; he stayed put for two days because his Father told him to; he learned of Lazarus' death from his Father; he eventually went to Bethany when his Father said "Go!"; he was able to assure Martha that Lazarus would rise again because that is what his Father said would happen; he called Lazarus out of the tomb when his Father said "Now!" All the time, Jesus said and did what his Father showed him (John 5:19–20).

As we watch, alongside those who were actually there, and who were amazed by the power of Jesus, able even to raise the dead, we are actually witnessing the outworking of Jesus' intimate relationship with God. The power was from God and the how, when and where to use that power was also given by God to Jesus, the Son whom he loves. Jesus' resources flowed out from his relationship with God as Father.

. . . under pressure

There is one incident in the Gospels that has particularly puzzled me: Jesus' handling of the Canaanite woman (or "the Syro-Phoenician woman", as she used to be called) (Matthew 15:21–8). She came to Jesus in need: her daughter was "demon-possessed and suffering terribly" (v. 22). Jesus appeared to ignore her; certainly, he did not reply. Apparently, she kept on asking and Jesus continued to ignore her. The disciples thought this meant Jesus was irritated by her—certainly they were!—and they urged Jesus to send her away. But he didn't respond to that request either.

The puzzling thing is this: Jesus seemed to show no compassion for this needy woman, which was so out of character. Why didn't he respond to her request? He had the power to; didn't he want to?

Jesus seemed to be struggling with the terms of his mission: "I was sent only to the lost sheep of Israel" (v. 24)—he was sent exclusively to God's chosen people, Israel. Therefore,

> he could not be at the beck and call of everyone, however deserving their requests might be. The privileges of the kingdom of God must be offered to the people of God, the children of the covenant . . . He would accept the limitations imposed upon him by his vocation; and he would make no exception in the case of this Canaanite woman . . .

The woman persisted and Jesus was impressed, yet he still didn't seem able to respond: "It is not right to take the children's bread and toss it to their dogs" (v. 26). Not very flattering, but the woman didn't argue the point: she was desperate, and she didn't mind being a dog providing she got a few crumbs—that was all she needed (v. 27). Apparently, at that point, Jesus' heart melted and, impressed by her persistent faith, he granted her request.

Could this be another example of "double action": that all the time the main action was being played out, Jesus was involved in a subsidiary action, communicating with his Father? Is the reality that Jesus' heart went out to her immediately, but then he began to struggle with what his Father wanted him to do? Perhaps it went something like this: "Father, as I understand my mission, I have been sent to the lost sheep of Israel. That doesn't include this woman. Yet she cries after me and my heart goes out to her. Father, is it ever right to give the dogs the children's bread? What do I do, Father?' And the Father replied: "Give her what she wants." And Jesus did.

This is pure conjecture on my part. But it fits the pattern that we have noticed in other parts of the Gospel accounts of Jesus' ministry: Jesus operated in each specific situation in close touch with his Father, always aware of what his Father was doing and what his Father wanted him to do.

The secret of success

If we were to ask the question: "What was the secret of Jesus' ability to foster that intimate relationship with his Father that enabled him always to know what his Father wanted?", the answer is not hard to find in the Gospel accounts. It is prayer.

Often it is recorded that Jesus went apart to pray. For example: "Very early in the morning, while it was still dark, Jesus got up, left the house and went off to a solitary place, where he prayed" (Mark 1:35). Again: "One of those days Jesus went out to a mountainside to pray, and spent the night praying to God" (Luke 6:12) And: "After leaving [his disciples], he went up on a mountainside to pray" (Mark 6:46). He was in prayer when he was transfigured in the presence of Peter, James and John (Luke 9:28–9); he was praying when the disciples asked him to teach them to pray (Luke 11:1); he prayed in the Garden of Gethsemane (Mark 14:32–42); and there is his great prayer (often called the "High-priestly Prayer") recorded in John 17.

Not only are we told that Jesus prayed, but at times we are given some insight into the content of his praying.

Clearly, an important part of prayer for Jesus was simply enjoying his Father; it was through prayer that the relationship was sustained—whenever the words of Jesus' prayers are recorded we find him addressing God as "Father". When the Seventy-two returned from their missionary journey, Jesus prayed: "I praise you, Father, Lord of heaven and earth . . . " (Luke 10:21); when he taught his disciples to pray, he began: "Our Father . . . " (Luke 11:2); at the grave of Lazarus, he prayed: "Father, I thank you that you have heard me . . . " (John 11:41); his great prayer in John 17 began: "Father, the hour has come . . . " (v. 1); in the Garden of Gethsemane, he prayed: "Abba, Father" (Mark 14:36); and as he died on the cross, he cried, in prayer: "Father, into your hands I commit my spirit" (Luke 23:46). For Jesus, enjoying his Father was the starting point for prayer.

There is another important feature of Jesus' praying which is hinted at in the Gospel records too: time and again, in effect, Jesus prayed: "Father, what do you want me to do next?" We have already seen that Jesus may well have prayed this kind of prayer behind the scenes in a number of the situations recorded in the Gospels. We can see the effect of this prayer and God's response to it particularly clearly in a little incident recorded in Luke 4:42–4.

Jesus had been enjoying some successful ministry in Capernaum: he taught the people and healed "various kinds of illness" (v. 40). Early the next morning he went out alone to pray, but he was disturbed by people coming looking for him—Mark tells us they were led by Simon Peter (Mark 1:36). They wanted him to go back and do some more teaching and healing. On the face of it, that was a perfectly reasonable and understandable request. But Jesus, emerging from a time of prayer, knew he had to say "No": he had to move on to other towns and preach there (Luke 4:43). God had shown him the next stage of his plan as he was in prayer, and he always did exactly what his Father wanted.

The same process is evident when Jesus chose the 12 apostles. Luke tells us that he spent the whole of the previous night in prayer (Luke 6:12). In the morning, he called his followers together and chose 12 of them to be special apostles. Why? Could it be that during the night, as he enjoyed his Father's presence in prayer, he posed the question: "What next, Father?" Then, when the Father told him to choose 12 special apostles from among his followers, did Jesus ask: "Whom shall I choose, Father?" This can only be conjecture, but we do know that at this important moment in his ministry, Jesus knew exactly what he had to do: he had discovered his Father's plan in prayer and then did what he saw his Father doing (John 5:19).

Inside information

If the secret of Jesus' success was prayer, then surely that is something that is available to us too. Or is it that, despite all we have said, Jesus was, after all, a special case, and that this kind of "inside information" is not available to us? If that were true it would let us off the hook! But the scriptures tell us otherwise: both before and after Jesus there were those who apparently knew what it was to have inside information.

Moses

The latter chapters of the book of Exodus tell in some detail about the Israelites building the tabernacle, a special tent where God would meet with his people. The account begins with Moses being called by God to climb Mount Sinai to meet with him (Exodus 24:12–18). As Moses went up the mountain, the glory of the Lord, in the form of a cloud, settled on the mountain top and God spoke to Moses from within the cloud. We are told that Moses stayed there for 40 days. It was there that Moses was told by God to build the tabernacle, and not only that; he was told how to provide the resources for its construction and given detailed plans for every part of it. God told Moses: "Then let them make a sanctuary for me, and I will dwell among them. Make this tabernacle and all its furnishings exactly like the pattern I will show you" (Exodus 25:8–9).

The people set to work. The following chapters of Exodus recount the building process; they are punctuated with the phrase "as the LORD commanded Moses". When they had finished, "Moses inspected the work and saw that they had done it just as the LORD had commanded" (Exodus 39:43). The principle operating here is important: God showed Moses what to do and Moses, with the help of the people, did it. He was able to do exactly what God wanted, and he found out what God wanted through intimate contact with him—in prayer.

Jeremiah

Jeremiah was called by God to be a prophet while he was still young; he was understandably scared and tried to get out of it. His excuse sounded reasonable enough: "Alas, Sovereign LORD, I do not know how to speak; I am too young" (Jeremiah 1:6). God replied: "Do not say, 'I am too young.' You must go to everyone I send you to and say whatever I command you . . . I have put my words in your mouth . . . Stand up and say to them whatever I command you" (Jeremiah 1:7,9,17). That is what happened for Jeremiah time after time. For example, "This is the word that came to Jeremiah from the LORD: 'Stand at the gate of the LORD'S house and there proclaim this message . . . '" (7:1–2); again, "This is the word that came to Jeremiah from the LORD: 'Go down to the potter's house, and there I will give you my message'" (18:1–2).

It happened so often that in the end people came to Jeremiah and asked him to consult God for them: "Pray that the LORD your God will tell us where we should go and what we should do" (42:3). Later, Jeremiah was able to give them an answer: "This is what the LORD, the God of Israel to whom you sent me to present your petition, says . . . " (42:9).

At times, this ability to have inside information from God was a lifesaver for him, particularly when enemies plotted against him. And he was quite happy to reveal his sources, too: "Because the LORD revealed their plot to me, I knew it, for at that time he showed me what they were doing" (11:18).

Jeremiah made it clear that intimacy with God in prayer is the only way to know the mind and purposes of God. It was through Jeremiah that God censured false prophets, who claimed to speak in God's name when God had not sent them. "I did not send these prophets, yet they have run with their message; I did not speak to them, yet they have prophesied. But if they had stood in my council, they would have proclaimed my words to my people . . . " (23:21–2). Here, in embryo, is the same principle we have seen in Jesus' ministry: resourcing for ministry out of relationship with God, knowing what to do and say as a result of standing in the council of God—and that is another way of talking about prayer.

Peter

Those who came after Jesus experienced the same kind of thing too. Peter, for instance, was praying one day when God spoke to him through a vision (Acts 10:9–23). God made Peter aware of the next phase of his plan: he wanted to bring non-Jews into the Christian family. Peter, being a staunch Jew, had always thought that impossible, so he argued with God about it. In the end, he was persuaded and found himself, just a couple of days later, preaching the gospel in the home of a non-Jew, where he witnessed God coming powerfully upon the whole household (Acts 10:24–48). God had showed Peter what he wanted to do next and Peter did it—and there was success. But note: it started in prayer.

And others

The five leaders of the young church in Antioch were worshipping together and fasting when God spoke to them, telling them what he wanted to do next (Acts 13:1–3). He wanted two of the five, Paul and Barnabas, to be commissioned for a new work. That must have been hard for them, but because they knew it was God's plan, they obeyed, praying for them and sending them off. That was the beginning of one of the most significant advances of the Christian Church in the whole of its history: the missionary journeys of Paul during which he travelled miles, preaching the gospel and founding numerous churches—and it began in prayer, doing what God wanted.

What about us?

The principle we have identified is this: discerning what God wants comes out of relationship with him in prayer. In prayer we are able to enjoy God and listen to God. That's how Jesus did it! That's how others in both Old and New Testaments did it!

But what about us? Can we really expect to enjoy such sharing of information? Isn't this first-division spirituality and therefore not for us? No! This is for all God's children. And it is the Holy Spirit who helps us to discover it for real.

The gift of God himself!

Paul understood this and he explained it to the Christians in the church at Corinth:

> The Spirit searches all things, even the deep things of God. For who knows a person's thoughts except their own spirit within them? In the same way no one knows the thoughts of God except the Spirit of God. What we have received is not the spirit of the world, but the Spirit who is from God, so that we may understand what God has freely given us (1 Corinthians 2:10–12).

In order to explain the work of the Spirit, Paul here uses the example of the human spirit. My spirit understands me completely, what I think, feel, hope, want—it knows how I tick! Similarly, says Paul, God's Spirit understands God completely, what he thinks, feels, hopes, wants—he knows how God ticks! (vv. 10–11).

Having said that, Paul then makes an amazing statement: we have received the Spirit who is from God (or "out of", the Greek word here is "*ek*") (v. 12). In other words, the Spirit who understands God completely is in me, and you—and in every child of God.

Here is our potential as children of God, that by the Spirit within us we can know what God thinks, feels, hopes and wants. It's as simple as that—but it's mind-blowing too!

The Father's promise

Just in case you are still not quite convinced that this includes you, remember that the gift of the Spirit is the gift of the Father for his children. Jesus called the gift of the Spirit "what my Father has promised" (Luke 24:49), and Peter reminded his hearers on the day of Pentecost that "The promise is for you and your children and for all who are far off—for all whom the Lord our God will call" (Acts 2:39). That means it's for you!

Also, when Jesus was encouraging his disciples to look forward to the coming of the Spirit, he said to them: "And I will ask the Father, and he will give you another advocate to help you and be with you for ever—the Spirit of truth" (John 14:16–17).

Notice, the Father will give the Holy Spirit—it's his gift for his children. What is more, all we have to do to receive this gift is to ask him for it. Jesus put it this way: "If you then, though you are evil, know how to give good gifts to your children, how much more will your Father in heaven give the Holy Spirit to those who ask him!" (Luke 11:13).

Have you ever asked the Father for the gift he has promised you? If not, why not pause right now and ask him?

It's all there!

We have enormous potential as God's children: not just the privilege of intimate relationship with him, but the possibility of knowing what is on his heart and mind, just as Jesus did: to be able to do what the Father is doing and to say what the Father is saying, just as Jesus did.

The potential is there; what we need to do is learn to tap it. That was certainly Paul's prayer for the Christians he wrote to: "I keep asking that the God of our Lord Jesus Christ, the glorious Father, may give you the Spirit of wisdom and revelation, so that you may know him better" (Ephesians 1:17). Again, "For this reason . . . we have not stopped praying for you. We continually ask God to fill you with the knowledge of his will through all the wisdom and understanding that the Spirit gives" (Colossians 1:9). And I don't think that Paul was in the habit of praying for things he didn't believe were possible. What was possible for first-century Christians is also possible for us, through the gift of the same Spirit.

Here is potential for each individual child of God to be effective for him: effective because he (or she) is sure about their relationship with God and is secure in him; effective because they have discovered the vast resources available to them from God through the Spirit; effective in living for God, effective in talking to others about God—in short, effective in mission, able to go and call others to be disciples.

Here, too, is potential for the Church of God and every local branch of it. What a difference it would make if we knew how to pray together in the way we have seen in this chapter! What if this kind of prayer were to become a central part of the meetings of church council, deacons or elders?

In churches where I have been in ministry, we have tried to take this seriously, spending time in our council meetings in prayer, often breaking off in the middle of our discussion to pray, asking God to show us what he is doing so that we can make the right decision. As we continue to do this, I think we shall find our agendas being changed and our priorities being adjusted as we discern what God wants to do. There will be adjustments in our evangelism as we begin to discover exactly where God wants us to go, and what he wants us to say when we get there. Our pastoral relationships will benefit, too, as we realize that God is able to tell us things about the person we are trying to help, things we would not know naturally.

More about these things later. For now, the truth we need to grasp is this: when Jesus said: "As the Father has sent me, so I am sending you", he intended that we should go knowing exactly what the Father wants and doing only what we see him doing—as Jesus did. And we pass this ability on to others as we call them to become disciples too.

3

Sent . . . In Love

"But why did he do it?" That is the question we may be prompted to ask when someone behaves in a strange way or does something unexpected— we want to know why. It's a question we might well ask of God too, with proper respect, of course!

Questions!

Why, for example, did God create us in the first place? Is it possible that he was somehow incomplete or unfulfilled without us? Did he need us?

Why did he specially adopt the nation Israel? (Or, as a certain W. N. Ewer has expressed it: "How odd of God to choose the Jews!") Reading the Old Testament you could be forgiven for gaining the impression that Israel was the most important nation, that world affairs revolved around her. But dipping into ancient history just a little shows that impression to be false: Israel was, in fact, pretty insignificant as far as world history was concerned, and scarcely appears in the records. So why did God choose Israel?

And when the people of Israel turned out to be so wayward and rebellious (the Old Testament makes no secret of their failings), why did God stick with them? Why did he not give them up as a bad job and find others who would be more responsive and reliable?

And why did God send Jesus into this world? More than that, having sent him, why did he allow him to be treated in the way he was and, in the end, let him die on a cross? Why did he do it?

Answers!

The answer to all these questions (or, at least, the beginning of an answer) can be summed up in one word: love.

Of our creation by God originally, Paul writes: "For he chose us in [Christ] before the creation of the world to be holy and blameless in his sight. In love he predestined us for adoption to sonship through Jesus Christ . . . " (Ephesians 1:4–5). He loved us: that's why he made us!

As for his choice of the nation Israel, God explains through Moses just why he did it:

> The LORD did not set his affection on you and choose you because you were more numerous than other peoples, for you were the fewest of all peoples. But it was because the LORD loved you and kept the oath he swore to your ancestors that he brought you out with a mighty hand and redeemed you . . . (Deuteronomy 7:7–8).

He loved them: that's why he chose them!

Through the prophet Hosea, God revealed why he could not give up the people he had chosen despite their waywardness. The eleventh chapter of Hosea offers us a marvellous glimpse of the heart of God, loving those whom he had chosen even though they continually refused and rebelled: here is the frustration and sadness of unrequited love. No one would have blamed him if he had given them up, but he couldn't do it: "How can I give you up, Israel? How can I abandon you? . . . My heart will not let me do it! My love for you is too strong" (Hosea 11:8, GNB). He loved them: that's why he didn't give them up!

And God sending Jesus is explained this way: "For God so loved the world that he gave his one and only Son" (John 3:16). More than that, "God demonstrates his own love for us in this: while we were still sinners, Christ died for us" (Romans 5:8). God loved us: that's why he sent Jesus; that's why Jesus died!

Here is an underlying, consistent theme throughout the Bible, Old and New Testaments alike. It is the heart-cry of God for his people: "I love you." Love explains all that God does, love is always his motive. But then that should be no surprise, for the Bible tells us: "God is love" (1 John 4:8,16).

"God is love"

This is one of the most fundamental statements about God in the whole of the Bible: it is central, crucial and foundational to any true understanding of God. If you will forgive a slightly crude analogy, it is as basic as saying "water is wet". Just as wetness is the very essence of water, so love is the very essence of God; just as wetness goes where water goes, so love is where God is. The whole of God's character is summed up in this simple yet profound truth. And New Testament scholars agree: "We should not regard love as simply one of the attributes of God among a list of others. It is the very central thing. Without it God would not be God—God is Love."[1] "To say that 'God is love' implies all his activity. If he creates, he creates in love; if he rules, he rules in love; if he judges, he judges in love. All that he does is the expression of his nature, which is—to love."[2]

Love in action

Despite such persuasive talk about God's love, some people may remain unconvinced. They may be tempted to challenge God: "If all this is true, prove it—show us!" And that is just what God has done: as if to forestall this challenge from the sceptics, he hasn't said it, he has demonstrated it—in Jesus.

John, in the introduction to his Gospel, writes: "No-one has ever seen God, but the one and only Son, who is himself God and is in the closest relationship with the Father, has made him known" (John 1:18). Later, John records the disciple Philip asking: "Lord, show us the Father and that will be enough for us" (John 14:8)—he wanted to know what God was like. Jesus replied: "Anyone who has seen me has seen the Father. How can you say, 'Show us the Father?' Don't you believe that I am in the Father, and that the Father is in me?" (John 14:9–10). If we want to know what God is like, if we want to understand what his love is like, we need look no further than Jesus: in Jesus God became man and lived on

---

[1] Leon Morris, "Love, Christian Style", an address quoted in Michael Harper, *The Love Affair* (London: Hodder & Stoughton, 1982), p. 67.

[2] C. H Dodd, *The Johannine Epistles* (London: Hodder & Stoughton, 1982), pp. 1–10.

earth; in Jesus God's love was translated into human life. So let's take a look—what is God's love like?

Everyone is "in"

Have you ever noticed how we naturally spend time with people we like, those who are like us, with whom we get on easily, but we have to make an effort to be with those with whom we don't naturally relate? We categorize people, albeit unconsciously: some are "in" and some are "out".

This behaviour was common in Jesus' day too. Even religious people did it, and the religious leaders were the experts. Because of their understanding of God's law, and all the petty rules and regulations they had introduced supposedly based on it, they had very definite categories of people—some were "in" and some were "out". For example, Jews were "in", non-Jews were "out"; men were "in", women were "out"; healthy people were "in", unhealthy people (like lepers) were out; good-living people were "in", those with dodgy morals were "out"—and so on.

Against this background, Jesus was vastly and noticeably different: he apparently had no time for such petty divisions and categories. His love was big enough for all: everyone was "in"; no one was "out".

The Samaritan woman

Jesus had been travelling with the disciples (John 4). They stopped to rest, and the disciples went off to the nearby village to get some food, leaving Jesus resting by a well. A woman came to draw water and Jesus engaged her in conversation. That may not seem anything very noteworthy to us, but in Jesus' social environment it was outrageous—that's why the disciples expressed surprise when they returned from shopping (v. 27). There were at least three very good reasons why Jesus should have had nothing to do with this woman. First, he was a Jew and she was a Samaritan. For generations, Jews and Samaritans had hated each other and would have no social contact with each other whatsoever. That's why the woman was surprised that Jesus actually spoke to her (v. 9).

Second, he was a Rabbi, a Jewish teacher, and she was a woman. Any self-respecting Jewish teacher would not talk to any woman in public, not even his own wife! If he was seen doing so, it would be the end of his reputation. In fact, some of the Pharisees, who were particularly strict about these things, were called "bruised and bleeding", because they would close their eyes rather than risk looking at a woman in public and as a result walked into things!

Third, he was a religious man and she was a woman of questionable morals. He ought to have avoided her completely—she was definitely "out".

So there was great social pressure stacked against Jesus, urging him not to have any contact with her; anything that could override such pressure and allow him to talk with her had to be powerful. And it was: he loved her. It didn't matter to him who she was or what she had done: he loved her and wanted to help her, which he proceeded to do. As far as Jesus was concerned, she was "in".

And the blind beggar

Jesus was visiting Jericho and had gathered a crowd as usual (Mark 10:46–52). A blind man was begging at the roadside. He heard the commotion and, learning that it was Jesus, cried out: "Jesus, Son of David, have mercy on me!" The reaction of the crowd was predictable; as far as they were concerned, he was "out", so they told him to shut up and kicked him back in the gutter. But he didn't give up that easily and continued to cry out. Jesus stopped and called him. He didn't need calling twice; Mark vividly tells us that "throwing his cloak aside, he jumped to his feet and came to Jesus" (v. 50).

There follows one of the most poignant moments in the whole of the Gospels: there, in the streets of Jericho, in full view of the heckling crowd, Jesus, the Son of God, asked a blind beggar: "What do you want me to do for you?" (v. 51). He asked for his sight and was healed.

But why is Jesus' attitude to him so different to that of the crowd? Why was Jesus willing to do anything for him when the crowd would do nothing for him? He loved him—as far as Jesus was concerned, he was "in".

And the leper

If Jesus' contemporaries had further categorized the "outs", then lepers would have been in the first division. If unhealthy people generally were out, lepers were "right out"—such was the fear of this particular disease, such was the stigma attached to it, that lepers were separated from the community, forced to live together apart from others. No healthy person would have any contact with them whatsoever.

It must have taken courage on the part of the leper to approach Jesus at all (Mark 1:40–5). He came, knelt down and begged Jesus to heal him: "If you are willing, you can make me clean" (v. 40). Jesus' response must have thrilled him: others avoided him, but Jesus didn't; most would have ignored him, but Jesus looked at him and answered him. More than that, Jesus actually touched him—he probably hadn't been touched by another person for a long time. "I am willing," Jesus said. "Be clean!"—and he was healed (vv. 41–2). But why was Jesus willing when others were unwilling? Mark tells us: Jesus was "filled with compassion" (v. 41). He loved him—he was "in".

Even the tax collector

Tax collectors were "out" for very different reasons. To begin with, they worked for the occupying power, the Romans, so they were seen as traitors. More than that, they were poorly paid; so they would extract from their clients more than the official amount (as much as they could) and pocket the difference—so they were cheats and thieves too. You may not be too fond of today's taxman; in Jesus' day they were hated—they were definitely "out".

It was, therefore, a frequent complaint of the religious leaders that Jesus spent time with such people. Did he not realize they were "out", lumped together with sinners and written off? What was worse, Jesus didn't just talk to them, but went to their homes and ate with them—at least, we know he went to the homes of Matthew and Zacchaeus, who were both tax-collectors (Matthew 9:10 and Luke 19:5–6)—and that was a sign of acceptance and friendship. Others despised and rejected them, Jesus loved and accepted them—they were "in".

Such selfless love

Jesus' love was big enough to embrace everyone—no one was "out"; it was also an utterly selfless love.

So much human love has strings attached: we love to achieve something, to get something in return, even if it is only the love of the one we love. Not so with Jesus. He loves for loving's sake, for him it is an end in itself, not a means to an end. "If you love those who love you," he said, "what credit is that to you? Even sinners love those who love them" (Luke 6:32).

Our love is often qualified, offered when it is convenient to us. As a husband and father, I have to admit, to my shame, that sometimes I love only when it is convenient to me—or rather, I don't offer love if it happens to be inconvenient.

Jesus was different: he loved, convenient or inconvenient. He offered love to children who were brought to him, even though it was apparently inconvenient for his disciples and they tried to send them away (Mark 10:13–16). He loved people enough to want to provide for their physical needs despite the inconvenience of the time and place—and the fact that there were five thousand of them! The disciples were all too aware of the inconvenience and urged Jesus to send them away to get something to eat. Jesus, however, told them to feed the crowd (Mark 6:35–7). Mind you, we can sympathize with the disciples: they had been so busy that they had not eaten themselves, and when Jesus did take them away to have a break, the crowds followed and they never got it (Mark 6:30–4). Note the contrast: the disciples were motivated by the inconvenience of the situation—they were selfish. Jesus was motivated by love, despite the inconvenience—he was selfless. Some years ago, a friend of ours was suffering with back trouble. She was admitted to hospital for treatment. Opposite her on the ward were a number of elderly ladies, some of whom were dying. Although in great pain herself, she was to be found at night sitting holding the hands of her dying fellow patients. That's selfless love, Jesus-style.

Such giving love

Human nature doesn't change: in Jesus' day and in our day alike, actions are often from mixed motives. "What's in it for me?" is a powerful factor; the selfish instinct is so strong. Jesus' disciples were no different. James and John, for example, on one occasion, asked for the best seats in heaven (Mark 10:35–40); and Peter, on another occasion, said indignantly to Jesus: "We have left everything to follow you! What then will there be for us?" (Matthew 19:27). And what about Judas? Was it when he realized there wasn't anything for him in following Jesus that he plotted to betray him for money?

The disciples didn't realize at that stage that in Jesus they were dealing with someone totally committed to loving unconditionally and therefore to giving "without counting the cost". Jesus had already let go of the perks of being God to become man, he had already given up the glory of heaven to live on earth (Philippians 2:6). His Father God had given him to the world freely out of love (John 3:16); he could do nothing else but give, give, and give again—and he would go on giving even if no one ever gave him anything. Such giving love!

Such costly love

A commitment like that it is bound to be costly. Too often we try to get away with "cheap" love, love that doesn't cost too much. Not so with Jesus. It doesn't cost much to love "nice" people; but what about blind beggars, untouchable lepers and immoral women—or today's equivalents? Those are the kind of people Jesus loved, and he invites us to love them too, to count them "in". Who might they be for us?

It's comfortable doing loving things for those who will probably return the favour one day; it's another thing to offer love to those who are unlikely ever to be able to return the favour. But that's what Jesus did, and he asks us to do the same: "If you do good to those who do good to you, what credit is that to you?" (Luke 6:33).

It's easy to love our friends; what about our enemies? "Love your enemies," said Jesus, "do good to them, and lend to them without expecting to get anything back" (Luke 6:35)—and he did just that!

There's no problem loving those who are with you and support you; but what about when they turn against you and betray you? Do you still love them then? Jesus did. His attitude to Judas at the Last Supper demonstrates that: Jesus spoke to Judas with tenderness even as he left the room to betray him (John 13:21–30; Matthew 26:20–5).

It's a pleasure to love those who applaud and affirm you; but what do you do when a friend and supporter, under pressure, denies they ever knew you—like Peter did to Jesus?

Do you still love then? Jesus did. There is that poignant moment during Jesus' trial when, immediately following Peter's denial, Jesus turned and looked straight at Peter—surely a look of love (Luke 22:61). Later, after his resurrection, Jesus reinstated Peter, calling him again to follow him (John 21:15–24). To love like that hurts—it's costly!

Such total love

In the end, of course, it cost Jesus his life: he gave everything because he loved. "Greater love has no one than this," said Jesus, "to lay down one's life for one's friends" (John 15:13). That's incredible enough! But Paul, reflecting on this truth later, realized the greater wonder still, that we were not exactly friends when Jesus died for us:

> . . . Christ died for the ungodly. Very rarely will anyone die for a righteous person, though for a good person someone might possibly dare to die. But God demonstrates his own love for us in this: while we were still sinners, Christ died for us (Romans 5:6–8).

There is no greater love than this: broad enough to count everybody "in"; utterly selfless, putting others first; always giving, never counting the cost; dying for those he loved. Total love!

From the heart!

As Jesus models this total love for us, he is in effect saying: "This is what God is like! This is what his love is like!" This is the love that moved him to send Jesus; this is the love that motivated Jesus as he carried out his Father's mission—it underlay every action, permeated every word. The same is true whether Jesus was dealing with needy individuals or aimless crowds.

When the leper asked Jesus to heal him, Jesus responded because he was "indignant" or "filled with compassion" (Mark 1:41). When he met the widow at Nain on her way to bury her son, "[Jesus'] heart went out to her" and he brought the young man back to life (Luke 7:11–17). When the blind men asked Jesus to heal them, we are told that "Jesus had compassion on them and touched their eyes"—they were healed (Matthew 20:34).

Jesus' reaction to crowds was similar. For example, "when he saw the crowds, he had compassion on them, because they were harassed and helpless, like sheep without a shepherd" (Matthew 9:36). Again "when Jesus landed and saw a large crowd, he had compassion on them and healed those who were ill" (Matthew 14:14). On another occasion, surrounded by great crowds, he said to his disciples: "I have compassion for these people; they have already been with me three days and have nothing to eat. I do not want to send them away hungry, or they may collapse on the way" (Matthew 15:32).

Behind each of these references in the original Greek there is a marvellous-sounding word: *splagchnizomai*. (Try saying it—it sounds great!) The root meaning of this word is "inward parts" or even "entrails". The love and compassion of Jesus for people came from the heart of his being—earlier generations would have said "from his bowels"! As Jesus himself said, "the mouth speaks what the heart is full of" (Matthew 12:34)—and we could add "and the hand acts". The words and actions of Jesus really were "heart-felt".

An important principle

In all this, we see a third all-important principle for mission. The first was: mission begins in relationship with God. The second was: within that relationship we discover what the Father wants us to do. The third is this: the Father's love must motivate our mission. That's how God did it; that's how Jesus did it; that's how we must do it. When Jesus said: "As the Father has sent me, I am sending you"; he was sending his followers in love just as his Father had sent him in love.

Mission that begins with anything other than love will be hard, formal and impersonal—and probably unfruitful too. It must be love that sends us, not just the response to Jesus' command to go! Love must precede mission.

The story is told of a man who became a Christian and then tried all kinds of ways to bring his wife to faith too, without success. Eventually she challenged him: "Do you love me because you want to convert me, or do you want to convert me because you love me?" Those are two very different attitudes: the first, if we are honest, is true of much of our mission; the second is true of Jesus—always! It needs to be true for us too. But how?

Loved by God

If we are daunted by this prerequisite of love, then we need to grasp, and be grabbed by, three great biblical truths. The first is this: God loved us first! In his first epistle, John writes: "This is love: not that we loved God, but that he loved us and sent his Son as an atoning sacrifice for our sins . . . We love because he first loved us" (1 John 4:10,19). Here is a simple but profound truth: we can love because we are loved.

Have you noticed how many hard, unloving people there are around? Have you ever wondered why? Time and again, in counselling people, the answer is clear: they don't know how to love because they have never really been loved. If a person has never been sat on a parent's knee and cuddled, if they have never heard the words "I love you", or they have heard them only from someone who has subsequently hurt them, then they will find it extraordinarily difficult to love, however much they want to.

What is true humanly is also true spiritually. So many Christians are not quite sure God loves them, they don't feel worthy of his love, they don't consider they have earned his love, they certainly don't feel his love. The truth is, none of us is worthy, none of us has earned it, and yet God does love us and he has proved it in Jesus. As that truth begins to dawn on us and we begin to know it is true, we will find ourselves released to love others. As John says: "We love because he first loved us" (1 John 4:19).

A wise spiritual counsellor was asked: "How can I love more?" He replied: "Let God love you more!" What a good answer. We need to let God love us more, to open ourselves up in prayer to receive God's love. The American writer, Philip Yancey, emphasizes this truth: "There is nothing we can do to make God love us more . . . and there is nothing we can do to make God love us less."[3]

---

[3]   Philip Yancey, *Where is God When It Hurts?* (Grand Rapids, MI: Zondervan, 1997), p. 70.

Some years ago, several members of the church where I was then the vicar went away for a conference. As well as the teaching, there was plenty of opportunity to wait on God in prayer, to invite him to come, to receive from him. One of the members, Rod, met with God several times during that conference; in particular, he was overwhelmed with the reality of God's love for him and for everyone. He came back more sure of God's love than ever before, with a broad grin on his face and a desire to tell others "Jesus loves you"—and those on the receiving end recognized the sincerity of it. What is even more significant is that during that same conference God called Rod to a ministry of evangelism among us.

Here is the principle in action: mission must begin in love. As Rod is involved in mission, he will be moved by love, having himself been moved by God's love for him. Remember, if you want to love more, let God love you more!

Grabbed by the cross

If it was John who grasped this first great truth about love, that God loved us first, then it is Paul who grasped the second. He expressed it like this: "For Christ's love compels us, because we are convinced that one died for all, and therefore all died" (2 Corinthians 5:14)—or as the New English Bible puts it: "For the love of Christ leaves us no choice . . .". "Compelled", "left no choice" by Christ's love-strong words! What is Paul saying? The Greek word here, *sunechei*, is a fascinating word with a number of different meanings which help us to understand what Paul is saying. It is used, for example, of a city being besieged, "[they will] hem you in on every side" (Luke 19:43); it can mean "guarded" or "held fast", as Jesus was at his trial (Luke 22:63); it describes the people around Jesus, "crowding him" or "pressing upon him" (Luke 8:45); it is used of someone "suffering from" or "afflicted by" a disease (Luke 4:38). It is a word which suggests constraint, a pressure to be or to do a particular thing. Most interesting of all are Jesus' own words about his mission: the same word appears. "I have a baptism to undergo, and what constraint I am under until it is completed!" (Luke 12:50).

Jesus knew he had a job to do, a mission to fulfil given him by his Father; he felt constrained, compelled to complete it. Paul experienced a similar compulsion. David Watson puts it like this:

Here Jesus felt a powerful motivating force urging him towards the cross. He had to go that way; he had to finish the work. Paul knew something of this compulsion too. The love of Christ pressed gently but firmly upon him; he felt surrounded and hemmed in by this love, as it constrained him in one clear direction. No matter what apathy or opposition he found, no matter how tiring or painful the work might be, "the love of Christ leaves us no choice."[4]

Paul was convinced that Jesus had died for everyone (2 Corinthians 5:14); what is more, "he died for all, that those who live should no longer live for themselves but for him who died for them and was raised again" (2 Corinthians 5:15).

And this was not just theology Paul was writing, this was not a nice theory: this was truth, reality—he knew it for himself. Writing to the Christians in Galatia, in the midst of a complicated theological passage (there are a few of them in Paul's writing!), Paul includes this simple word of personal testimony: "I have been crucified with Christ and I no longer live, but Christ lives in me. The life I now live in the body, I live by faith in the Son of God, who loved me and gave himself for me" (Galatians 2:20). No wonder Paul felt compelled by Christ's love! This personal experience of the love of Christ shown in the cross is crucial: it's where the desire to be involved in mission is kindled. Clearly that was so for Paul. It has also been so for me; it began when, at the age of 17, I realized that God loved me and Jesus died for me.

Let the cross of Christ grab you!

Filled with the Spirit

"God loved us first", "the love of Christ compels us". Even when we begin to grasp these two great truths, we may well ask: "How can I love like that?"

A third truth offers us hope: "God's love has been poured out into our hearts through the Holy Spirit, who has been given to us" (Romans 5:5).

---

[4] D. C. K. Watson, *I Believe in Evangelism* (London: Hodder & Stoughton, 1976), p. 91.

Here again is the crucial role of the Holy Spirit in mission. As we have already seen, these mission principles we have identified are not meant to be true just in theory but in practice too; it is the desire of the Spirit to make them work for us and in us. It is the Spirit, Paul explains, who brings to us God's love; indeed, to use Paul's extravagant language, he causes God's love to be poured out into us. The love that God is, the love which Jesus modelled throughout his life and supremely in his death, is made available to us in full measure.

If the Father's love must motivate our mission, this is where it begins to happen: when the Holy Spirit fills our hearts with God's love. That's what happened for the first Christians on the Day of Pentecost: they were filled with the love of God as they were filled with the Spirit (Acts 2:4). That's why they didn't give up talking about Jesus when they were opposed by the people and threatened by the authorities: the love of Christ compelled them, the Father's love filled them. That's why Peter could reply to those who threatened him: "We cannot help speaking about what we have seen and heard" (Acts 4:20).

I still remember the first time I was aware of the Father's love within me. I was a student in York and stopped to talk to a young woman who was selling a revolutionary newspaper in the street. I enquired about her political views and asked her whether she would be prepared to kill to achieve them. When she answered "Yes", I was horrified; but I was also aware of a great love welling up within me for her. At that moment, I believe, I was experiencing God's love poured out in my heart; I knew something of Jesus' compassion for one person who was "lost". On numerous occasions since then I have had similar experiences, even finding myself weeping over people, God's tears of compassion for those he loves so much.

The Spirit resources us with the Father's love so that we can move out in love to tell others the good news of Jesus. No wonder we are urged to go on being filled with the Spirit (Ephesians 5:18); there needs to be a daily, refreshing experience of the Spirit in our hearts if we would be effective in mission.

The way of love—a warning!

If love is our motive, the way of Jesus our model, then there are things we need to realize as we embark on mission.

Love never forces. Because we operate in love, we shall never be able to force anyone to accept Christ and enter his kingdom. Love offers and waits to be accepted. That's how Jesus did it, and that's how we must do it.

Love always respects. Whoever we reach out to in love is an individual created by God, loved by God. Love will never violate that but will always respect the other person. That's how Jesus did it—even with Judas, and that's how we must do it.

Love never condemns. Whatever reaction we may get, whatever is done to us as a result of our involvement in mission, we must never write off the other person or condemn them. Pilate washed his hands of Jesus, but Jesus washed his hands of no one, not even Peter. That's how Jesus did it, and that's how we must do it.

Love risks rejection. Hardest of all, perhaps, is the risky element of getting involved in Jesus' mission. We can speak and act in love, making an offer in the name of Jesus, but there has to be the freedom for the other person to refuse. That's the way of love. That's the way Jesus did it—and the rich young ruler walked away sad (Mark 10:17–23). That's the way we must do it.

That's the way!

When Jesus said: "As the Father has sent me, I am sending you", he was sending his disciples out into mission in love, to love all to whom they reached out. As his Father loved him and motivated him through love, so they would enjoy the Father's love poured out into their hearts. And so will we as we invite others to be disciples.

4

Sent . . . Into the World

I was working at my desk. It was just before Christmas and I was preparing a sermon on a suitable pre-Christmas theme. As I was thinking, half-praying, some striking words came into my mind. I didn't remember ever reading them or hearing them before: I think they came from God. They certainly made me think and I have often reflected on them since. They went something like this: "It was easy for Jesus to be Son of God in heaven—love, unity and no opposition. The trouble started for him when he came into the world—there he was opposed, hurt, abused and crucified."

God became human

The incarnation lies at the heart of Christianity and therefore at the heart of Christian mission. But what does that mean? What is the "incarnation"? For many, even within the church, it will be little more than a bit of theological jargon. Some will be familiar with the word, if only because they are Anglicans and say in the Creed at Communion: ". . . [Jesus] was incarnate from the Holy Spirit and the Virgin Mary." But how many Christians are able to explain what it means or appreciate its significance?

The incarnation is that mystery (and by "mystery" I mean, whatever others may mean, something which we accept as true without fully understanding it) which we remember and celebrate at Christmas each year: it has to do with the birth of Jesus.

If you look up "incarnation" in a dictionary, you will find a definition of "embodiment in flesh". For Christians, therefore, incarnation is about

God being embodied in human flesh, God becoming a man, in Jesus. That is what John says in the opening verses of his Gospel, verses often read at carol services. Verse 14 sums it up: "The Word became flesh and made his dwelling among us . . . " Paul put it like this: "For in Christ all the fullness of the Deity lives in bodily form" (Colossians 2:9). And the writer of Hebrews says: " . . . in these last days [God] has spoken to us by his Son, whom he appointed heir of all things, and through whom he made the universe. The Son is the radiance of God's glory and the exact representation of his being . . . " (Hebrews 1:2–3).

These are all different ways of saying the same thing; the Message version of the Bible puts it simply and strikingly: "The Word became flesh and blood, and moved into the neighbourhood" (John l:14)—that's the wonder of Christmas, that's incarnation!

But why is it so significant? You and I are human beings living on Planet Earth (at least I am—I assume you are!). The incarnation tells us that God became a human being and lived on Planet Earth. If that is true, then it has to be significant for us; indeed, there can scarcely be anything more significant. That is why Jesus is so important—he is God become one of us.

The God-Man

The belief that Jesus is both fully God and fully human is central to the Christian faith, and unique among world religions. Both Matthew and Luke, in telling the story of Jesus' birth, are careful to explain that although Mary was Jesus' mother, God, through the working of his Holy Spirit, was his father. Matthew records the angel reassuring Joseph: " . . . what is conceived in her is from the Holy Spirit" (Matthew 1:20). Luke describes how Mary asked the angel how she could possibly conceive a child since she was still a virgin, to which the angel replied: "The Holy Spirit will come on you, and the power of the Most High will overshadow you. So the holy one to be born will be called the Son of God" (Luke 1:34–5).

And this emphasis is reflected in the Creeds too; for example, in the Nicene Creed we say of Jesus that he is "true God from true God" and "he was made man".

Down the years this belief has been challenged in various ways. There have been those who have questioned whether Jesus was God.

For example, some have believed that Jesus was really the son of Joseph and Mary, and that divine attributes were given to him at his baptism, when the Holy Spirit came on him. Those who believe this are usually called "adoptionist". Others, like the Gnostics who came into prominence in the latter part of the first century AD, doubted whether Jesus was fully human, usually because they couldn't accept that God can get involved with sinful human things. So for them, Jesus neither was fully human, nor did he really die.

Many sects and groups have arisen during the 2000 years of Christian history with incomplete understandings of Jesus: incomplete, that is, compared to the orthodox Christian view that he was both fully God and fully human. Today, two such prominent groups are Jehovah's Witnesses and Mormons. Jehovah's Witnesses speak of Jesus as divine but deny that he was God; thus, they have no room for the incarnation. Mormons believe that Jesus is no more divine than any other human person: he is in no sense unique.

Even mainstream Christianity is not immune from alternate views about the Incarnation: over the years numerous Church leaders and theologians, including bishops, have expressed doubt about this central strand in Christian doctrine, but the Church has usually closed ranks and found a compromise along the lines of accepting the theological meaning of the virgin birth, but not necessarily accepting it as proven historical fact.

We may well ask: does it matter? Is it worth arguing about? I believe it is, for if the incarnation is not true, then the wonder has gone not only out of Christmas, but out of the Christian gospel—indeed, the heart has been cut out of Christianity. Because of the incarnation, we have an amazing message to pass on, a wonder-full truth to share with our fellow human beings: that God, in order to fulfil his mission to humankind, became involved with them, became one of them—he became a human being and lived among them.

And how is this relevant to mission? The incarnation is not only the heart of the message we have to preach; it also offers us a model for mission: to carry out his mission God sent Jesus as a human being living in the world. When Jesus says to us: "As the Father has sent me, I am sending you", he is sending us into mission in the same way—as human beings in the world.

A real man!

Jesus was a human being—a real man! The writers of the New Testament do their best to communicate that. The trouble is: ecclesiastical art and stained-glass windows have not helped us. How many of us, if we have any visual impression of Jesus at all, think of him as a fresh-complexioned young man, perhaps with blue eyes, even with a halo round his head?

I suspect the reality was rather different. He was a Jew and probably looked like most other Middle Eastern men in the first century AD; he was a carpenter and therefore his hands, rather than being "soft as your face" (having done the washing-up with the best washing-up liquid!) were presumably hard, damaged and even a little dirty; rather than fresh-complexioned, his outdoor life may well have given him a weather-beaten appearance, and it's quite likely that he had a beard (he may have had hairs on his chest too for all we know!).

The point I am making is this: when God became a human being, he became a real man that other men would respect and relate to, rather than writing him off as different and even soft. Wasn't that part of his attraction: other human beings found him real, open, approachable—human? He was good to know.

Born like a human being

There are a number of ways in which Jesus' humanity is shown. To begin with, he was born just like any other human being. His conception may have been unusual, a miraculous act of God, but there was nothing unusual or miraculous about his birth—except, perhaps, that his first bed was a manger in a stable. He fully experienced being born. Psychologists and counsellors today are very aware how significant are the nine months in the womb and the circumstances of our birth: that we can be damaged while still in the womb or during the birth process. We hear about babies being born with withdrawal symptoms because their mothers were taking drugs; we know, too, how a difficult birth can harm a child, the effects of which may emerge only much later. In other words, right from conception, through development in the womb and birth, there is an element of risk; but it's all part of the human experience.

Jesus has experienced it—he can say: "I know what it's like."

Grew like a human being

Although we know very little about Jesus' early years, we do know that he grew up in a family like most other human beings. He had to learn to walk and talk like the rest of us, to dress himself, brush his teeth and comb his hair (or whatever they did in those days!). Luke tells us that Jesus "grew and became strong" (Luke 2:40). Luke also tells us a little of his religious upbringing, in particular of his visit to Jerusalem for the Feast of the Passover when he was 12 (Luke 2:41–50), when he took the opportunity to sit and listen to the religious teachers, impressing them with his knowledge. The remainder of his early years Luke sums up like this: "And Jesus grew in wisdom and stature, and in favour with God and man" (Luke 2:52).

We also know that he had brothers and sisters (Matthew 13:55–6), that his human father, Joseph, was a carpenter and that, according to the custom of the day, Jesus probably learned the family trade. Jesus had an upbringing very similar to that of any other man: he knew what it was to grow up as part of a family, to be obedient to parents, to relate to brothers and sisters and to learn a trade. Indeed, his upbringing was so ordinary that when he started saying and doing amazing things in his own hometown, the people who knew him and had seen him grow up were puzzled:

> "Where did this man get this wisdom and these miraculous powers?" they asked. "Isn't this the carpenter's son? Isn't his mother's name Mary, and aren't his brothers James, Joseph, Simon and Judas? Aren't all his sisters with us? Where then did this man get all these things?" (Matthew 13:54–6).

Jesus experienced all the struggles and strains of growing up from childhood to adulthood like anyone else—he can say, "I know what it's like."

Felt like a human being

Jesus knew the whole range of human experience at first hand. For example, he loved going with others to celebrate such happy events as weddings (John 2:1–11); he appreciated having a place where he could relax with friends and be himself, such as the home of Mary and Martha (Luke 10:38–42; John 12:1–3; Matthew 21:17); he knew the pain and sadness of losing a dear friend and weeping with the family (John 11). He also experienced all the normal physical human feelings of tiredness (Mark 4:38), thirst (John 4:7), and hunger (Mark 6:31). He knew, too, how much other people can be hurtful; he had to cope with the misunderstanding of his family, who even thought him mad (Mark 3:21); with the constant and increasing harassment of other religious leaders, those who ought to have known better; with the treachery of one of his followers, Judas, and the failure of an even closer friend, Peter. And there was the harsh treatment from those who arrested him, accused him, condemned him, whipped him, executed him, and all the physical pain that went with it.

"He doesn't know what it's like!" is the accusation that some who have a hard life fling at Jesus. But he does! Jesus has known at first hand every kind of human experience; he has plumbed the depths of human suffering.

Tempted like a human being

Another insight into Jesus' humanity is offered us by the writer of Hebrews. He tells us that in Jesus "we have one who has been tempted in every way, just as we are—yet he did not sin" (Hebrews 4:15). We are all surrounded by temptation, under pressure to do wrong. Jesus was no exception: there is nothing we experience by way of temptation that Jesus hasn't also handled.

In fact, Jesus has been tempted more than any of us. Does that seem a strange thing to say? William Barclay explains it like this:

> Think of it in terms of pain. There is a degree of pain which the human frame can stand—and then when that degree is reached a person faints and loses consciousness; he has reached his limit. There are agonies of pain he does not know, because there came

collapse. It is so with temptation. We collapse before temptation; but Jesus went to our stage of temptation and far beyond it and still did not collapse. It is true to say that He was tempted in all things as we are; but it is also true to say that never was man tempted as He was.[1]

Coping with temptation is an integral part of being human in this world, and Jesus did it successfully.

Died like a human being

The ultimate human experience is death, and Jesus experienced that too. His death was as real and total as everyone's, and more painful than most. John, in his Gospel, adds a detail about the crucifixion which confirms Jesus' death: he tells us that when a soldier stuck a spear in Jesus' side, his blood was already beginning to separate (John 19:34)—with his limited medical knowledge John actually described it as blood and water. It was only when Pilate was satisfied that Jesus really was dead that he gave permission for his body to be buried (Mark 15:43–5). Dead and buried: that was Jesus, the man!

Fully human

The New Testament makes it clear: Jesus was fully human, born like a man, grew up like a man, felt like a man, was tempted like a man, died like a man. And that, incidentally, is why he prayed.

I have often been asked: "If Jesus was God, why did he pray? Did he talk to himself?" Jesus prayed not because he was God but because he was human. Like the rest of us he had to learn how to live human life in contact with God, communicating with God, so he prayed. And he did it successfully too—he models it for us. When God became a human being in Jesus, he became completely human. His mission in the world was achieved as a human being among human beings.

But why have I bothered to spell this out in such detail? What is its relevance to our mission? Simply this: that when Jesus calls us to continue

---

[1]   William Barclay, *The Letter to the Hebrews* (Edinburgh: St Andrew Press, 1975), p. 38.

his mission in the world, he invites us to do so as men and women. He calls us to mission with a human face.

What a strange lot!

Have you noticed how reluctant people are to come to church? They take an awful lot of persuading to join us. They seem to think that churchgoers are a funny lot, that we are somehow different. To hear some talk you would think we had three legs and two heads!

But why is this so? Because that is the impression we give: that being "religious" means being not quite human, not wholly normal. Churchgoing teenagers have at times struggled with their parents over this. "Why do you want to spend so much time at church?" "Why can't you be normal teenagers?" But who gave them the idea that being involved in church is abnormal and not good for their teenage children?

We need to learn from Jesus: he was different, but he remained thoroughly human, so people didn't think him abnormal, but were able to relate to him naturally. We need to seize every opportunity to demonstrate to those outside the church that we are normal after all—well, almost!

Church house groups sometimes have social gatherings for the group and their families, including those who don't come to church. I remember at one such gathering, one of the members, a father of two, was off work with "miner's knee", not because he'd been praying but because he is a painter and decorator by trade and has to kneel a lot at work—that's pretty normal! Another of the men, also a father of two, is a rugby player and was recovering from having his ear nearly torn off in a match—that's pretty normal too! I would like to think that any non-churchgoers who were there at least got the message that Christians are normal human beings.

What about the clergy?

If Christians generally have given the gospel a bad press, we clergy haven't helped. The media love to caricature the clergy: so often we are depicted as wet, or soft, or dozy, or incomprehensible, or out of touch, or effeminate—or any combination of these things. And they say there is always an element of truth in caricature!

Certainly, we often give the impression of being different. But then we are programmed to be different: our church upbringing and theological training have encouraged it. We dress differently, speak differently, behave differently, live differently (or some of us do); many of us are even given extra bits on the front of our names. I remember, years ago, soon after arriving in a new parish, having coffee with a few of the older ladies. During our conversation one of them said to us: "Of course, we shall call you Mr and Mrs Marsh, because you're different, aren't you?" I wanted to cry out "No, we're not!", but I held my peace. Ministers or not, between us we have given the impression that we are somehow different, and that does not help us in our mission. We need to learn from Jesus: he was far more effective in mission than ever we shall be, and he was natural, normal, human, approachable. In our mission, we need to be thoroughly human and completely natural too—like Jesus.

Sharing ourselves

I get the impression that Paul grasped this and modelled himself on Jesus. He speaks of his strategy in mission in these terms:

> . . . we put up with anything rather than hinder the gospel of Christ . . . Though I am free and belong to no one, I have made myself a slave to everyone, to win as many as possible. To the Jews I became like a Jew, to win the Jews. To those under the law I became like one under the law (though I myself am not under the law), so as to win those under the law. To those not having the law I became like one not having the law (though I am not free from God's law but am under Christ's law), so as to win those not having the law. To the weak I became weak, to win the weak. I have become all things to all people so that by all possible means I might save some (1 Corinthians 9:12,19–22).

These are not the words of one who has remained aloof and separate from those he seeks to win: Paul has got involved with them, wherever they are—just like Jesus did. "Just as a nursing mother cares for her children, so we cared for you. Because we loved you so much, we were delighted to share with you not only the gospel of God but our lives as well" (1 Thessalonians 2:7–8). That's it, they shared their lives. No wonder Paul was so successful in mission: he followed the example of his master, Jesus. He didn't just preach, he gave himself. That is mission with a human face, Jesus-style mission, and effective—but it's also costly.

Personal testimony

Earlier (in Chapter 2), I referred to a "milestone experience" of mine at a Prayer Counselling School some years ago. It was very significant, but painful too. I was helped to see that my ministry, especially in teaching, although apparently a blessing to many, was in fact distancing me from people. I was comfortable up-front preaching to hundreds, but uncomfortable face to face with one; and those whom I was teaching found me aloof and unapproachable. That is not the Jesus model. I realize that now and am trying to be more like him—though it's taking time. It has meant not hiding my humanity, the man that I am, behind the safe facade of "the minister"; it has also meant being honest about myself when it would be easier to be less than honest.

I remember, for example, taking the funeral of a young man, killed in a car accident. During the service I commented that many were probably asking the question "Why?". I then admitted that I didn't know the answer. Afterwards, a neighbour of the young man wrote to me; it was an untidy note on a rough scrap of paper. She wrote:

> Over the years we have attended funerals . . . In all the other funeral services I have not heard the vicar or priest . . . say they did not know why someone we love is taken from us and when you said you could not answer that question either as to why, you levelled yourself to the mourners. I do not mean any disrespect— more respect of putting into words what everybody felt.

That was a timely reminder: that being human involves being honest, and being honest means being vulnerable, but approachable, like Jesus.

Samuel Chadwick, a well-known Methodist preacher of the early twentieth century, tells of the time when he discovered that his minister was a man:

> I have never forgotten the dread that gripped me when, as a youth, I was invited to go for an interview at the manse. I walked past the door several times before I had the courage to ring the bell, and as I stood at the door my heart throbbed in my ears. Imagine my surprise when shown into the room to find the great man on all-fours, giving a ride to riotously happy children, who turned his long beard into driving-reins! He was their father![2]

That minister was not afraid to let a young member of his church see that he was human, a father of children, normal and therefore approachable.

I happen to be a minister, but I am also a man, a husband and a father. I want people to relate to me in all those roles, to know the whole "me". That's what I see Jesus doing as he gave himself in ministry to others, and that's what I see Paul doing as he shared his life with others. That's mission with a human face.

In the footsteps of the master

As we face up to the challenge of being involved in Jesus' mission, we shall probably be only too aware of our humanity and the size and opposition of the world into which we are sent. In no way does that disqualify us or let us off the hook, for that's precisely where God started when he embarked on his mission to humankind. He came as a human being among human beings and lived alongside them in this world. That's our calling too: "As the Father has sent me, I am sending you." And this is the environment in which we call others to join us as disciples.

---

[2]   Samuel Chadwick, *The Path of Prayer* (London: Hodder & Stoughton, 1936), p. 47.

The big, bad world

If the call to mission with a human face is a challenge, then the arena in which that mission is meant to happen is an even greater challenge: the world. Jesus was sent into it, and so are we.

The incarnation, as I have already suggested, offers us a model for mission, a pattern to follow. It means identification: Jesus identified himself with all that it means to be human, and so must we. It means involvement: Jesus involved himself in all the messiness of human life and relationships, and so must we. The world didn't thank him or applaud him for doing so: they may not treat us any better. People often misunderstood Jesus and criticized him: we risk the same treatment. They dubbed him "friend of sinners" because of the company he kept; they may call us worse names than that.

Jesus made no secret of the toughness of his call to mission; he was fully aware of the dangers. When he sent out the disciples in mission, he was honest with them: "I am sending you out like sheep among wolves" (Matthew 10:16). When he talked with them about their future mission, he warned them what to expect:

> If the world hates you, keep in mind that it hated me first. If you belonged to the world, it would love you as its own. As it is, you do not belong to the world, but I have chosen you out of the world. That is why the world hates you. Remember what I told you: "A servant is not greater than his master." If they persecuted me, they will persecute you also. If they obeyed my teaching, they will obey yours also. They will treat you in this way because of my name, for they do not know the one who sent me (John 15:18–21).

To follow Jesus in mission is to risk hatred and persecution from the world. That's why Jesus prayed for them like this:

> I have given them your word and the world has hated them, for they are not of the world any more than I am of the world. My prayer is not that you take them out of the world but that you

protect them from the evil one. They are not of the world, even
as I am not of it. Sanctify them by the truth; your word is truth.
As you sent me into the world, I have sent them into the world
(John 17:14–18).

He sends them just as he was sent; he prays for their protection, and
he recognizes the underlying cause of the world's opposition. Those he
sends will be noticeably different—they are not of this world. And that's
the problem!

Salt and light

Jesus often talked about this call to be different. It is perhaps most clear
when he speaks of his followers as salt and light:

> You are the salt of the earth. But if the salt loses its saltiness, how
> can it be made salty again? It is no longer good for anything,
> except to be thrown out and trampled underfoot. You are the light
> of the world. A town built on a hill cannot be hidden. Neither do
> people light a lamp and put it under a bowl. Instead they put it on
> its stand, and it gives light to everyone in the house. In the same
> way, let your light shine before others, that they may see your
> good deeds and praise your Father in heaven (Matthew 5:13–16).

We are all familiar with salt and its uses today, particularly in adding
flavour to food. In Jesus' day it was even more important, not least as
a preserving agent in the absence of refrigeration; it prevented meat
and other food going off. The point of Jesus' picture is clear: followers
of Jesus are called to affect the world in which they live for good, to
be a moral and spiritual preservative in a world which increasingly
has little time for spiritual things and is constantly lowering its moral
standards. "God intends the most powerful of all restraints within sinful
society to be his own redeemed, regenerate and righteous people."[3]

---

3   John Stott, *Christian Counter-Culture: The Message of the Sermon on the
Mount* (Leicester: InterVarsity Press, 1982), p. 59.

If we are to do this effectively, we have to make sure we maintain our distinctiveness from the world as Jesus did—and that's hard!

Jesus' second picture, of light, is even more difficult to put into practice. Salt can be effective without being seen and heard—you hardly know it's there. That's not so with light: by its very nature it has to be seen to be effective; everyone should be aware of it. When Jesus speaks of his followers as "light", he is reminding them that they need to be seen and recognized by the world if they are to affect the world. Sadly, over the years I have met too many Christians who "keep their heads down". No one knows they are Christians at work, down the street, or in the club. But the challenge of Jesus is to "let the light shine".

I remember some years ago a member of the church where I was then vicar spoke of her last visit to the hairdresser. She got into conversation there and, in response to a question, found herself openly admitting to being a Christian—in the hairdresser's! And it was so natural, she said. But many would have kept quiet. If we take Jesus' challenge seriously, we cannot; we must let the light shine.

Another member of the same church was a miner. He got plenty of stick from his fellow miners for being a Christian, but as a result of "letting his light shine", he had a number of opportunities to speak about Jesus down the mine. That really is being light in the darkness!

Paul picks up this theme in his writing. Encouraging the Christians in Philippi, he urges them to "become blameless and pure, 'children of God without fault in a warped and crooked generation'. Then you will shine among them like stars in the sky as you hold firmly to the word of life . . ." (Philippians 2:15–16). Similarly, he challenges the Christians in Rome: "Do not conform to the pattern of this world, but be transformed by the renewing of your mind" (Romans 12:2). Or as J. B. Phillips expressed it in his paraphrase of the New Testament: "Don't let the world around you squeeze you into its own mould." And that is the crux of the challenge: not to go along with the patterns, attitudes, standards and ways of the world, but to live like Jesus in the world, with *his* patterns, attitudes and standards. It's the call to be different, and none of us likes to be different. But it's part of the call to mission.

Working it out

Many of the early Christians knew very keenly the reality of this: they took seriously Jesus' call to mission and suffered for it. Acts tells something of their struggles, of the opposition and persecution the Christians experienced from both the Roman authorities and the Jewish communities. But nothing deterred them.

For example, Peter and John were arrested and imprisoned for preaching; they were questioned, threatened and ordered to stop (Acts 4). But they continued to preach and were arrested again (Acts 5:18). Questioned a second time, Peter responded: "We must obey God rather than human beings!" (Acts 5:29)—they believed they had a God-given mission to preach Jesus and would not be stopped. This time they were flogged and ordered to stop again; but "they never stopped teaching and proclaiming the good news that Jesus is the Messiah" (Acts 5:42).

Stephen, also, a man "full of God's grace and power" (Acts 6:8) quickly fell foul of the authorities when he got involved in mission. He refused to compromise the message and ended up as the first Christian martyr (Acts 7:54–60). And Paul, in all his missionary travelling, preaching, teaching and founding churches, was never far from trouble. In both Antioch and Iconium, for example, there was organized opposition and physical attack against Paul and his companions; when they moved on to other towns, the troublemakers simply followed and stirred things up again (Acts 13:49—14:20). And yet in all these towns people believed in Jesus and churches were established. Paul visited them on his way home and he urged them to keep going: "We must go through many hardships to enter the kingdom of God" (Acts 14:22)—he knew what he was talking about! Later, looking back on his experiences of mission, Paul catalogued some of the things that happened:

> Five times I received from the Jews the forty lashes minus one. Three times I was beaten with rods, once I was pelted with stones, three times I was shipwrecked, I spent a night and a day in the open sea, I have been constantly on the move. I have been in danger from rivers, in danger from bandits, in danger from my fellow Jews, in danger from Gentiles; in danger in the city, in danger in the country, in danger at sea; and in danger from

false believers. I have laboured and toiled and have often gone
without sleep; I have known hunger and thirst and have often
gone without food; I have been cold and naked (2 Corinthians
11:24–7).

Here is someone totally committed to the mission of Jesus and who has
experienced at first hand the opposition of the world to that mission,
just as Jesus promised.

Growing the church the hard way . . .

. . . at Corinth

In those early days, churches were planted in some of the most unlikely
places, and grew remarkably well considering the circumstances.

Take the church in Corinth, for example. Reading Paul's letters you
might be surprised at the problems that were rife in the church: divisions,
immorality, taking each other to court, and even the Communion
services becoming more like drunken orgies. In fact, when you appreciate
something of the background, it is amazing that the church was planted
at all, let alone that it became as effective as it was.

Corinth was a great city, a prosperous trading and commercial centre,
and the home of the Isthmian Games (second only to the Olympic Games).
It was also an evil city, renowned for its drunkenness and debauchery, its
immorality and filth, no doubt encouraged by the presence on the hill
behind the city of the Temple of Aphrodite (the goddess of love), to which
were attached 1,000 priestesses who were cult prostitutes.

It was in that "world" that Paul preached the gospel and founded a
church; it was in that environment that the church grew so that Paul
could say of its members that they did not lack any spiritual gift (1
Corinthians 1:7). What is more, before Paul arrived many of them had
been fully involved in the wicked "world" of Corinth. Paul writes:

Do not be deceived: Neither the sexually immoral nor idolaters
nor adulterers nor men who have sex with men nor thieves nor
the greedy nor drunkards nor slanderers nor swindlers will

> inherit the kingdom of God. And that is what some of you were.
> But you were washed, you were sanctified, you were justified in
> the name of the Lord Jesus Christ and by the Spirit of our God
> (1 Corinthians 6:9–11).

Now they had come out of the world and were the church in Corinth; they knew all about being in the world but not of it; they knew at first hand the challenge of fulfilling the mission of Christ in an antagonistic world.

. . . at Thessalonica

The church in Thessalonica was planted in difficult circumstances too. When Paul arrived there and began preaching, the local Jews were so incensed that they rounded up a mob and started a riot. It became so dangerous for Paul that local Christians had to rescue him and Silas, and get them out of the city under the cover of night (Acts 17:1–10).

Later, when writing to the church in Thessalonica, Paul referred back to those experiences:

> You became imitators of us and of the Lord, for you welcomed
> the message in the midst of severe suffering with joy given by
> the Holy Spirit . . . We had previously suffered and been treated
> outrageously in Philippi, as you know, but with the help of our
> God we dared to tell you his gospel in spite of strong opposition
> . . . For you, brothers and sisters, became imitators of God's
> churches in Judea, which are in Christ Jesus; you suffered from
> your own people the same things those churches suffered from
> the Jews . . . (1 Thessalonians 1:6; 2:2,14).

This church was planted in the midst of opposition but, apparently, quickly grew into an attractive church, an example to others. "We ought always to thank God for you, brothers and sisters," Paul wrote to them, "and rightly so, because your faith is growing more and more, and the love all of you have for one other is increasing. Therefore, among God's churches we boast about your perseverance and faith in all the persecutions and trials you are enduring" (2 Thessalonians 1:3–4).

Here is effective mission in a hostile world: a church born and growing in difficult circumstances, just as Jesus said it would be.

. . . at Pergamum

The same was true of the church at Pergamum. Pergamum was a city in Asia Minor (now Turkey); the church was one of seven for which the risen Christ had a message, revealed to John in a vision and recorded by him in Revelation (Chapters 2 and 3).

Pergamum was a great capital city, an administrative centre, a cultural centre (it had, for example, a great library), and a centre of religion. The hill on which the city was built was covered with pagan temples, crowned by an altar to the god Zeus—this temple is possibly what is referred to as "Satan's throne" (Revelation 2:13). Emperor worship was also strong there; that meant everyone was supposed to say "Caesar is Lord!" In that unpromising situation a church was born, probably during the time when Paul was based in Ephesus for two years (Acts 19:1–10). It grew and, despite certain shortcomings, remained true to Jesus in the face of great opposition, even to the extent of one of their number being put to death (Revelation 2:13). Here again is faithfulness to the mission call of Jesus in a hostile world.

. . . in every generation

And this pattern has been repeated time after time through church history. The church has sadly been far from perfect in its attitudes and activities on numerous occasions, but whenever and wherever followers of Jesus have responded to his call to mission in the world, the gospel has been preached, people have believed and churches have been planted. Those churches have often survived and grown remarkably, sometimes in the midst of fierce opposition. Many have lost their lives for the sake of Christ and his mission, and still do today—indeed, it is reckoned that more have died for Christ in the twentieth and twenty-first century than in all 19 previous centuries put together. Didn't Jesus say: "If they persecuted me, they will persecute you also" (John 15:20)? That is the risk we take when we engage in his mission.

In the twentieth century, when this book was first written, the focus of concern was chiefly on the church in Russia and the other Communist states of Eastern Europe, together with China: church leaders were arrested, church property confiscated and the church survived largely underground and hidden. Today, in the twenty-first century, as I revisit and revise the text of the book, the focus is entirely on countries in Asia and Africa; 360 million Christians experience persecution in at least 50 countries, and it is said that Christianity receives more persecution than any other of the world religions. Persecution is extreme in countries like North Korea, Afghanistan, Libya, Iran and India. And yet, just as in its early days, the church doesn't just survive but grows. In India, for example, despite the government policy of making it a Hindu nation, the church is underground and Christianity is spreading; in Israel, despite Christians being called worse than Hitler, Christian influence is growing; and in Iran, officially a Shiite Islamic state, the young people are searching for truth and finding it in the gospel. Our fellow Christians in these countries know the reality of being sent into the world and the cost that can be involved. I, for one, am both encouraged and challenged by them.

What about us?

The call of Jesus remains: "Go into all the world and preach the gospel to all creation" (Mark 16:15), "go . . . make disciples" (Matthew 28:19) But where do we start? Just where we are, each of us has a "world" in which to go in mission; it begins on our doorstep, or possibly even in our own front room, among our relations, neighbours and friends. Of course, we find home the hardest place of all to "let the light shine"—the people we live with know us too well, with all our faults! Yet, in obedience to Jesus, we need to start there.

I remember, some years ago, speaking to a young couple looking forward to their upcoming marriage. The girl's mother had started coming to the church and had recently been confirmed. According to the daughter, her mum had changed, becoming more peaceful, more content, nicer to know—and her dad had noticed the difference too. It's not surprising that both dad and daughter started attending church with mum. And that's the beginning of mission: being a Christian at home so that other members of the family notice the difference.

Then there's your friends. Do they know you are Christian? Have they noticed the difference? Or are all your friends Christians? Sadly, that seems be true of many Christians, and yet there is great potential for mission here. Perhaps your mission field is the friends you have, the people you know, the acquaintances around you: that's your little bit of "world" into which you are sent.

There are opportunities in the community too: in our schools to serve as a parent governor or to play an active part in parent associations— these are opportunities for the Christian voice to be heard. There are similar openings for involvement in local hospitals, prisons, homes for the elderly, disabled or children. I reckon Jesus would have been involved in these places—it's all part of mission in the world.

And what about where you work? Or do you keep your head down there? Does Jesus ever get a look in at the office, is he ever talked about on the shop floor, other than using his name as a swear word? Many are members of unions and therefore have the right to speak and vote about matters concerning work. But how many Christians actually attend union meetings? Even if a meeting were scheduled for the same time as the morning service at your church, the union meeting could be the right place to be. From my reading of the Gospels, I think that might well have been the decision Jesus would have made. I am always encouraged when I hear of Christians who "come out" in their workplace: in politics, science, media, sport, industry, and so on.

And where you play? Are there not opportunities to be involved in the decision making of the club or society to which you belong? Do you take them, or do you just complain (or even leave!) when decisions are made that are not right, not Christian?

So many opportunities to follow the example of Jesus and get involved, so many situations in which to be salt and light, and nowhere out of bounds! Sadly, the Christian voice is often silent when it should be heard because Christians are absent when they should be present. The incarnation of Jesus, our model for mission, urges us to be identified, to get involved! "As the Father has sent me, I am sending you."

Looking at the world

Some of us never actually get started in mission because we never really believe we can do anything that will be effective in this "big, bad world". One reason for this is the way we look at the world we live in. Let me try to explain.

In the West, we have been brought up and educated in a particular way: most of us have scarcely noticed it, but we have taken it in "with mother's milk". It means that we view the world in a particular way; we have been programmed to have a particular "worldview".

Our worldview can be summed up with three words:

It is scientific: we may know very little about science, but basically we have a scientific attitude to the world. We tend to accept those things which can be understood and explained, and reject the unexplained.

It is logical: everything that happens has a logical cause. Where a cause is lacking we tend to doubt.

It is materialistic: those things we can experience with our senses (sight, smell, sound, touch) we accept. We tend to be sceptical about things which are not physical or material and can't be examined in the normal way.

Thus, the world as we see it is closed, conforming to certain fixed patterns. Anything other than that is suspect; any suggestion that the pattern can be broken and the situation changed is beyond belief.

However, the message of Jesus is just that kind of message: God has broken into the world and changed things in ways which are not fully explicable in "normal" ways. And as Christians, whenever we tell the good news of Jesus, we are in effect saying that God can and does break in today—and he will if we give him a chance.

The question is: do we really believe that? There has been theological debate in recent years as to whether or not God is an "interventionist God", that is, whether or not he does "break in" to his world. Some within the church find the idea hard to accept; many outside the church are sceptical. Doubt from Christians and scepticism from non-Christians: two of the greatest hindrances to effective mission in the world today. Both are caused, in part at least, not so much by apathy or ignorance but by our particular closed view of the world. There is an amusing incident in the life of Paul which highlights the effect of a particular fixed world view. Paul had been shipwrecked and ended up on the island of Malta (Acts 28). As he was gathering sticks to make a fire, a snake bit him. The islanders who saw it interpreted the situation immediately: Paul must be a murderer and was receiving his just punishment (v. 4). But Paul didn't die as they expected; he simply shook the snake off into the fire and was unaffected by it. Realizing he wasn't a murderer after all, the people hurriedly reached the only other conclusion that was possible: Paul was a god! (v. 6).

We may find that amusing, but it was perfectly consistent with people's particular worldview at that time. Sometimes we respond to situations as a result of our way of seeing the world which might be equally ridiculous if we did but know it!

Taking a second look at the world

There are other ways of looking at the world besides ours. People in Jesus' day certainly viewed things rather differently, and we need to remember that when we try to understand the Bible. Today, too, some have very different worldviews from us, often rather closer to that of Jesus' day.

Shortly after the Second World War, some sociologists carried out a fascinating experiment in the Far East to find out how Eastern attitudes differed from those in the West. Several thousand people were interviewed and asked logic questions like this: "Cotton doesn't grow in cold-weather countries. England is a cold-weather country. Does cotton grow in England?" The answers surprised them; the majority said that they were not qualified to answer the question because they had never been to England.

That may be a rather different way of responding to the world from ours, but it is reasonable: why should they rule out the possibility of growing cotton in England? It is also more open: there is more room for the inexplicable happening, for the supernatural event, and there is more recognition given to the spiritual dimension of life as opposed to the purely physical. In a word, there's more room for God.

The New Testament also challenges us to take a second look at our world in preparation for mission. Time and again we read of God breaking into the world. He did in the incarnation: Mary and Joseph recognized it even if no one else did. Every time Jesus performed a miracle, God broke in and the people recognized it in their response; for example, "God has come to help his people" (Luke 7:16). God broke in at the resurrection too: the Christians emphasized it in their preaching: "God raised him from the dead" (Acts 2:24). And God continued to break in through the ministry of the first Christians: when Peter told the lame man at the gate of the Temple to get up (Acts 3:6); when Paul told the disabled man at Lystra to stand on his feet (Acts 14:10); and many other times.

God does not change (Malachi 3:6): he is just as able to break into the world of people in twenty-first-century western Europe as he did in first-century Middle East. The challenge is for us to believe it, expect it and look for it. This, too, is part of what Jesus promised when he said: "As the Father has sent me, I am sending you."

Overcoming the world

There is one other truth we need to grasp as we move out into the world in mission: we have the potential in Christ to overcome the world. How? John explains: "Everyone born of God overcomes the world. This is the victory that has overcome the world, even our faith. Who is it that overcomes the world? Only he who believes that Jesus is the Son of God" (1 John 5:4–5).

That doesn't mean we shall need to fight physical battles in our mission. Paul makes it clear that our concern is not with human, or even political, enemies but with spiritual ones: "For our struggle is not against flesh and blood, but against the rulers, against the authorities, against the powers of this dark world and against the spiritual forces of evil in the heavenly realms" (Ephesians 6:12). It is these battles for which we are equipped: "For though we live in the world, we do not wage war as the world does. The weapons we fight with are not the weapons of the world. On the contrary, they have divine power to demolish strongholds" (2 Corinthians 10:3–4).

In case we are scared by the prospect of this kind of battle and are intimidated into inactivity as a result, John reminds us that although we have an enemy in the world (he calls it "the spirit of the antichrist"), "You, dear children, are from God and have overcome them, because the one who is in you is greater than the one who is in the world" (1 John 4:4). And that's the secret of success in mission in the face of a hostile world:

relationship with God as Father and the indwelling of the Spirit of Jesus, who has himself overcome the world (John 16:33).

Review

So now we have added a fourth mission principle. The first was: mission begins with relationship to God as children to father, just like Jesus. The second was: out of that relationship we discover what God wants to do and say. The third was: the Father's love must motivate our mission. The fourth is this: the setting for our mission is as human beings in the world of human beings with all its opposition, just as it was for Jesus. That's what Jesus meant when he said: "As the Father has sent me, I am sending you." This is the context in which we are called to go and make disciples.

5

Sent . . . To Save

"Are you saved, brother?" It was my first Saturday as a student in York. I had taken my friend's advice back home to find St Cuthbert's Church when I got to York and that's what I had set out to do. It wasn't an easy place to find—York's narrow streets are bewildering to a stranger—but eventually I discovered it, tucked just inside the city walls. It was open, so I walked in and was greeted by a middle-aged man with grey hair and a welcoming smile. It was he who asked if I was saved.

But what did he mean?

Clarifying our aim

If we are to be involved in any activity, it helps to have a clear idea of what our aims. are. In football it's scoring goals (and stopping your opponents doing so!); in archery it's hitting the target. The aim of God's mission in this world is equally clear: it is "to save".

It was for this precise purpose that God sent Jesus. Even before Jesus' birth, the purpose of his coming was clearly explained. The angel told Joseph: "[Mary] will give birth to a son, and you are to give him the name Jesus, because he will save his people from their sins" (Matthew 1:21). Jesus was even given a name to go with the task—"Jesus" means "the Lord saves".

Time and again Jesus confirmed this purpose in his ministry. For example, Zacchaeus, as a result of his meeting with Jesus, became a changed man and showed it by giving away his money. Jesus commented: "The Son of Man came to seek and to save the lost" (Luke 19:10). Again, to the woman who anointed his feet in the home of Simon the Pharisee,

Jesus said: "Your faith has saved you; go in peace" (Luke 7:50). For Jesus, the purpose of his mission was clear: to save people.

We need to register that loud and clear before we go any further. Mission is talked about in so many ways, even within the church. Sometimes it is in terms of being the presence of God in the world, sometimes in terms of prayer for the world, sometimes in terms of influencing the world for good, sometimes in terms of compassionate involvement in the suffering of the world. All these things are part of Christian mission, but the mission Jesus invites us to be involved in is more radical: it is to save people and the world in which they live. That, of course, will mean changing things; but that is precisely what Jesus did most of the time.

It's urgent too!

So our aim in mission is to save. But we also need to grasp this: that when salvation is necessary, there is usually an element of danger and urgency involved. The word "rescue" (which means the same as "save") possibly helps us to get the feel of this better. Think, for example, of a house on fire and a firefighter going into the burning building at great risk to him or herself to rescue someone trapped inside. That's salvation! Or think of a lifeboat crew risking stormy seas to go the rescue of people afloat in a life raft after their yacht has sunk. That's salvation!

The element of danger and urgency is obvious in both those examples. Jesus often communicated a similar urgency in his teaching: it is as if people are in great danger and there is no time to lose. For example, when he urged his disciples: "The harvest is plentiful, but the workers are few. Ask the Lord of the harvest, therefore, to send out workers into his harvest field" (Luke 10:2); or when he explained to them: "As long as it is day, we must do the works of him who sent me. Night is coming, when no one can work" (John 9:4).

That same note of urgency is there whenever he sends others out in mission, too. For example, to the Seventy-two he said:

> Go! I am sending you out like lambs among wolves. Do not take
> a purse or bag or sandals; and do not greet anyone on the road
> . . . When you enter a town and are not welcomed, go into its

> streets and say, "Even the dust of your town we wipe from our feet as a warning to you. Yet be sure of this: The kingdom of God has come near." I tell you, it will be more bearable on that day for Sodom than for that town (Luke 10:3–4,10–12).

Again, in all Jesus' teaching about the coming judgement on the Last Day, not least in the many stories he told to illustrate the point, there is that clear message that time is limited: that if people are not ready for the coming of the harvester (Matthew 13:24–30,36–43), if they are not prepared for the arrival of the bridegroom (Matthew 25:1–13), then they may find themselves left out. Jesus shows us that people are in danger, and the mission to rescue them is urgent. We need to capture something of that same urgency in our own approach to mission; we need to see the danger that people are in socially, morally and spiritually, and we need to act to save them.

But what is that danger? It takes many different forms today: there is apathy, the "can't be bothered" syndrome; violence, often the result of frustration; selfishness, the root cause of so many evils in society; broken relationships, both personal and corporate; boredom, the feeling that nothing is worth doing, nothing has any point; loneliness, the feeling that nobody knows or cares; guilt, the "if-only" syndrome; and many other symptoms too. And they are dangerous because they so often result in damage or destruction, either of the individual or some other person or thing. In addition to all this, there is a spiritual hunger, the desire for "something more", some spiritual reality and power, a desire which often leads people into the occult or extremist activities.

Jesus' call to mission is a call to act, to rescue those who are living dangerously. That's just what God did: he sent Jesus because he loved the world so much but also saw the danger in which people were living. He came to the rescue in Jesus, coming right into that dangerous situation and offering salvation: believe in Jesus and so enjoy life rather than death (John 3:16).

Paul picks up this theme in his writings:

> As for you, you were dead in your transgressions and sins, in which you used to live . . . But because of his great love for us,

> God, who is rich in mercy, made us alive with Christ even when
> we were dead in transgressions . . . For it is by grace you have been
> saved, through faith . . . (Ephesians 2:1–2,4–5,8).

Here is a picture of a desperate situation in response to which God has acted to save.

Today, people are still living dangerously. Many are hopeless, many are desperate. God's response is still the same: to seek and to save. That must be our response too. And because the task is urgent, it must be a major priority in our lives and in our churches: we need to channel much of our time, money, human and spiritual resources into this all-important activity. As someone has said: "Everything else happening in the church is like rearranging the furniture while the house is on fire."

It's good news!

So the aim of our mission is to save, and the task is urgent. Let us also note, however, that the message we have to share is marvellously positive. This emphasis is clear in the Gospels. John, for example, having explained that Jesus was sent into the world because God loved the world so much, goes on to explain: "For God did not send his Son into the world to condemn the world, but to save the world through him" (John 3:17). It would be so easy for us to respond to the wickedness and selfishness of those around us negatively, frowning upon their activities and condemning them, with a shake of the head and a "tut-tut"! But that is not the model Jesus gives us: he is not in the business of condemning but of rescuing, and his response is always positive.

Of course, in responding positively, Jesus never condones sin, rather he exposes it in order to forgive and change the sinner. This balance is demonstrated clearly in the case of the woman accused of adultery who was brought to Jesus so that he could pass judgement on her (John 8:1–11). When her accusers slunk away without condemning her, Jesus said to her: "Neither do I condemn you." But he added: "Go now and leave your life of sin." She went away saved, not condemned.

Later, in dialogue with religious leaders, Jesus said: "If anyone hears my words but does not keep them, I do not judge that person. For I did not come to judge the world, but to save the world" (John 12:47). Here is the same emphasis: Jesus' mission is to save people, not judge them; it's positive, not negative.

Jesus confirmed this in his response to James and John when they wanted to call down fire from heaven to destroy people who refused to welcome Jesus or his followers (Luke 9:51-6). Jesus "rebuked" them. The word used is a strong one: it was a good "ticking off", because they had got it wrong. What they wanted to do was not Jesus' style. A footnote in some biblical texts tells us that some manuscripts include Jesus explaining: "You do not know what kind of spirit you are of, for the Son of Man did not come to destroy human lives, but to save them" (v. 55). Whether or not he actually said it, it was implied in his rebuke and is in line with his attitude to mission.

We need to hear this emphasis in Jesus' mission, because, sadly, the church's attempts at mission often come across as largely negative, emphasizing the "thou-shalt-nots" and generally taking all the fun out of life. People often seem to hear our negative message (for example, confronting evils in society), and have failed to register the good news of the gospel. The positive tone of Jesus' mission was established that first Christmas night when the angel proclaimed: "Do not be afraid. I bring you good news that will cause great joy for all the people. Today in the town of David a Saviour has been born to you; he is the Messiah, the Lord" (Luke 2:10-11).

Jesus the Saviour is good news of great joy for all people, so let's make sure that our mission for Jesus sounds like good news and looks joyful! The message is summed up well in these words of Jesus: "I have come that they may have life, and have it to the full" (John 10:10). Life to the full—that's our message!

Our aim in mission is to save, that task is urgent, and our message is good news: you don't have to stay in that desperate and dangerous state; God can save you!

An old hand

Of course, God's desire to save didn't start with Jesus. He had been active in saving people long before that; in fact, almost as long as there have been people to save.

Noah and the ark

There was Noah, for example. Society had gone seriously astray in his day: Genesis tells us that "the LORD saw how great the wickedness of the human race had become on the earth, and that every inclination of the thoughts of the human heart was only evil all the time" (Genesis 6:5). God was grieved and decided that he had no option: "I will wipe from the face of the earth the human race I have created" (Genesis 6:7).

But Noah was different. We are told: "Noah was a righteous man, blameless among the people of his time, and he walked with God" (Genesis 6:9). So Noah and his family were exempted from God's punishment. The story of how this was carried out is well known: how, instructed by God, Noah built an ark and took his family and the animals into it. While everything around them was destroyed, they were safe. Or saved! That's how the New Testament talks about it.

In Hebrews we read: "By faith, Noah, when warned about things not yet seen, in holy fear built an ark to save his family" (Hebrews 11:7). Peter refers to it also: "In [the ark] only a few people, eight in all, were saved through water" (1 Peter 3:20); and again: "[God] did not spare the ancient world when he brought the flood on its ungodly people, but protected [the word also means "rescued"] Noah, a preacher of righteousness, and seven others" (2 Peter 2:5). In the story of Noah, then, we find, very early in the Bible, the theme of God working to save.

Moses and the Red Sea

There is another well-known story early in the Bible which also demonstrates the saving activity of God. God's people, the Israelites, had been in slavery in Egypt for years. Now, led by Moses, they had escaped and were heading for a new life in a country of their own—the Promised Land. Unfortunately, Pharoah, the king of Egypt, regretted his permission to let them go and came after them with his army. Eventually, the Israelites were trapped with the Red Sea in front of them, uncrossable, and the Egyptian army behind them, getting closer. What could they do, except moan to those in charge? (Yes, they did it in those days, too!) (Exodus 14).

That's when God launched his rescue bid. He told Moses to stretch out his hand over the sea. The water divided, the ground dried out, and the people crossed safely. (Some of us may remember the epic 1956 film *The Ten Commandments*, which included a memorable attempt to depict the scene.) Then the sea moved back, drowning the pursuing Egyptian army. The Israelites were safe—they were saved. It is summed up like this: "That day the LORD saved Israel from the hands of the Egyptians" (Exodus 14:30). To celebrate the event and to give thanks to God for his action, Moses and the Israelites sang: "I will sing to the LORD, for he is highly exalted. Both horse and driver he has hurled into the sea. The LORD is my strength and my defence; he has become my salvation" (Exodus 15:1–2).

God our Saviour

Time and again through the years that followed, the Israelites experienced God's saving activity. For example, in the time of King Saul, in their frequent battles with the Philistines, they saw the hand of God in each victory: "so on that day the LORD saved Israel" (1 Samuel 14:23). Later, in the days of King Jeroboam, we read: "[The LORD] saved them by the hand of Jeroboam son of Jehoash" (2 Kings 14:27).

The writers of the Psalms often referred to God's saving activity too: "Now this I know; the LORD gives victory to [saves] his anointed; he answers him from his holy heaven with the victorious power [saving power] of his right hand" (Psalm 20:6); "This poor man called, and the LORD heard him; he saved him out of all his troubles" (Psalm 34:6); "Then they cried to the LORD in their trouble, and he saved them from their distress" (Psalm 107:13).

So the saving power (or salvation) of God became a prominent theme in the life and worship of God's people. This is reflected in the writings of the prophets. In Isaiah, for example, we read: "For I am the LORD your God, the Holy One of Israel, your Saviour . . . I, even I, am the LORD, and apart from me there is no saviour" (Isaiah 43:3,11). And in Hosea, this: "But I have been the LORD your God ever since you came out of Egypt. You shall acknowledge no God but me, no Saviour except me" (Hosea 13:4).

The Saviour comes!

As time went on, God's people began to look forward to the future more and more. They had known God saving them many times, most recently when, following the destruction of Jerusalem (587 BC) and the resulting 70-year exile of God's people in Babylon, God brought them back to live in Jerusalem. (Nehemiah and Ezra were among those whom God used to effect this: we read about it in the biblical books named after them.)

But God's people were not satisfied: they believed there was more. They looked forward to another great day when God would demonstrate his power to save again, another great rescue act by God rather like the escape from Egypt through the Red Sea. They were convinced that someone greater than Moses would come to do it, and that the salvation he would bring would be greater than that brought by Moses.

It isn't always clear exactly what they expected. Some apparently looked for political rescue, to be set free from occupying powers. Certainly, that expectation was current in Jesus' day, even among his disciples. Nevertheless, the stage was set for the coming of a Saviour, for God's great saving act. That Saviour came in Jesus, that saving act was his coming into the world.

For those who had eyes to see and ears to hear, the coming of God to earth as a man called Jesus, meaning "God saves", should have been no surprise: that the thrust of his mission on earth was to save should have been expected—that's our God. Paul, writing of the coming of Jesus, put it like this: "But when the kindness and love of God our Saviour appeared, he saved us . . . " (Titus 3:4–5).

The second exodus
But what was the great saving act that Jesus brought? It was, of course, his death on the cross. The great demonstration of the salvation of God in the Old Testament had been the Exodus: in the New Testament it is the cross.

These two great salvation events are linked together by Luke in his account of the transfiguration when, on a mountain, in the presence of his three closest friends, Jesus' appearance was transformed, and they caught a glimpse of his glory (Luke 9:28–36). Moses and Elijah appeared and talked with Jesus, and Luke tells us: "They spoke about his departure, which he was about to bring to fulfilment at Jerusalem" (v. 31).

What strange talk! "Fulfilling his departure"—what on earth does that mean? It makes more sense when we realize that the Greek word translated "departure" is *exodos*. They were speaking of Jesus' "exodus", his great saving act, his death on the cross.

Certainly, for the writers of the New Testament the cross was central. One quarter of the Gospels is given over to telling the story of the last week of Jesus' life, culminating in his death; the crucifixion itself is told with greater detail than any other event in the action-packed life of Jesus. The cross features in the preaching of the first leaders of the church recorded in Acts; it is referred to in almost all the Epistles, and is particularly prominent in some (for example, Romans and Hebrews). The cross of Jesus is the great theme of the New Testament.

What did he do?

So Jesus is the Saviour, his mission was to save, and the cross was his great saving act. But in what way does Jesus' death on the cross save us? The Bible explains this in a number of different ways, rather like different facets of one precious jewel. Let's take a look at some of those facets.

The lawcourt
One way in which the salvation of Jesus is talked about in the New Testament is in legal language and the setting of a lawcourt. The big theological word which is at the heart of this is "justification", which means "to declare righteous"—or as the pidgin-English version of the Bible amusingly puts it: "God say, 'im all right." To be justified is to be acquitted by the court. The picture is of God as judge presiding over the court in which I, along with all other people, am in the dock, guilty.

Guilty of what? Of rebelling against God, of breaking his laws, of falling short of his standards.

Paul spells it out in his letter to the Christians in Rome. Having explained that we are all in the same boat, whether Jew or Gentile, whether we claim to believe in God or not, he sums up the situation like this, quoting from the Old Testament: "There is no one righteous, not even one; there is no one who understands, no one who seeks God. All have turned away, they have together become worthless; there is no one who does good, not even one" (Romans 3:10–12). Paul adds: "There is no difference between Jew and Gentile, for all have sinned and fall short of the glory of God" (Romans 3:22–3).

If that were the end of the story, then there would be no hope for us: we would be found guilty, sentenced and condemned in God's court. But God the judge is also God the Saviour, and he loves us. So he has done something about it: he has launched a rescue bid. "But God demonstrates his own love for us in this: while we were still sinners, Christ died for us" (Romans 5:8)—in other words, he died "on behalf of us". Jesus' death for us was God's way of seeing that justice was done: the punishment due because of our sin was paid by Jesus.

Many years before Jesus, when God's people were looking forward to the coming of their God-Saviour, this particular aspect of salvation was part of their expectation. One of their prophets wrote: "But he was pierced for our transgressions, he was crushed for our iniquities; the punishment that brought us peace was upon him" (Isaiah 53:5). Because Jesus carried the can for us, we have been "saved from God's wrath" (Romans 5:9)—the wrath of a holy God sitting in judgement on sinful people.

The outcome of all this is (in Paul's words again): ". . . all are justified freely by his grace through the redemption that came by Christ Jesus" (Romans 3:24). And because we are justified, declared righteous, we may leave the courtroom free from guilt with nothing to pay—and we cannot be tried again for the same offence!

This emphasis is very relevant today. There are so many people who struggle with feelings of guilt because of things they have done and wished they hadn't, or things they didn't do which they wish they did. Must they carry that burden of guilt for the rest of their lives, or can they really be forgiven and have the guilt lifted? The good news is: God has forgiven you through Jesus. You may walk free of any guilt—you may be "saved".

The slave market

The salvation of Jesus is also spoken about in terms of a "ransom". For the people of Jesus' day, the most familiar setting for this idea would have been the slave market: a slave could be set free from his master on the payment of a price, a ransom.

The New Testament also uses the word "redemption" or "being redeemed" to express the same idea. This would once have been familiar language to people who knew the pawnbroker's shop in the high street. If you were hard up you could go there and sell something of value. Then when your financial circumstances improved, you could return and buy back your valuable at a higher price—you could "redeem" it. Sadly, such are the financial struggles of many in the twenty-first century as I revisit the text of this book that pawnshops are again evident in our high streets.

Today, too, this idea is all too familiar because of international terrorism and the seizing of hostages by various groups of extremists. Influential people are kidnapped in the street, planes are hijacked in mid-flight, and a "price" is fixed (sometimes money, sometimes other people), which will ensure the safe release of those held hostage. That is a "ransom". (The word has passed into popular language in the phrase "a king's ransom" when we refer to something of great value.) Jesus himself spoke of his death in this way: " . . . the Son of Man did not come to be served, but to serve, and to give his life as a ransom for many" (Mark 10:45). Jesus saw himself as the ransom price paid so that others may go free. "The sinner is a slave. He is in bondage to his sins. Christ has paid the price, His life, which brings release to the sinner. As a result he is a free man."[1] This theme is taken up by Paul: "[Christ] redeemed us . . . " (Galatians 3:14). "In him we have redemption through his blood, the forgiveness of sins . . . " (Ephesians 1:7). "For there is one God and one mediator between God and mankind, the man Christ Jesus, who gave himself as a ransom for all people" (1 Timothy 2:5–6). Through Christ we are

---

[1]   Leon Morris, *The Cross in the New Testament* (London: Paternoster Press, 1965), p. 53.

released, he has fully paid the ransom price, and two things follow. First, we are set free from sin and all that binds us, and are able to enjoy "the freedom and glory of the children of God" (Romans 8:21). Second, we are indebted to the one who has paid the ransom price, Jesus. As a result, "you are not your own; you were bought at a price" (1 Corinthians 6:19-20). So we are still "in service", but with a new master; "You have been set free from sin and have become slaves to righteousness" (Romans 6:18). We now live our lives for God, we serve God; but his service, says the Collect in the Prayer Book, "is perfect freedom".

Again, this message of freedom in Jesus is most relevant today. It is good news particularly to those who feel bound by sin, by habit, by attitude. Is there no way out of this prison, they ask? Because of Jesus, the answer is "Yes!" He has paid the price for your freedom—you may be "saved".

The Temple sacrifice

The pattern of worship in the Temple offers another helpful picture of the salvation offered by God through Jesus, though it is, for us, an unfamiliar picture. When John the Baptist first saw Jesus, he pointed him out to his followers with these words: "Look, the Lamb of God, who takes away the sin of the world!" (John 1:29).

Those who heard John speak of the Lamb of God would immediately think of the worship at the Temple and, in particular, of people coming to worship with an animal which the priest would take and sacrifice on the altar. The idea was that the life of the animal was offered to God, the sacrifice was accepted by God, and the worshipper could go on his way forgiven by God of all sin. In calling Jesus "the Lamb of God", John was implying that Jesus had come himself to be that sacrificial animal which deals with human sin.

This is a prominent theme in the New Testament, and particularly so in Hebrews, where it is fully developed. There it is explained that in making this sacrifice for us, Jesus is really fulfilling two roles.

First, he is the priest, the one who stands between human beings and God: "For this reason he had to be made like them, fully human in every way, in order that he might become a merciful and faithful high priest in service to God, and that he might make atonement for the sins of the people" (Hebrews 2:17). Second, he is also the sacrifice which is offered to God for the sins of the people: "but now [Christ] has appeared once for all at the culmination of the ages to do away with sin by the sacrifice of himself" (Hebrews 9:26). John picks up this theme in his writing: "But if anybody does sin, we have an advocate with the Father—Jesus Christ, the Righteous One. He is the atoning sacrifice for our sins, and not only for ours but also for the sins of the whole world" (1 John 2:1–2).

The perfect sacrifice has been made by the perfect priest, and that sacrifice has been accepted by God. Thus, there is forgiveness for all. In effect, what this means is that as far as God is concerned, Jesus has done all that is necessary to deal fully with all sin of all people of all time—no person, no sin is beyond the scope of the sacrifice of Jesus. And that is good news for those who wonder, "Can God possibly forgive me? I'm so bad." "Can God possibly forgive my sin? It's so great." The answer to both those questions is "Yes." "If we confess our sins, [God] is faithful and just and will forgive us our sins and purify us from all unrighteousness" (1 John 1:9)—you may be "saved".

I am reminded of Brian, a member of the church where I was vicar, who made a commitment to God at Spring Harvest, the Christian holiday conference. The next morning, at the final Communion service, I happened to catch sight of him during the time of worship. He was singing with great enthusiasm, there was a broad grin on his face, and there were tears in his eyes: we were singing the chorus that has the simple refrain, "I'm forgiven, I'm forgiven, I'm forgiven." It was obvious that he knew the reality of it; it was written all over his face—he was saved!

Personal relationship

The fourth picture of the salvation of Jesus is much more familiar: unless we live the life of a recluse, we all have to relate to others. Salvation is to do with our relationship with God.

When God first created human beings, his plan was that they should enjoy relationship with him—that is implied in the words, "Let us make mankind in our image" (Genesis 1:26). When God chose the nation Israel, it was so that he could have a people to call his own: "I will take you as my own people, and I will be your God" (Exodus 6:7).

When Jesus came into the world, the heart of his message was relationship with God as Father, with an invitation to become children of God (John 1:12). Creatures and their Creator, a nation and its God, children and their Father—relationship with God is the consistent message of Old and New Testaments.

But there is another theme too: that when the creature, or the nation, or the child rebels, the relationship is spoiled. When human beings forget God, go their own way, do their own thing, relationship with God is broken: "But your iniquities have separated you from your God; your sins have hidden his face from you, so that he will not hear" (Isaiah 59:2). And that, the Bible explains, is a situation that we are powerless to do anything about. Only God can do it, and God has, in Jesus!

When God sent Jesus to save us, it was not just to deal with our sin (though he did that totally), but to restore the relationship between us and God which had been broken by that sin. It was an act of reconciliation: "God was reconciling the world to himself in Christ, not counting people's sins against them" (2 Corinthians 5:19). The Good News Bible puts it simply: "We rejoice because of what God has done through our Lord Jesus Christ, who has now made us God's friends" (Romans 5:11). Relationship restored, made God's friends, reconciled—that's salvation.

There are so many who feel God can't possibly want them as his friends; they feel unworthy and unacceptable. The good news is that God wants you so much he has restored the broken relationship, he offers you his friendship now—you may be "saved".

"We preach Christ crucified"

These four facets of salvation are not the whole story, but they show something of the scope of God's act of salvation in Jesus. We are found "not guilty" and acquitted; we are set free as a result of the ransom being paid; sacrifice for our sin has been made which is completely acceptable to God; our relationship to God is restored and we are reconciled. And all that was achieved when Jesus died on a cross outside Jerusalem that first Good Friday.

But how does all this relate to our mission? As we have seen, God's mission is to save. He sent Jesus to do just that, and he achieved it at the cross. The focal point of God's saving mission is the cross: that must be ours too.

Paul grasped this very clearly. Writing to the Christians in Corinth, he reminded them: "For I resolved to know nothing while I was with you except Jesus Christ and him crucified" (1 Corinthians 2:2). Of course, that message will not always be understood and accepted. At Corinth, Paul was apparently laughed out of court: some who heard him demanded a miraculous sign to prove that the message was true, while others wanted a thorough, rational explanation. Paul's answer to both was the same: "We preach Christ crucified: a stumbling-block to Jews and foolishness to Gentiles, but to those whom God has called, both Jews and Greeks, Christ the power of God and the wisdom of God" (1 Corinthians 1:23–4).

Paul knew that the cross was the key to salvation: "For the message of the cross is foolishness to those who are perishing, but to us who are being saved it is the power of God" (1 Corinthians 1:18). The heart of Paul's message was the cross of Christ: that must be the heart of our message too.

Preaching the cross today

However, when we preach the cross today we will find resistance, for a number of reasons. First, the message of the cross assumes that we are sinful. But people don't like being called "sinners". Nevertheless, as far as the Bible is concerned, we all are. One vicar, some years ago, put a notice up outside his church which read: "This church is for sinners only!" The community was up in arms and he was forced to take it down. Did the truth hurt? The problem is that many still see sin in terms of robbing banks, mugging old ladies, being cruel to children and animals. The truth is, according to the Bible, that to sin is simply to fall short of God's high standards—and we all do that. None of us is good enough: we all sin and that sin spoils our relationship with God, which is why we need Jesus the Saviour.

A blow to our pride

And that is the second aspect of the cross which people often resist: that God had to send Jesus, and Jesus had to die on the cross to rescue us from our sin, because we were unable to help ourselves, unable to put ourselves right with God. That hits us where it hurts the most, at the point of our pride. Most of us have been brought up to be independent, needing no one, relying on no one, with the determination to make it on our own. The cross says, "You can't make it on your own, not into right relationship with God, you can't!" We have to let God do it for us through Jesus, we have to depend on God. Paul was brought up to believe that you could be saved by living a good life, by keeping God's rules, but he had to learn something different. He wrote: "[God] saved us, not because of righteous things we had done, but because of his mercy" (Titus 3:5). And again: " . . . a person is not justified by the works of the law, but by faith in Jesus Christ" (Galatians 2:16).

So many people today have not understood this. Frequently I have conversations with people who tell me in some way or other that they reckon they are Christian and that God will accept them because they are decent people—it all depends on how you live. This understanding is deeply imbedded in people, and it means that the message of the cross is hard to accept. If we would be right with God, we have to depend on Jesus to do it for us; we have to swallow our pride.

Something for nothing!

If that hurdle is crossed there is another not far ahead, another point of resistance to the message of the cross. If someone asks: "OK, then, what do I have to do to be saved?", the answer is often unacceptable.

Paul was asked this question by the jailer in his prison cell in Philippi. His answer was: "Believe in the Lord Jesus Christ, and you will be saved" (Acts 16:31). In other words, believe that Jesus has done all that is necessary for you to be saved; or, accept all that God offers you in Jesus. To that, many will respond: "But what can I do?", usually meaning: "But what can I contribute?" "Nothing" is the answer—and that is the problem! For so many of us have an inbred scepticism about anything that's offered free, there has to be a catch in it somewhere. The Yorkshire folk, among whom I live and work, have a memorable expression, that you don't get "owt for nowt". (For the benefit of the uninitiated, that means "anything for nothing"!) But from God you do: " . . . the gift of God is eternal life in Christ Jesus our Lord" (Romans 6:23). And all you can do with a free gift that's offered is accept it—or reject it!

RSVP

And that brings us to a fourth point of resistance to the message of the cross: that if God's act of salvation is going to be effective for me, I have to receive it. There needs to be a personal response.

If you are thirsty and I offer you a glass of water, it is not enough for you to know I have water to quench your thirst; you have to receive it and drink it, otherwise you will remain thirsty. Similarly, it is not enough to know that God loves us and has acted to save us, not enough to know that Jesus died on a cross to take away all our sin: we need to respond to that act of salvation and take it for ourselves. That was the challenge of Jesus to Nicodemus in John 3 (see Chapter 1), the need for personal response to God. And it is this personal response that lies at the heart of Paul's theology too. Remember his words: " . . . the Son of God, who loved me and gave himself for me" (Galatians 2:20).

The power of the cross

The message of the cross, which is that "God saves", is an uncomfortable and unwelcome one today. But whenever we have the courage of our convictions and preach the cross as Paul did, we shall find it is still both powerful and relevant. It speaks to the person riddled with guilt feelings: "I forgive you." It speaks to the person who feels unloved and unwanted: "I love you." It speaks to the person who is aware of the enormity of their sin: "I am the perfect sacrifice for all sin." It speaks to the person who feels a million miles from God: "Come and know me."

One of the Post-Communion Prayers in the Church of England Common Worship Communion Service captures something of the wonder of all this: "Father of all, we give you thanks and praise, that when we were still far off you met us in your Son and brought us home. Dying and living,

he declared your love, gave us grace, and opened the gate of glory . . . "[2]
The cross, then, must be at the heart of our mission.

> The cross . . . brings everything else together and reduces
> them to their proper proportions. From its perspective we can
> evaluate the true tasks of the church. As we look down on the
> seemingly endless business of church organizations, committee
> meetings and church services we can begin to see their relative
> unimportance as compared with the task of proclaiming the
> riches of the cross. As we look down on the many problems of
> the world we are reminded that Christ has redeemed mankind
> and he has accomplished what he set out to do . . . [Let us] put
> the cross back into the centre of our work and witness—where
> it properly belongs, pre-eminent in both our lives and in the
> church's preaching. Just as Jesus himself lived under the shadow
> of the cross, so must his disciples.[3]

That's not all!

But the cross on a hill outside Jerusalem was not the end, nor was the
tomb in the nearby garden where his friends buried Jesus' body. Two
days after he died, not only was the cross empty but the tomb was empty
too. He had risen from death, at least, that's what his followers claimed.
And the New Testament makes it clear that Jesus' resurrection is of first
importance; because without it there could be no salvation. If Jesus had
stayed dead we would still be hopelessly lost.

Paul hints at this in his letter to the Christians in Rome: "[Jesus]
was delivered over to death for our sins and was raised to life for our
justification" (Romans 4:25). He spells it out more fully writing to the
Corinthian Christians: "If Christ has not been raised, our preaching is
useless and so is your faith . . . And if Christ has not been raised, your

---

[2] Church of England, *Common Worship: Services and Prayers for the Church
of England* © Archbishops' Council 2000.

[3] George Carey, *The Gate of Glory* (London: Hodder & Stoughton, 1986), pp.
220–1.

faith is futile; you are still in your sins" (1 Corinthians 15:14,17). That's clear enough!

Whenever the first Christians preached the good news of Jesus, they talked about the resurrection. Peter, for example, preaching on the day of Pentecost, having reproached the people for crucifying Jesus, went on: "But God raised him from the dead, freeing him from the agony of death . . . " (Acts 2:24). Again, on trial for preaching and healing a disabled man, Peter said: "It is by the name of Jesus Christ of Nazareth, whom you crucified but whom God raised from the dead, that this man stands before you healed" (Acts 4:10). Paul, similarly, preaching in Pisidian Antioch, spoke of Jesus' death and burial, and went on: "But God raised [Jesus] from the dead" (Acts 13:30). At Thessalonica, we are told that Paul went into the synagogue and "reasoned with them from the Scriptures, explaining and proving that the Messiah had to suffer and rise from the dead" (Acts 17:2–3). In fact, Paul was so persistent in preaching about the resurrection that in Athens, when a group of philosophers took him to task for his preaching, they actually accused him of preaching foreign gods—Jesus and the resurrection! (Acts 17:18).

So the resurrection is crucial to salvation, the cross is incomplete without it. That's why it is a serious matter when some within the church raise questions about the resurrection, suggesting that it is unimportant whether or not Jesus actually rose from death, that it wouldn't change anything if his bones were found tomorrow in a tomb in Jerusalem. That is not the testimony of the New Testament: the truth is, if Jesus didn't rise, it would change everything! To deny the resurrection is actually to undermine the cross and to render ineffective the salvation of God.

Salvation is through the cross and resurrection of Jesus: that is what the first Christians believed and preached, that is what Christians down through the centuries have believed and preached, that is what we must believe and preach if we would be faithful to the mission of Jesus.

Work out your salvation

Our mission to save is not complete when we have introduced people to Jesus, crucified and risen, nor when we have persuaded them that this is "the power of God that brings salvation to everyone who believes"

(Romans 1:16), nor even when we have helped them to believe and so be saved. This is only the beginning.

The story is told of a young Salvation Army officer travelling in a train. Opposite her was a bishop. She began to do what she had been trained to do: to talk about Jesus. She leant forward and asked the bishop: "Sir, are you saved?" His reply must have surprised her: "My dear, I have been saved, I am being saved, and I shall be saved." That is an excellent answer, and a thoroughly biblical one, too. For the Bible shows us clearly that salvation is not only to do with what Jesus has done for us, but also what he is doing still and will do in the future. Paul puts it like this: "Therefore, since we have been justified through faith [past], we have peace with God through our Lord Jesus Christ, through whom we have gained access by faith into this grace in which we now stand [present]. And we boast in the hope of the glory of God [future] (Romans 5:1–2). The same Jesus who died to save us and who rose from death is alive today, and is at work in those who have believed in him. His chief work is to make us like himself, to make us holy—the big word for that is "sanctification", the process of being made holy.

Paul recognizes the need for us to co-operate in this process: writing to the church in Philippi he urges them: ". . . continue to work out your salvation with fear and trembling, for it is God who works in you to will and to act in order to fulfil his good purpose" (Philippians 2:12–13).

The finer details
"Work out your salvation": the latter parts of most of Paul's letters are full of practical guidelines as to what is involved. Among other things, being "saved" should make a difference to our human relationships.

In marriage, for example, we now have an example to follow—the love of Jesus. For husband and wife to love each other as Jesus loved us provides the best possible basis for building strong, healthy marriages. There are guidelines for family life too: children are encouraged to honour and obey their parents, while parents are urged not to exasperate their children but to bring them up in God's ways. Similarly, at work, both employee (slave) and employer (master) should respect each other, the employer being fair in all his dealings, the employee working conscientiously (Ephesians 5:22—6:9; Colossians 3:18—4:6).

Then there are those we don't get on with naturally, those with whom there are barriers or prejudices: we are urged to discover our unity in Christ, realizing that "you are all one in Christ Jesus" (Galatians 3:28). And we are encouraged to be sensitive to those who see things differently from us: we are to accept them rather than argue with them (Romans 14:1–6).

There should be a change in our personal lives too, old habits going, new attitudes appearing:

> But now you must also rid yourselves of all such things as these: anger, rage, malice, slander and filthy language from your lips. Do not lie to each other, since you have taken off your old self with its practices and have put on the new self, which is being renewed in knowledge in the image of its Creator (Colossians 3:8–10).

To be saved is to be loved, so we should love others (1 John 4:19); it is to be forgiven, so we should forgive others (Ephesians 4:32); it is to be accepted, so we should be accepting of others (Romans 15:7).

In all these things, the Holy Spirit is at work within us: he makes salvation real for us, and he helps us "work it out"—without his help it would be a real struggle (even with him it's a struggle at times!).

It is always exciting to see people meeting with Jesus, discovering the significance of his cross and receiving God's gift of eternal life—being "saved". It is even more exciting watching them change as a result, to see the fruits of salvation develop in them: relationships put right, attitudes changing, bad habits dying, new abilities blossoming. I have often seen this kind of change in people over the years; it is a vital part of salvation, the present outworking of it in our daily lives. The German atheist philosopher Friedrich Nietzsche once said: "Christians need to look a lot more saved before I will believe in their Saviour." That's a fair challenge!

For ever and ever, amen

But even this is not the end of the story. The New Testament makes it clear that God's salvation is good not just for this life but for the next too. Jesus himself said:

> For my Father's will is that everyone who looks to the Son and believes in him shall have eternal life, and I will raise them up on the last day . . . I am the resurrection and the life. The one who believes in me will live, even though they die; and whoever lives and believes in me will never die (John 6:40; 11:25).

As if to prove the point, and to forestall the sceptics, God brought Jesus back to life after his death. That resurrection, the New Testament emphasizes, is like a guarantee of life beyond death for us too:

> . . . for we have testified about God that he raised Christ from the dead. But he did not raise him if in fact the dead are not raised. For if the dead are not raised, then Christ has not been raised either. And if Christ has not been raised, your faith is futile; you are still in your sins . . . But Christ has indeed been raised from the dead, the firstfruits of those who have fallen asleep (1 Corinthians 15:15–17,20).

This is the "future tense" of salvation, the looking forward to sharing the glory of God (Romans 8:17)—the big word for it is "glorification".

While I was working on this chapter, a member of the church where I was vicar died after some years of illness. In life, he often assured his wife that he was not afraid of death, that dying was simply going through a doorway; thus, the body he would leave behind would be merely a shell. So at his funeral, although there was sadness, there was a note of joy too: we were able to focus our attention on Jesus' promise of eternal life, on his victory over death through the resurrection, and we were able to sing "Thine be the glory, risen, conquering Son, endless is the victory thou o'er death hast won!"

The purpose of God's salvation is not just concerned with this life, but life beyond death too. As Paul wrote: "If only for this life we have hope in Christ, we are of all people most to be pitied" (1 Corinthians 15:19). And how relevant is this part of our message today. So many are fearful of death and unsure about life beyond death. Jesus the Saviour removes the fear and the uncertainty: ". . . he too shared in their humanity so that by his death he might destroy him who holds the power of death—that is, the devil—and free those who all their lives were held in slavery by their fear of death" (Hebrews 2:14–15).

Rescue complete!

One thing is clear: when God acted in Jesus to rescue us, he did a thorough job; nothing was left to chance, nothing overlooked, complete provision was made for every eventuality, past, present and future. Our mission is to proclaim Jesus the Saviour, who is "good news that will cause great joy for all the people" (Luke 2:10).

We noted earlier in this chapter that the mission of Jesus is a radical one, because it involves change. The power for that change lies in the cross and the resurrection; and many are in desperate need of it. Some are bound by the past, they have no knowledge of forgiveness; some are bound by the future, they have no hope; while others are bound by the present, their circumstances seem to paralyse them and there is no escape. But all may be saved through Jesus, and it is our privilege to be involved in that mission.

Our aim in mission, then, is to save, in the fullest sense of that word, and that salvation is in the cross of Jesus. Looking forward, Jesus spoke often about his death; looking back, the early Christians spoke often about the cross. So we must make the cross the focal point of our mission, the heart of our message. As Peter rightly stated in one of his court appearances: "Salvation is found in no one else, for there is no other name under heaven given to mankind by which we must be saved" (Acts 4:12).

"As the Father has sent me, I am sending you." As we seek to respond to the call to go and make disciples, the cross needs to be at the heart of our response, because disciples are sent to save.

6

Sent . . . To Heal

I still remember very clearly the first time I laid hands on someone and prayed for them to be healed—I guess we often remember our "firsts", particularly if they are successful!

I was a student, home on holiday and visiting a friend's church. After the service, we adjourned to someone's house for coffee. There was a young man there in great pain: he had an abscess in his mouth. What made it worse for him was the prospect of important exams the next day. Two of us took him aside to another room.

We had both only recently experienced a new release of the Spirit (the baptism of the Spirit some would call it), and so the whole idea of receiving and exercising gifts of the Spirit was new to us. Neither of us had ever prayed for anyone to be healed before; we were complete novices. Yet to pray seemed the right thing to do. So, hesitantly, we placed our hands on the side of his face and prayed, claiming the promise of Mark 16:18 that "they will place their hands on people who are ill, and they will get well". After a short while we felt a gentle vibration under our hands as we prayed, which we assumed was the power of God—it was exciting! When we had finished, the pain had gone and there was just a gentle tingling feeling inside his mouth, rather like people feel after dental treatment. A visit to the dentist the next morning confirmed his healing, and after another 24 hours there was no sign of the abscess at all.

A complete job!

The Christian tradition in which I grew up had little place for healing—at least, it was never mentioned. The salvation God offered us through Jesus, so I was taught, was wholly spiritual: it was saving from sin, from spiritual death, from the wrath of God—saving the soul for eternal life. Any references to healing in the Bible were either glossed over or dismissed as happening then but not now, or "spiritualized"—so, for example, blindness, imprisonment or sickness were merely pictures of spiritual conditions. I now know that won't do, that such an understanding does not do justice to the teaching of the Bible. Wherever salvation appears, healing is often not far behind; salvation and healing are much more closely connected than I used to think, two aspects of one great saving activity of God. We see this confirmed in the word often translated "save" in the New Testament, the Greek work *sozo*. This word has a breadth and depth of meaning: it can mean to preserve or rescue from some natural danger, or from some human affliction; it can mean to save or free from disease or to preserve in good condition; it can also be translated as to prosper or to get on well. All this refers to the human, physical dimension of life. But the word has a second meaning that refers more to the spiritual dimension: hence, it also means to save or keep from eternal death, and from all that might lead to it, particularly sin. What is more, it would appear that often in the New Testament the use of the word is meant to imply both physical and spiritual meanings.

For example, to the blind beggar Jesus said: "Go, your faith has healed you" (Mark 10:52); to the healed leper who came back to say thank you, Jesus said: "Rise and go; your faith has made you well" (Luke 17:19); and to the woman in the crowd who touched his clothes and was healed he said: "Daughter, your faith has healed you" (Mark 5:34). Although in each of these cases there is physical healing, the use of the verb *sozo* may well suggest more than just physical healing—some English translations actually have "Your faith has saved you."

Clearly, then, salvation and healing are closely related in Jesus' mission, showing us that God's salvation is not just spiritual but physical—and, as we shall see in due course, there are social, moral and even political implications of that salvation too. It is "so great a salvation" (Hebrews

2:3), with power to reach, to touch, to change every part of a person's life and make them whole.

It's nothing new!

As with God's saving activity, so with his healing activity: it's not new! God has been in the business of healing as long as there have been people who get sick. What about Abraham's wife Sarah, for example? She was childless until the age of 90, and then, suddenly, she became pregnant and produced a son, Isaac (Genesis 21:1–7). Of course, God had some special interest in this particular conception but presumably it was the result physically of some miraculous working within her reproductive organs—a healing!

Something similar happened for Rachel two generations later. Rachel was Jacob's favourite wife (of two), but, while the other women in his life were producing children galore (at least ten sons and a daughter between them!), Rachel remained childless (Genesis 29:31—30:21). Then, we are told, "God remembered Rachel; he listened to her and enabled her to conceive" (Genesis 30:22), and she produced two more sons for Jacob. Another act of healing?

God heals

Several generations later, when God's people were on their travels between Egypt and the Promised Land, having just crossed the Red Sea, God spoke to them:

> If you listen carefully to the voice of the LORD your God and do what is right in his eyes, if you pay attention to his commands and keep all his decrees, I will not bring on you any of the diseases I brought on the Egyptians, for I am the LORD, who heals you (Exodus 15:26).

This is one of those special moments in the story of God's dealings with his people when he revealed to them something about himself, a facet of his character which would always be true. This time it is this: "I am the LORD who heals you." In the ensuing years, there were many times when his actions were as good as his word, and some of the specific incidents are recorded for us. For example, through Elijah he brought to life the widow of Zarephath's son (1 Kings 17); through Elisha he restored the life of the son of a woman from Shunem (2 Kings 4), and healed the commander of the Syrian army, Naaman, from leprosy (2 Kings 5); and in the time of Isaiah, God healed the king, Hezekiah (2 Kings 20).

In view of this, it is no wonder that alongside the theme that "God saves" in the worship and writings of God's people, there was also the theme that "God heals". Psalm 103 expresses that twin belief clearly: "Praise the LORD, my soul; all my inmost being, praise his holy name. Praise the LORD, O my soul, and forget not all his benefits—who forgives all your sins and heals all your diseases, who redeems your life from the pit and crowns you with love and compassion" (vv. 1–4). More than that, as time went on, the poor moral and spiritual state of God's people was increasingly spoken of as sickness, their great need being healing. For example: "Why do you cry out over your wound, your pain that has no cure? Because of your great guilt and many sins I have done these things to you . . . But I will restore you to health and heal your wounds, declares the LORD . . . " (Jeremiah 30:15,17). Again "Come, let us return to the LORD. He has torn us to pieces, but he will heal us; he has injured us, but he will bind up our wounds" (Hosea 6:1), and: "It was I who taught Ephraim to walk, taking them by the arms; but they did not realize it was I who healed them" (Hosea 11:3).

In those parts of the Old Testament which look forward to the coming of the great Saviour-figure, there is again reference to his coming to heal as well as to save. The best-known passage is Isaiah 53:

> Surely he took up our pain and bore our suffering, yet we considered him punished by God, stricken by him, and afflicted. But he was pierced for our transgressions, he was crushed for our iniquities; the punishment that brought us peace was on him, and by his wounds we are healed (vv. 4–5).

In other places, too, there is the promise that God will come to rescue and heal those who have rebelled, such as this: "I will not accuse them for ever, nor will I always be angry, for then they would faint away because of me . . . I have seen their ways, but I will heal them; I will guide them and restore comfort to Israel's mourners . . . " (Isaiah 57:16,18). And in the very last chapter of the Old Testament, in words which again look forward to a time when God will act, God says: "But for you who revere my name, the sun of righteousness will rise with healing in its rays. And you will go out and frolic like well-fed calves" (Malachi 4:2).

The coming of the healing Saviour

So, for those who were at all familiar with the content of the Old Testament, as many of Jesus' contemporaries claimed to be, there should have been no surprise that the coming of "God our Saviour" was not just for the rescuing of the soul but for the complete healing of people. And if we read the small print carefully—that is, all the Old Testament says about the coming of the Saviour—we shall realize that his coming means restoration for humanity, corporately as well as individually, physically and socially as well as spiritually.

In fact, the aim of God's saving activity is to bring to his people nothing less than *shalom*. That is a lovely Hebrew word usually translated as "peace", but it has a much richer, fuller meaning than our word "peace" usually suggests. It means so much more than the absence of "aggro", for example, because the kids have gone to bed! It means the complete wellbeing of the whole person, body, soul and spirit, personally, socially and economically—setting people free to be the whole people God has always intended them to be. Thus, Jesus' title "Prince of Peace (*Shalom*)" is very significant—he comes to bring health and wholeness as well as salvation. Here too is the significance of those well-known words spoken by the angels at the time of Jesus' birth: "Glory to God in the highest heaven, and on earth peace to those on whom his favour rests" (Luke 2:14). The birth of the Saviour, in David's town of Bethlehem, is the coming of *shalom*—no wonder it is good news! Peter grasped this truth later when, in one of his sermons, he spoke of "announcing the good news of peace through Jesus Christ, who is Lord of all" (Acts 10:36). Jesus is not just the Saviour but the peace-bringer; he is Prince of Peace and brings healing, health and wholeness. That's salvation!

Healing as he goes

It is no wonder, then, that when we turn to the Gospels and look at the life and ministry of Jesus, we find that healing has a very prominent place: wherever we find him preaching and teaching we usually find him healing the sick as well. Someone has said that wherever you dip into the Gospels you will find Jesus either on his way to heal, or healing, or coming back from healing, or talking about healing. That may be a slight exaggeration, but it is true that roughly one fifth of the Gospels is given over to recording or discussing Jesus' healing ministry, which suggests it is quite important.

Luke's Gospel, in particular, is full of healing—hardly surprising when you remember that he was a doctor. We were made aware of this in one of the churches where I was vicar when we set about preaching our way section by section through Luke's Gospel at the morning services. By the time we had got to the end of Chapter 8, we had already preached about healing about ten times, not because of any pet theme of ours but because of the emphasis in the Gospel. We found we could not escape it: healing is important in the mission of Jesus.

In the Gospels, there are some 28 recorded instances where Jesus healed specific individuals or groups. Many of these are the well-known "stories of Jesus" some of us know from Sunday-school days: like the giving of sight to blind Bartimaeus (Mark 10:46–52), the healing of the man with a withered hand (Mark 3:1–6), the restoring of the paralytic lowered through the roof by his friends (Mark 2:1–11), and many more. In addition to these specific instances there are some 13 other occasions described in the Gospels when Jesus healed people; sometimes, it would appear, very many people.

For example:

> Jesus went throughout Galilee, teaching in their synagogues, proclaiming the good news of the kingdom, and healing every disease and illness among the people (Matthew 4:23).

Again:

> [Jesus] went down with them and stood on a level place. A large crowd of his disciples was there and a great number of people from all over Judea, from Jerusalem, and from the coastal region around Tyre and Sidon, who had come to hear him and to be healed of their diseases. Those troubled by impure spirits were cured, and the people all tried to touch him, because power was coming from him and healing them all (Luke 6:17–19).

And again:

> When Jesus had finished saying these things, he left Galilee and went into the region of Judea to the other side of the Jordan. Large crowds followed him, and he healed them there (Matthew 19:1–2).

Reading these accounts I sometimes wonder just how many people Jesus did heal during his short public ministry. Hundreds? Thousands? More?

It's all part of mission!

It is also significant that whenever Jesus spoke in general terms about his mission, healing was usually mentioned. For example, early in his public ministry Jesus visited his hometown of Nazareth and went to the synagogue service on the Sabbath. He was invited to read the second lesson, a reading from the prophecy of Isaiah—we know it as the beginning of Isaiah 61 (Luke 4:16–21). For Jesus, it summed up what his mission was all about; it included "recovery of sight for the blind" (v. 18).

Later, John the Baptist, in prison, was eager to learn whether Jesus really was the promised Messiah, the God-Saviour, or whether they should continue to look for another. So he sent two of his disciples to ask Jesus: "Are you the one who was to come, or should we expect someone else?" (Luke 7:19). Jesus' reply must have been a bit of a surprise: he didn't offer John a reasoned, theological argument, quoting the Old Testament to back up his argument, which is what he may have expected. Instead, Jesus said to John's messengers: "Go back and report to John what you have seen and heard. The blind receive sight, the lame walk, those who have leprosy are cured, the deaf hear, the dead are raised, and the good news is preached to the poor" (Luke 7:22).

Apparently, as Jesus saw it, the best proof that he was the Messiah, the promised Saviour, was the fact that people were being healed—they were being made whole, finding peace (*shalom*) through him. In other words, the healing ministry of Jesus was an integral, vitally important part of his mission to save.

The Saviour heals

So let's take a closer look at Jesus' healing ministry. First, why did he heal? There are a number of answers to that question, one of which we have just been talking about: healing is an integral part of saving, so Jesus the Saviour is also Jesus the healer.

We have also already noted in Chapter 2 how Jesus was keenly aware of what his Father wanted and did only what he saw his Father doing (John 5:19). Healing was part of his Father's will for him. We see this in Jesus' conversation with his disciples in the presence of a blind man (John 9:1–12). Jesus explained why he was going to heal him: "As long as it is day, we must do the work of him who sent me. Night is coming, when no one can work" (v. 4). We see this, too, when the Jews complained that Jesus healed the lame man at the Pool of Bethesda on the Sabbath (John 5:1–18). Jesus replied: "My Father is always at his work to this very day, and I too am working" (v. 17). In other words, he was doing no more and no less than his Father was doing, even if it was the Sabbath! God was in the healing business, so Jesus was too.

There is another reason why Jesus got involved in healing: Jesus saw it as victory over Satan, reclaiming ground that Satan had illegitimately claimed, putting right what Satan had spoiled. We shall consider this more fully in Chapter 8; for now, consider one incident where this is seen clearly. Jesus was teaching in the synagogue one Sabbath; there was a woman there whose back was badly bent, rendering her disabled—she had been like it for 18 years (Luke 13:10–17). Jesus put his hands on her, and she straightened up, praising God (v. 13). But the synagogue ruler was not pleased and complained (typical, isn't it!): you're not supposed to heal on the Sabbath! Jesus' response to that is both strange and significant:

> You hypocrites! Doesn't each of you on the Sabbath untie his ox or donkey from the stall and lead it out to give it water? Then should not this woman, a daughter of Abraham, whom Satan has kept bound for eighteen long years, be set free on the Sabbath day from what bound her? (vv. 15–16).

Notice, Jesus describes her condition as "bound by Satan". Thus, he healed her to undo Satan's damage.

Jesus also healed because he was moved by the suffering and disease he met with time and again. We looked in Chapter 3 at that marvellous Greek word *splagchnizomai* and saw how Jesus was moved from deep within in his mission. What is true of his ministry generally was true of his healing ministry particularly. Jesus was filled with compassion for the leper who came and knelt in front of him and asked to be healed (Mark 1:41); he had compassion on blind men begging at the roadside and he healed them (Matthew 20:29–34); his heart went out to the woman who was about to bury her only son and he brought him back to life (Luke 7:11–17); and he had compassion on the crowds and healed those who were sick (Matthew 14:14). Jesus was moved by people's needs; that's why he healed.

But how did he do it?
The Gospels offer us a number of reasons why Jesus healed. The answer to the question "How?" is not so clear. There is no one pattern of healing that Jesus always used; rather there is variety.

Sometimes Jesus took the initiative, sometimes the sick person did; sometimes there was faith in action on the part of the one who was healed, at other times it was not evident; sometimes Jesus touched the sick person, sometimes he didn't, and at other times the sick person touched Jesus; sometimes he prayed, sometimes he simply spoke a word of command like "Get up!" or "Be clean!"; at times he would use some physical agent such as spittle (Mark 7:33) or mud (John 9:6); sometimes the sick person was asked to do something like "Go and wash" or "Stretch out your hand" or "Go, show yourselves to the priests"; often Jesus healed publicly, but occasionally he chose to take people away to a more private place; mostly he healed directly, occasionally he did it indirectly, from a distance (e.g. John 4:46–52). However Jesus chose to act in each specific situation, this much is clear: he healed with power (Luke 5:17), with authority (Mark 1:27), and therefore with great effectiveness—"People were overwhelmed with amazement. 'He has done everything well,' they said. 'He even makes the deaf hear and the mute speak'" (Mark 7:37).

All or some?

A third question we could ask is "Whom did Jesus heal?" A superficial reading of the Gospels might suggest the answer to that question is "everyone"; however, a closer study shows that this is not so. We know, for example, that Jesus only healed one sick person at the Pool of Bethesda, although there were probably many sick around the pool that day (John 5:1–13); it is quite likely there were other beggars at the roadside in Jericho the day Jesus visited, besides blind Bartimaeus (Mark 10:46–52); we are told that when he visited his hometown Jesus could do very few miracles because of their lack of faith, except to heal a few sick people (Mark 6:5). In addition, when he was handling the crowds, although many were healed, were there some, perhaps on the fringes of the crowd, who were not healed? Who knows?

What is more significant is the wide range of sickness which we know Jesus dealt with. He gave sight to the blind (John 9:1–12), hearing to the deaf (Mark 7:31–5), and speech to the dumb (Matthew 9:32–3); he straightened malformed limbs (Luke 6:6–10), straightened out a bent back (Luke 13:10–13), and enabled the lame and paralysed to walk (Luke 5:17–25; Matthew 21:14); he healed those with a high fever (Luke 4:38–9), those suffering from leprosy (Luke 5:12–13), a man with dropsy (called oedema today) (Luke 14:1–4), a woman with a chronic internal haemorrhage (Luke 8:43–8); he set free those who were affected by evil (Luke 4:31–5), and even brought back to life those who had already died (e.g. John 11). Matthew's brief reports of Jesus' healing activity read like a medical catalogue:

> News about him spread all over Syria and people brought to him
> all who were ill with various diseases, those suffering severe pain,
> the demon-possessed, those having seizures and the paralysed,
> and he healed them . . . Great crowds came to him, bringing the
> lame, the blind, the crippled, the mute and many others, and
> laid them at his feet; and he healed them (Matthew 4:24; 15:30).

All this should be no surprise: Jesus is the bringer of *shalom*, and
therefore he is bound to want to deal with anything and everything in
people's lives that robs them of that wholeness. Legitimately he may make
the claim: "I have come that they may have life, and have it to the full"
(John 10:10)—he deals with everything that spoils life. Jesus' mission is
to bring life and wholeness.

Careful diagnosis

If we take a closer look still at Jesus' healing ministry, we discover another
significant feature; that Jesus apparently saw the root cause of each
person's condition and acted accordingly.

Sometimes he simply dealt with the physical symptoms and spoke
healing to the person: for example, to the man with leprosy he said, "Be
clean!" and he was cured (Matthew 8:3), and to the blind man he said,
"Go, your faith has healed you", and he received his sight (Mark 10:52).

On other occasions, however, Jesus handled things very differently.
The best-known example of this is the man lowered through the roof
by his friends to the feet of Jesus (Mark 2:1–11). Everyone could see
what was wrong with him: he was paralysed. Yet, Jesus did not deal
immediately with his paralysis; instead, he said to the man: "Son, your
sins are forgiven" (v. 5). That probably surprised many who were there
that day; it certainly annoyed the religious teachers who reckoned that
Jesus was overstepping the mark—only God was supposed to forgive sins!

But what was Jesus actually doing? Apparently, he recognized that this
man's physical condition was caused by sin in his life. Only when that
was dealt with could there be healing: forgiveness of sin first, physical
healing second.

This is very significant, especially in view of those, perhaps with
only a superficial knowledge of the Gospels, who are quick to dismiss

the healing ministry of Jesus as primitive and insignificant because he lacked the insights of modern medical science. The truth is that Jesus was in many ways centuries ahead of his time: for it is only in relatively recent years that medical science has fully and openly come to terms with the fact that psychological problems can cause physical sickness. For example, feelings of guilt or bitterness or anger can result in some physical conditions, and if the root cause is not recognized and dealt with, then relief from the symptoms will often only be partial and temporary.

Jesus' handling of the paralysed man is an important model for us in our ministry of healing; first he recognized and dealt with the cause, then he healed the symptoms. In our experience, albeit limited, we often find it is necessary to follow this pattern.

I think, for example, of a woman with whom Ron, a member of the healing ministry team in one of my churches, prayed: she had suffered with pain across her chest for about seven or eight years, a condition for which her doctor could find no cause. As they prayed, Ron was prompted to ask her whether there was any situation within her family that caused her hurt. Apparently there was, for she began to weep. Eventually Ron was able to lead her in prayer for release and healing of the hurt, in the course of which she was encouraged to forgive those who had caused it. Even as they prayed the pain in her chest eased, and when Ron met her the following evening, she was radiant. The pain had completely gone.

This ministry is not just for those within the church either; there is great need of it in the wider community too. It is an all-important part of our mission. How many hurting people in our communities need not so much a pill from the doctor, or counselling from the psychiatrist, but the "*shalom*-wholeness" from Jesus, the great physician? In his mission that's what Jesus offered, and we must offer it too.

Down with the devil!

There is a third way in which Jesus confronted sickness and brought healing: he saw it as a spiritual matter. We have already noted the incident of the woman with a bent back whom Jesus described as having been bound by Satan for 18 years (Luke 13:10–17). There was also the occasion when a dumb man was brought to Jesus: although his physical problem was obvious, Jesus handled it spiritually, driving out the demon (Matthew

9:32–3). (It is worth noting that another time Jesus handled a dumb man very differently, spitting and touching the man's tongue, as a result of which he began to speak, in Mark 7:31–5.) Again, there was the epileptic boy brought to Jesus by his father: Jesus healed him by rebuking a demon in him (Matthew 17:14–18).

This "spiritual" approach to healing is also very significant and we need to learn from it. Although there are many today who dismiss any talk of "demons" as primitive superstition, it is quite clear that some illnesses have spiritual causes. This should not be surprising when today there is increasing interest and involvement in occult subjects, from full-blooded Satanism to the supposedly harmless (though that is far from the case) dabbling with Ouija boards and the like. People are being exposed to harmful spiritual powers and may become infected by them; when that happens spiritual ministry is necessary, whatever medical help may also be needed.

Towards the end of one meeting at our church a man was literally rolling around in the aisle, which was somewhat alarming for those who were nearby. He was escorted to a back room. He had physical problems, he would at times behave strangely and irrationally, but, most significantly, he spoke of being aware of something evil and powerful inside him. In prayer, that evil was dealt with. Once free of that, the other symptoms cleared up. Today he is a changed man, and is happy to tell you so—he is enjoying the *shalom* of Jesus.

Bringing wholeness of body, mind and spirit was an integral part of Jesus' mission: our mission must be the same. "As the Father has sent me, I am sending you." But can we justify that? I believe we can.

Sending others out

There are several places in the Gospels where Jesus commissions others to go out in mission in his name. In every case, healing is part of the commission, either explicitly or implicitly. Let's take a look.

When Jesus sent the Twelve out in mission, we are told: " . . . he gave them power and authority to drive out all demons and to cure diseases, and he sent them out to proclaim the kingdom of God and to heal those who were ill" (Luke 9:1–2). And that is exactly what they did: "So they set out and went from village to village, proclaiming the good news and healing people everywhere" (Luke 9:6).

Later, he sent the Seventy-two out in mission; his instructions to them were similar to those he gave to the Twelve. When they entered a town, they were to "heal those who were ill and tell them, 'The kingdom of God has come near to you'" (Luke 10:9). The Seventy-two came back excited, telling Jesus: "Lord, even the demons submit to us in your name" (Luke 10:17).

John includes neither of these two specific commissions in his Gospel, but he does record this promise from Jesus as he talked with his disciples: "Very truly I tell you, whoever believes in me will do the works I have been doing, and they will do even greater things than these, because I am going to the Father" (John 14:12). That is mind-blowing! Jesus is telling his disciples that they will do all the things he has been doing. Does that include giving sight to the blind, causing the lame to walk, growing limbs, straightening backs, opening ears and mouths, curing diseases, and even raising the dead? Apparently, it does: that's what Jesus had been doing, and he said they would do the same.

Jesus spelled this out a little more after his resurrection, as he talked with his disciples. His words are recorded at the end of Mark's Gospel (though they are not part of the original Gospel and were probably not written by Mark):

> Go into all the world and preach the gospel to all creation . . . And these signs will accompany those who believe: in my name they will drive out demons; they will speak in new tongues; they will pick up snakes with their hands; and when they drink deadly poison, it will not hurt them at all; they will place their hands on people who are ill, and they will get well (Mark 16:15,17–18).

Again, healing is prominent in his instructions.

The best-known commission for mission is recorded at the end of Matthew's Gospel. It doesn't specifically refer to healing, but is it implied? Consider Jesus' words carefully: "All authority in heaven and on earth has been given to me. Therefore go and make disciples of all nations, baptizing them in the name of the Father and of the Son and of the Holy Spirit, and teaching them to obey everything I have commanded you . . ." (Matthew 28:18–20). At first, it might seem that he is instructing the disciples to teach others the same things he has taught them. However, he is actually telling them to teach others to obey (literally "to observe strictly") everything he had commanded them—the Greek actually says "all things whatsoever" as if to emphasize the point. Since Jesus had previously commanded them to go and preach the kingdom of God, heal the sick and drive out demons (Luke 9:1–2), presumably these things were included. Certainly, the disciples understood it to include these things, if Acts is anything to go by. There we find them busy doing those things Jesus had commanded them to do: preaching, healing, driving out demons. What is more, it is quite clear that they not only took to heart the command of Jesus to heal, but they had also watched him carefully so that they knew exactly what to do—Jesus had modelled healing for them.

Take Peter, for example: he had never healed a lame man before when he met one at the gate of the Temple, but he had seen Jesus do it and so he knew what to do—and it worked! (Acts 3:1–10). He had never brought a dead person back to life when he was taken into the room where the dead body of Dorcas was lying. But he had been present when Jesus had healed Jairus' daughter, so he followed that pattern—and it worked! (Acts 9:36–43). But it wasn't just Peter: all the early Christians apparently took seriously the command of Jesus to continue his work and the promise of Jesus that they would do what he did. Peter, Stephen, Philip, Paul and Barnabas—they all did it; it was part of Jesus' mission.

Healing today?

So it's clear that the first followers of Jesus continued to heal as well as preach when they continued Jesus' mission. But can we be sure that those of us who follow Jesus 2000 years later are still meant to heal? I believe that the teaching of scripture clearly implies that the answer to that question is "Yes".

God is the same

To begin with there is the character of God, who says of himself: "I the LORD do not change" (Malachi 3:6). Whatever God is committed to and longing for in the Bible, he is still committed to it and longing for it today. When God made the world and human beings in it, the whole set-up was good (Genesis 1:31). Even human beings, at first, enjoyed wholeness. The account of "the Fall" in Genesis 3 suggests that when human beings first sinned, that wholeness began to disintegrate, and something wholesome and healthy was lost: "Then the eyes of both of them [Adam and Eve] were opened, and they realized that they were naked" (v. 7). In a relatively short period of time following that incident, struggle, pain, frustration, jealousy and murder entered into the experience of human life (Genesis 3, 4)—the wholeness was spoiled.

It is also clear, however, that God's intention for the end of things, when he will end the world as we know it, is that all should be well again: that everything that spoils and destroys will be finished:

> God's dwelling-place is now among the people, and he will dwell with them. They will be his people, and God himself will be with them and be their God. He will wipe away every tear from their eyes. There will be no more death or mourning or crying or pain, for the old order of things has passed away (Revelation 21:3–4).

When our world began it was perfect and one day it will be perfect again—that is the desire of God, our Creator.

Of course, as a result of sin, things are far from perfect now: the whole of creation struggles and will continue to do so until the final day when "the creation itself will be liberated from its bondage to decay and brought into the freedom and glory of the children of God" (Romans 8:21). But in the midst of that struggle in which we all live, God still desires that perfection he originally designed for us; he is still "the LORD, who heals you" (Exodus 15:26); he continues to bring *shalom* wherever and whenever he can; he is committed to health and healing, and he longs for wholeness.

If this is what God wants and works for, then it must be what we want and work for, too—it's part of the mission to which we are called.

In practice, I think that means that whenever someone who is sick or suffering in some way asks me to pray for them, unless I feel specifically that it is inappropriate, then I should pray. And I shall pray knowing that healing is God's will in general, even if I don't know that it is his specific will for this particular person at this particular time (which is often the case). I hope, through prayer, to discern God's specific will, though this does not always happen. Yet I still pray.

If we would be involved in God's mission, we need to be committed to the ministry of healing too, because God is and his mission does not change!

Jesus is the same

Not only is God unchanging, Jesus, as Hebrews reminds us, is "the same yesterday and today and for ever" (Hebrews 13:8). The phrase has often been a slogan text for evangelical enterprise of all kinds: it has often been seen, for example, emblazoned across the stage of large auditoria where evangelistic missions have been held. However, in practice we have really believed and preached that Jesus is only partly the same today as yesterday: he still saves today, but he doesn't heal any more.

But that won't do. Healing is so inextricably bound up with salvation that you cannot have one and not the other. Indeed, I believe it is not unreasonable to suggest that if Jesus does not heal today then Jesus cannot save today either! Commitment to God's mission involves preaching Jesus; the Jesus we preach must be the Jesus of the Gospels, and that Jesus is a healing Jesus as well as a saving Jesus.

The early Christians got hold of that firmly and acted accordingly. Just occasionally, I feel sorry for the political and religious leaders in the early days of the church. They had found the things Jesus said and did embarrassing and threatening, so they did away with him, thinking that would be the end of all those strange events. But it wasn't! Just a few weeks later, it all started again: challenging preaching, amazing miracles and the inevitable crowds. All that Jesus did, his followers did. Why not today too?

The resources are the same

Fortunately for us, not only is God unchanging and Jesus the same as ever, but the resources for mission which Jesus enjoyed are also available to us—we may be filled with the same Spirit. Paul speaks of the Spirit of him who raised Jesus from the dead, living in us (Romans 8:11); and the power of that Spirit is the same power which raised Jesus from death—that's powerful! (Ephesians 1:19–20). What is more, the Spirit brings us gifts and abilities which enable us to do things we would otherwise struggle to do.

We shall look more fully at this in Chapter 11, but among the gifts the Spirit brings are the significant "gifts of healing" (1 Corinthians 12:9). We have no excuse for opting out because we lack resources: they are all there for us through the Spirit, so that we can do what Jesus did.

Healing in the church

Down the centuries, the church has never completely lost sight of this aspect of mission, though the history of the Church's healing ministry is inconsistent, sometimes strong, sometimes scarcely visible. Today, in some parts of the Church, particularly in developing countries, healing is a prominent and effective tool in mission: healings are no longer considered extraordinary but simply an ordinary, natural part of the everyday outreach of the church. Not surprisingly, in those places the church is growing, and growing fast!

Meanwhile, here in the West, things are rather different: we still struggle with scepticism and unbelief, still seeing healing as "supernatural" and therefore to be handled with great caution, certainly not accepting it as the norm. But there are encouraging signs too: the church is rediscovering its heritage and recognizing healing as part of its mission. Thus, there have been numerous initiatives in recent years seeking to put healing back on the church's agenda and to resource the church for this ministry.

It is also encouraging that an increasing number of books have been written on the subject of healing. Maybe the day will come here, too, when healing is so completely integrated into mission that healings are ordinary rather than extraordinary, miracles natural rather than supernatural. Then, perhaps, we shall be as effective in mission as our fellow Christians in other parts of the world already are.

Count me in!

But what about you and me? I think there is no escape: mission inevitably includes healing. So I am committed to the healing ministry of the church, not because I believe God has specifically gifted me for that ministry, but because he has called me to be involved in his mission.

Of course, being committed doesn't solve all the problems: there are still plenty of unanswered questions, not least why some of those I pray for don't recover their health. I don't know the answer to that question, but I am wrestling with it, trying to understand. What I have realized is this: even if I see no one healed, that doesn't let me off the hook.

The call to mission is a call to pray for healing. Over the years, as a church leader, I have been committed to this ministry, often offering prayer at services and also at other times. A few people have been healed in various ways and made more whole—it would have been great to see more. But our feet have been kept firmly on the ground in this ministry, particularly in the church where I was vicar some years ago, when each Sunday night a number of young people in wheelchairs, with physical and mental disabilities, joined us for worship. It was encouraging to see some of them becoming more "whole"; of course, we would love to have seen one of them leave their wheelchair and walk, though that didn't happen.

Soon after writing about this, one of those young people died. I was reminded of Paul's words: "Therefore, since through God's mercy we have this ministry, we do not lose heart" (2 Corinthians 4:1). That's just how we felt!

The call to mission is a call to heal and we must respond; it is part of the call to discipleship.

"As the Father has sent me, I am sending you."

7

Sent . . . With Signs Accompanying

We had just finished the evening service at the church in Cambridge where I was curate, and I had gone to the door to talk with people as they left. Just outside on the pavement I found a small group of young adults, obviously concerned about something. It was apparent that the two women in the group were particularly distressed. They began to explain that they had been playing with a Ouija board and some frightening things had begun to happen. The women were very scared and realized that they were out of their depth. So, although none of them were Christians, they ended up at the church asking for help.

We invited them inside; some came, others declined and chose to wait outside. Inside, one of the women reacted quite violently to the cross which stood on the Communion table. If there had been any doubt in our minds before, now we knew what we were dealing with: these people had been infected by evil spiritual power.

In the end, just one of the women responded to our offer of help and came, with one of the young men, into a side room. There we talked with her about Jesus, about her need to turn to him, to repent of her sin, to commit her life to him—the only place of spiritual safety. Then we prayed with her and, in the name of Jesus, asked that she should be set free from every evil spiritual influence. As we prayed, her body became tense and then she slumped onto the floor. That was a little alarming, until we remembered that something similar had happened when Jesus was dealing with a young boy who had an evil spirit: the crowd thought he was dead until Jesus took him by the hand and helped him up (Mark 9:26–7). We did the same and helped the woman up. All the tension and anxiety had gone and so had the frightened look in her eyes—there was a sense of peace about her.

The young man had been watching the whole thing, and when we had finished, he let out a "Wow!" and then said: "Who needs words when you can see something like that!" When we went back outside to rejoin the others, he boldly announced: "We've just seen God deliver Jeanette!" He knew it, he could not deny it, and he was prepared to tell the others—he had seen God in action.

God in action . . .

"Actions speak louder than words" so the old proverb goes. God apparently believes it, too. Throughout the pages of the Bible, Old and New Testaments alike, we find that he is not just a talking God but a doing God. Time after time God spoke to his people, Israel, through prophets; but frequently, too, God did amazing things among his people. Through what he said and what he did they learned about him.

You could say that God has always been in action, busy doing things. The opening chapters of the Bible speak of the most amazing burst of activity that there has ever been, when "God created the heavens and the earth" (Genesis 1:1). This is not the place to discuss in detail how it actually happened; for now, let us simply note that, according to the Bible, the world is here as a result of God's initiative, and was formed as a result of his action.

This is certainly the testimony of the writers of the Old Testament: "The earth is the LORD'S, and everything in it, the world, and all who live in it; for he founded it on the seas and established it on the waters" (Psalm 24:1–2); "He set the earth on its foundations; it can never be moved" (Psalm 104:5).

> He stretches out the heavens like a canopy, and spreads them out like a tent to live in . . . Lift up your eyes and look to the heavens: who created all these? He who brings out the starry host one by one, and calls forth each of them by name. Because of his great power and mighty strength, not one of them is missing (Isaiah 40:22,26).

And the writer of Hebrews says: "By faith we understand that the universe was formed at God's command, so that what is seen was not made out of what was visible" (Hebrews 11:3).

Thus, the whole universe points us to God, revealing to us, if we have eyes to see, something of the power, the splendour, the glory of God. That's how the Psalm writers saw it: "LORD, our Lord, how majestic is your name in all the earth! You have set your glory in the heavens" (Psalm 8:1); "The heavens declare the glory of God; the skies proclaim the work of his hands" (Psalm 19:1). Much later, Paul, in his no-nonsense way, declared that no one had any excuse for not knowing God: the fact of God shouts at them from the world around them. "For since the creation of the world God's invisible qualities—his eternal power and divine nature—have been clearly seen, being understood from what has been made, so that people are without excuse" (Romans 1:20).

Already we see here an important principle: that when God acts, when he does amazing things, we are not simply to see the action and be amazed, but we are to look behind the action to the one who has caused it to happen, and worship him. Every action of God is a "sign" pointing us to God: the right reaction to which is worship. In all the signs and wonders and miracles we read about in the Bible, this is God's clear intention: that people shall see and worship. Let's take a look at that principle at work.

... through Moses

The Israelites were on their travels. They had crossed the Red Sea and were now in the Desert of Sin (what an unfortunate name!) (Exodus 16). There the people resorted to their favourite pastime, which was to grumble at the leadership, although they did have grounds for complaint; they had no food (v. 3). Moses told them that God would miraculously provide for them, morning and evening: "At twilight you will eat meat, and in the morning you will be filled with bread" (v. 12). We can read exactly how God provided for them in this chapter; it's fascinating reading! But notice, God had a very important reason for acting in this way. Of course, he was concerned for their physical needs and wanted to provide for them, but the real reason for his miraculous action was to remind the people about their God: "Then you will know that I am the LORD your God" (v. 12).

. . . through Joshua

The Israelites were nearing the end of their travels, about to enter the Promised Land. Moses was dead and Joshua was now their leader. The last barrier between them and their new home was the River Jordan, but there was no bridge. Joshua apparently had an inkling that God was going to help them by one of his amazing acts. He told the people: "Consecrate yourselves, for tomorrow the LORD will do amazing things among you" (Joshua 3:5). And that is what happened: miraculously, the people crossed the Jordan not only safely but without getting their feet wet—you can read the whole story in Joshua 3 and 4. God had done it again!

But Joshua tried to make sure the people understood the real purpose of this miracle. Even as he told them what was going to happen, he explained: "This is how you will know that the living God is among you . . . " (Joshua 3:10). Once safely across, Joshua reminded them:

> For the LORD your God dried up the Jordan before you until you had crossed over. The LORD your God did to the Jordan what he had done to the Red Sea when he dried it up before us until we had crossed over. He did this so that all the peoples of the earth might know that the hand of the LORD is powerful and so that you might always fear the LORD your God (Joshua 4:23–4).

In other words: "Don't just be amazed at what has happened, worship God who has caused it to happen!" And that was not confined just to the Israelites but included people of other nations who happened to see what happened: it should cause them to look to the God of Israel too.

Notice what was happening: Israel's God acted miraculously for them, they acknowledged it and worshipped him; others, looking on, saw what happened and also recognized it was the God of Israel who had done it. Maybe it wouldn't be too long before the "outsiders" asked to know more about Israel' s God. That's mission!

... through Elijah

Elijah the prophet had no food or drink. God told him to go to the home of a widow living in the village of Zarephath, and she would provide for him—the story is in 1 Kings 17:7-24. She had only a small amount of flour and oil and was about to make a last meal for herself and her son. Elijah told her that if she fed him first, God would make sure she didn't go without food—and that's exactly what happened (vv. 13-16).

Shortly afterwards her son died. Elijah prayed for him and returned him to his mother alive. Two miraculous acts of God in a poor widow's home! But notice her response: "Now I know that you are a man of God and that the word of the LORD from your mouth is the truth" (v. 24). Wouldn't it be great if people said that about us: that they recognize us to be men and women of God and that they are convinced that what we say is truth? For Elijah, that happened when God worked "wonders" through him. Is there any reason why God cannot do similar things today with similar results? That would be effective mission!

If that wasn't enough, God acted even more dramatically through Elijah some years later. Things had deteriorated in Israel: many people were worshipping other gods, in particular Baal. What made it worse was that Ahab the king was ineffective, and affairs were directed largely by his wife, Jezebel, a nasty piece of work! Elijah wanted to call Israel back to God; so he initiated a challenge which would demonstrate to the people once and for all who really was God: the God of Israel or Baal. Two altars were built and sacrifices placed on them. The prophets of Baal would call on their god and Elijah on his, asking for a bit of spontaneous combustion, or fire without striking a match. The god who answered with fire was the real god. (The whole story is recorded in 1 Kings 18:16-40.)

Guess who won? Israel's God, of course: he is the real God. But notice, once again, the purpose of all this was not simply to show that Israel's God could produce better firework displays than Baal, but rather that the people would see, believe and worship the God who answered with fire. And they did: "When all the people saw this, they fell prostrate and cried, 'The LORD—he is God! The LORD—he is God!'" (v. 39).

. . . through Elisha

Elijah's successor as a prophet was Elisha, for whom God continued to do amazing things. For example, there was a commander in the Syrian army called Naaman who was ill with leprosy, a dreaded incurable disease. He was told that the prophet Elisha in Israel might be able to heal him so, prepared to try anything, he set off to find him—this story is in 2 Kings 5. To his dismay, Elisha told him to go and bathe seven times in the River Jordan and when, reluctantly, he did so, he was healed (vv. 8–14). His response is significant: "Now I know that there is no God in all the world except in Israel . . . " (v. 15). So convinced was he, he asked to take some of Israel's soil back with him so he could worship Israel's God back home (v. 17).

It's the principle that's important. God acted in a miraculous way: this time the recipient was an "outsider", but he believed as a result of what he saw God do. Again, that's mission!

. . . through Shadrach, Meshach and Abednego

God's people were in exile in Babylon. Daniel and his three friends Shadrach, Meshach and Abednego had been appointed to responsible positions by King Nebuchadnezzar. Even in exile, they were still devoted to God and worshipped him daily. But Nebuchadnezzar set up a golden image and instructed everyone to worship it, to the exclusion of all other gods. It was out of the question for Shadrach, Meshach and Abednego to go along with that, even though the threatened punishment was to be thrown in a fiery furnace, and they told the king so—the story is in Daniel 3.

The king was furious; he had them tied up and thrown into the furnace. But God was with them to help. They emerged unharmed, without so much as a hair singed. The king was amazed and realized who was responsible: "Praise be to the God of Shadrach, Meshach and Abednego, who has sent his angel and rescued his servants! . . . no other god can save in this way" (vv. 28–9). Subsequently, he sent a decree throughout his kingdom; after the usual greetings, it began:

> It is my pleasure to tell you about the miraculous signs and wonders that the Most High God has performed for me. How

great are his signs, how mighty his wonders! His kingdom is
an eternal kingdom; his dominion endures from generation to
generation (Daniel 4:2–3).

God acted and Nebuchadnezzar, another "outsider", believed!

. . . through Daniel

The story of Daniel in the lions' den is one of the best-known Old
Testament stories—it's recorded in Daniel 6. Darius was king in Babylon
and Daniel had become his second-in-command. The officials were
jealous of him and plotted his downfall; they persuaded King Darius
to issue a decree that everyone was to worship him and only him; any
dissenters would be thrown to the lions.

As expected, Daniel responded in just the same way as Shadrach,
Meshach and Abednego had done: he refused to stop worshipping his
God. So he was reported to the king who was urged to stand by his decree
and, against his better judgement, Daniel was thrown into the lions' den.

The next morning, Darius came early to the den and called out to
Daniel: "Daniel, servant of the living God, has your God, whom you
serve continually, been able to rescue you from the lions?" (v. 20). It
was a silly question really, of course he had! In fact, Daniel was totally
unscathed. Darius was thrilled and wrote to all his people:

> May you prosper greatly! I issue a decree that in every part of
> my kingdom people must fear and reverence the God of Daniel.
> For he is the living God and he endures for ever; his kingdom
> will not be destroyed, his dominion will never end. He rescues
> and he saves; he performs signs and wonders in the heavens and
> on the earth. He has rescued Daniel from the power of the lions
> (vv. 25–7).

Darius had been converted to belief in God, and all as a result of God's
action. That's mission!

. . . again and again

There are many more instances of God's action in the pages of the Old Testament. Its writers agree that this miraculous activity was one effective way in which God made himself known, showed himself to be the living God.

Moses talked about it like this:

> Has any god ever tried to take for himself one nation out of another nation, by testings, by signs and wonders, by war, by a mighty hand and an outstretched arm, or by great and awesome deeds, like all the things the LORD your God did for you in Egypt before your very eyes? You were shown these things so that you might know that the LORD is God; besides him there is no other (Deuteronomy 4:34–5).

The Psalmist testified:

> I will remember the deeds of the LORD; yes, I will remember your miracles of long ago. I will consider all your works and meditate on all your mighty deeds. Your ways, O God, are holy. What god is so great as our God? You are the God who performs miracles; you display your power among the peoples (Psalm 77:11–14).

The prophet, Jeremiah, in prayer, reflected on the greatness of God:

> Great and mighty God, whose name is the LORD Almighty, great are your purposes and mighty are your deeds . . . You performed signs and wonders in Egypt and have continued them to this day, in Israel and among all mankind, and have gained the renown that is still yours (Jeremiah 32:18–20).

United testimony: God's action encourages belief!

Jesus takes over the action

When we turn to the New Testament and in particular to the life and ministry of Jesus, we find the same pattern: that Jesus came to do as well as to speak; his ministry is full of action. Of course, that should be no surprise: if God was a God of action, and Jesus is God's Son, committed to doing only what he saw his Father doing, then it is only to be expected that there will be action.

We have already noted in Chapter 6 that there are 28 specific instances in the Gospels of Jesus' healing activity, together with 13 brief accounts of many being healed. But healing was by no means his only activity: there are also ten other specific references in the Gospels to Jesus acting "miraculously". Many of these are well known: the stilling of the storm, when Jesus spoke directly to a raging storm on the Sea of Galilee and it ceased (Mark 4:35–41); the feeding of the five thousand, when Jesus fed a crowd with a few loaves of bread and a couple of fish—and there was a lot left over (Matthew 14:13–21); when Jesus walked on water, and invited Peter to join him—though Peter wasn't entirely successful (Matthew 14:22–33); when Jesus went to a wedding reception where the wine ran out, and he turned 180 gallons of water into the best vintage (John 2:1–11).

In the final chapters of his Gospel, John implies that there were many more miraculous happenings during the ministry of Jesus that have not been recorded. He writes:

> Jesus performed many other signs in the presence of his disciples, which are not recorded in this book ... Jesus did many other things as well. If every one of them were written down, I suppose that even the whole world would not have room for the books that would be written (John 20:30; 21:25).

Getting the point

Jesus didn't do miracles just for fun, or simply to draw a crowd. There was a more important purpose, similar to that which we saw in the Old Testament. His intention was that people should see beyond the miracles to God whose power caused them to happen. But even in Jesus' day people often missed the point and he rebuked them for following him for the wrong reasons: "Very truly I tell you, you are looking for me, not because you saw signs I performed but because you ate the loaves and had your fill" (John 6:26).

However, sometimes they did get the point. When Jesus healed the paralytic lowered through the roof, the people praised God—they recognized that it was God's power they had seen at work (Luke 5:26). When he brought back to life the widow of Nain's son, the crowd "were all filled with awe and praised God. 'A great prophet has appeared among us,' they said. 'God has come to help his people'" (Luke 7:16). Those who witnessed Jesus heal the boy with an evil spirit and return him to his father well were all "amazed at the greatness of God" (Luke 9:43); and on an occasion when many were healed, the crowd "praised the God of Israel" (Matthew 15:31).

There was a similar response to some of the non-healing miracles too. John tells us that the crowd of five thousand who experienced the miraculous feeding said: "Surely this is the Prophet who is to come into the world" (John 6:14). John also comments that through the miracle of changing water into wine, Jesus "revealed his glory, and his disciples believed in him" (John 2:11). When Jesus stilled the storm, the disciples in the boat were prompted to ask important questions: "Who is this? Even the wind and the waves obey him!" (Mark 4:41); and later, when Jesus came walking on water, their reaction was even more definite: "Truly you are the Son of God" (Matthew 14:33).

The God of miracles

Here is the same pattern we identified in the Old Testament: people are made aware of God through signs and wonders. It is John particularly, in his Gospel, who highlights this: he refers to miraculous happenings as "signs", because their significance is not in the action itself, but in what it reveals about the one who performs it.

Jesus claimed that the miracles supported his teaching, they were corroborating evidence: "For the works that the Father has given me to finish—the very works that I am doing—testify that the Father has sent me" (John 5:36). As far as Jesus was concerned the miracles said everything, at least that appeared to be his response to a direct question from the Jews: "The works I do in my Father's name testify about me" (John 10:25). Later in the same conversation, Jesus urged them to believe in his miracles even if they found it difficult to accept what he said: "Do not believe me unless I do the works of my Father. But if I do them, even though you do not believe me, believe the works, that you may know and understand that the Father is in me, and I in the Father" (John 10:37–8). His response was similar when Philip, one of the disciples, was asking questions: "Believe me when I say that I am in the Father and the Father is in me; or at least believe on the evidence of the works themselves" (John 14:11).

It is quite clear from the Gospels, particularly John's Gospel, that to wonder at the miracles of Jesus and not believe in him was to miss the point. Jesus would surely have enthusiastically endorsed this comment of John's:

> Jesus performed many other signs in the presence of his disciples, which are not recorded in this book. But these are written that you may believe that Jesus is the Messiah, the Son of God, and that by believing you may have life in his name (John 20:30–1).

Signs and wonders are intended to point us to God: they invite us to believe and worship.

The action continues . . .

We have already seen in Chapter 6 that Jesus clearly intended his disciples to continue his mission in every respect, including the "miraculous part". His instructions to the Twelve and to the Seventy-two included the command to act as well as to preach (Luke 9:1–6; 10:1–12); his commission to the disciples after his resurrection was to pass on to others everything he had commanded them to do—and that included the action (Matthew 28:19–20). According to John, Jesus told his disciples that they would do everything that he had been doing (John 14:12).

Acts tells us that this is exactly what happened: the first followers of Jesus went out and continued the mission of Jesus in action as well as word. It is significant that Luke (the writer of Acts) begins his account by referring back to "all that Jesus began to do and to teach" (Acts 1:1). In effect, the rest of the book is an account of how the first Christians continued "to do and to teach". The action started immediately. The first "miracle" involved language: the Holy Spirit gave Jesus' followers new languages in which to speak and praise God. The people were staggered:

> Aren't all these men who are speaking Galileans? Then how is it that each of us hears them in our own native language? . . . we hear them declaring the wonders of God in our own tongues! Amazed and perplexed, they asked one another, "What does this mean?" (Acts 2:7–8,11–12).

Peter answered that question when he spoke to the crowd: "This is God in action" is, in effect, what he told them. And many believed as a result, three thousand of them!

Thus, the first Christian church was inaugurated as a result of a "wonder". And Luke, describing that church's activities, included this comment: "Everyone was filled with awe at the many wonders and signs performed by the apostles" (Acts 2:43). So, right at the start of the story of the Christian church, we find the same pattern again that we have observed in the Old Testament and in the Gospels: a sense of awe among the people in the face of miraculous happenings.

. . . in all kinds of ways

We have already looked at some of the healings in Acts (Chapter 6). Apparently, all kinds of other miraculous events occurred too, through the action of God.

For example, Peter and John, having been arrested, threatened and then released (Acts 4:1–22), returned to the other Christians, and they had a praise and prayer meeting (Acts 4:23–31). One of the specific things they asked God to do was: "Stretch out your hand to heal and perform signs and wonders through the name of your holy servant Jesus" (v. 30). Luke tells us that afterwards "With great power the apostles continued to testify to the resurrection of the Lord Jesus" (v. 33). No mention of miracles there, you might say, but many commentators think that the implication is the apostles had the power to work miracles: as they gave public testimony to the risen Christ, "the power of God, shown in mighty works, attended their preaching—the very thing for which they had prayed."[1]

Certainly in the next chapter, we are told that "the apostles performed many signs and wonders among the people" (Acts 5:12). The result was many more believers (v. 14) and many more healings (v. 16). There was even the slightly weird phenomenon of Peter's shadow passing over sick people (v. 15).

What is more, the original followers of Jesus didn't have a monopoly on the "action" either. There was Stephen, for example: he was "a man full of God's grace and power, [who] performed great wonders and signs among the people" (Acts 6:8). Then there was Philip: "When the crowds heard Philip and saw the signs he performed, they all paid close attention to what he said. For with shrieks, impure spirits came out of many, and many who were paralysed or lame were healed" (Acts 8:6–7). And, of course, Paul and Barnabas: "[They] spent considerable time there, speaking boldly for the Lord, who confirmed the message of his grace by enabling them to perform signs and wonders" (Acts 14:3). Later, when Paul was in Ephesus, we read: "God did extraordinary miracles through Paul, so that even handkerchiefs and aprons that had touched him were taken to those who were ill, and their illnesses were cured and the evil spirits left them" (Acts 19:11–12)—you can't get much more extraordinary than that!

Time and again, through the pages of Acts, we see the action of God as he causes miraculous things to happen. All the chief characters whom we normally think of as evangelists were involved: Peter, Stephen, Philip, Paul and Barnabas. Almost every time, the pattern is the same: there is a miraculous happening, the people who witness it are amazed and wonder at it, and many of them believe. As we have already seen, that is always the purpose of miracles: that people might believe in the God of miracles. And that's mission!

---

[1]   F. F. Bruce, *The Book of Acts* (London: Marshall, Morgan & Scott, 1954), p. 109.

It's all part of the strategy

If we were able to take Paul aside and ask him how he did it, that is, what was his strategy for mission, how would he answer? It is clear from the New Testament records that whenever he preached, things happened! One bishop, impressed by this, is reported to have asked: "Why is it that when Paul preached things happened, and that when I preach all that happens is a cup of tea?"

For example, in his first letter to the Christians in Corinth, he reminded them: "My message and my preaching were not with wise and persuasive words, but with a demonstration of the Spirit's power, so that your faith might not rest on human wisdom, but on God's power" (1 Corinthians 2:4–5). It looks as though things happened when he went to Thessalonica too: "For we know, brothers and sisters loved by God, that he has chosen you, because our gospel came to you not simply with words, but also with power, with the Holy Spirit and deep conviction" (1 Thessalonians 1:4–5). The power to work miracles was there again. And in Galatia, where the Christians were beginning to fall away, he challenged them:

> Are you so foolish? After beginning by means of the Spirit, are you now trying to finish by means of the flesh? Have you experienced so much in vain—if it really was in vain? So again I ask, does God give you his Spirit and work miracles among you by the works of the law, or by your believing what you heard? (Galatians 3:3–5).

He sums it all up for us in his letter to the Christians in Rome; here is his mission strategy in a nutshell:

> I will not venture to speak of anything except what Christ has accomplished through me in leading the Gentiles to obey God by what I have said and done—by the power of signs and wonders, through the power of the Spirit of God . . . I have fully proclaimed the gospel of Christ (Romans 15:18–19).

Paul is probably the greatest Christian missionary there has ever been (except for Jesus himself, of course). We would do well to learn from him: if signs and wonders were important for him, maybe we should make room for them in our mission too—we could do with a bit of God's action!

Does God's action continue?

We have seen that God continued his miraculous activity both through the ministry of Jesus, and in the ongoing mission of the first Christians. But did he continue the action beyond that, or did he give up working that way? Is he still doing it today?

This question has been hotly debated in the Christian church over the years, and many books have been written on both sides of the argument. In general, there are four views of the matter that have been expressed.

Some have claimed that signs and wonders died out with the first apostles, and any supposedly miraculous happening since is therefore not of God.

Some think that signs and wonders were only intended for the first years of Christianity; they were like "divine credentials" but were no longer needed once the church was established and the Bible officially accepted. Those who support this view would also say that in those places where it is claimed there are signs and wonders today, it is because the church is young; in time, when it is established, signs and wonders will no longer be needed there either and will die out.

Some have suggested that signs and wonders declined because the condition of the church deteriorated—the spiritual environment was no longer conducive for them to happen.

On the other hand, others have believed that signs and wonders have never ceased and that consistently, throughout Christian history, God has worked "with signs accompanying" amongst his followers, and still is doing so today.

A key passage in this debate is 1 Corinthians 13. Many know this as Paul's famous chapter on love, but towards the end there is reference also to supernatural things. Tongues, prophecy and knowledge are specifically mentioned (vv. 8–9), three of the gifts of the Spirit which Paul has listed in Chapter 12 (vv. 8–10). Paul explains that these things, "the imperfect", will disappear when perfection comes (13:10).

The question is, what is "perfection"? Some have understood perfection to be the completed scriptures, the Bible as it is now: with that in place, these supernatural things are no longer needed and not to be expected. Others understand perfection to be the end of all things, when we are in the presence of God himself and will therefore understand fully: the imperfect spiritual gifts will then be redundant.

The latter seems to me to be the better understanding of perfection: in verse 12 Paul is talking about seeing face to face and knowing fully, which is surely a reference to being with God at the end of all things. If this is right, then it follows that spiritual gifts, the raw material of signs and wonders, are still available today. "It is not until our pilgrimage comes to an end that spiritual gifts will cease. Whoever teaches that they cease before then, is irresponsibly anticipating the end."[2]

According to the writer of Hebrews, these spiritual gifts and miraculous happenings are God's way of emphasizing the truth of the gospel: "God also testified to [this salvation] by signs, wonders and various miracles, and by gifts of the Holy Spirit distributed according to his will" (Hebrews 2:4). If that is true, and if God does not change, then we can expect to find God confirming the preaching of the gospel in the same "supernatural" way both throughout church history and today.

The testimony of church history

A careful reading of church history confirms that signs and wonders did not cease either with the death of the first generation of Christians, or with the completion of the Bible. There is evidence of miraculous happenings in every period of church history, although it is somewhat patchy: miracles appear to be more in evidence at certain times than others, more numerous in certain places than others. In general, the principle seems to be that whenever God's people (particularly the leadership) were open to his action and expected him to do things, then

---

2   Arnold Bittlinger, *Gifts and Graces* (London: Hodder & Stoughton, 1967), p. 90.

signs and wonders happened; when that expectancy was lacking, they
didn't happen.

Often, God apparently worked other than through the normal
channels and the official ministers; as a result, church history is
sadly littered with occasions when God worked miraculously among
a particular group of Christians and the official church disapproved,
dismissing them as heretics, excommunicating them, even persecuting
them. Nevertheless, through all this, we can see that the God of action
whom we have observed in both Old and New Testaments has continued
to be in action throughout church history, confirming his word "by the
signs that accompanied it" (Mark 16:20).

God's action experienced . . .

It would be good to look at a few examples of God's action from the pages
of church history. (For this material I am indebted to John Wimber, both
for his painstaking research and his permission to use it.)

. . . by Justin Martyr

Justin Martyr lived in the early part of the second century. In one of his
books, he wrote:

> For numberless demoniacs throughout the whole world, and in
> your city, many of our Christian men exorcising them in the
> name of Jesus Christ, who was crucified under Pontius Pilate,
> have healed and do heal, rendering helpless and driving the
> possessing devils out of the men, though they could not be cured
> by all the other exorcists, and those who used incantations and
> drugs.

He was quite clear that spiritual gifts were to be expected:

> For the prophetical gifts remain with us, even to the present time.
> And hence you ought to understand that [the gifts] formerly
> among your nation have been transferred to us.

. . . by Irenaeus

Irenaeus lived in the latter part of the second century and was Bishop of Lyons. Apparently, spiritual gifts were much in evidence in his day:

> . . . those who are in truth His disciples, receiving grace from Him, so in His name perform [miracles], so as to promote the welfare of other men, according to the gift which each one has received from Him. For some do certainly and truly drive out devils, so that those who have thus been cleansed from evil spirits frequently join themselves to the church. Others have foreknowledge of things to come: they see visions, and utter prophetic expressions. Others still, heal the sick by laying their hands upon them, and they are made whole. Yea, moreover, as I have said, the dead even have been raised up, and remained among us for many years.

. . . by Augustine

Augustine was one of the most important figures in early Christian history. He lived from 354 to 430 and was Bishop of Hippo in North Africa. There was plenty of "action" in his day, too:

> Actually, if I kept merely to miracles of healing and omitted all others, and if I told only those wrought by this one martyr, the glorious St Stephen, and if I limited myself to those that happened here at Hippo and Calama, I should have to fill several volumes and, even then, I could do no more than tell those cases that have been officially recorded and attested for public reading in our churches . . . It is a simple fact that there is no lack of miracles even in our day. And the God who works the miracles we read in the Scriptures uses any means and manner He chooses.

. . . by Francis of Assisi

Francis (1182–1226) is probably the best-known saint of church history, remembered for his love of nature (depicted memorably in the film *Brother Sun and Sister Moon*). He also had a remarkable healing ministry:

One of the brothers suffered frequently from a very serious infirmity and one horrible to see; I do not know what name it is called, though some think it is an evil spirit. Frequently he was cast upon the ground and he turned about foaming at the mouth and with a terrible look upon his face; at times his limbs were drawn up, at other times they were extended; now they were folded up and twisted, again they were rigid and hard. Sometimes, when he was stretched out and rigid, he would be raised up into the air to the height of a man's stature, with his feet even with his head, and then would fall back to the ground. Pitying his grievous illness the holy father Francis went to him and, after praying, signed him and blessed him. Suddenly he was cured and he did not again suffer in the least from the tortures of this illness.

. . . by Martin Luther

Martin Luther (1483–1546) is best known for his role in the Reformation, not least for nailing to the church door at Wittenberg in Germany his "Ninety-Five Theses", a detailed challenge to the corrupt practices of the church. But he also knew something of the ministry of healing, as this letter reveals:

> The tax collector in Torgau and the counsellor in Belgern have written to ask me that I offer some good advice and help for Mrs John Korner's afflicted husband. I know of no worldly help to give. If the physicians are at a loss to find a remedy, you may be sure that it is not a case of ordinary melancholy. It must, rather, be an affliction that comes from the devil, and this must be counteracted by the power of Christ with the prayer of faith. This is what we do, and what we have been accustomed to do, for a cabinet maker here was similarly afflicted with madness and we cured him by prayer in Christ's name.

There follows detailed instructions of how to minister to the sick person and what to pray. He then goes on:

Then, when you depart, lay your hands upon the man again and say, "These signs shall follow them that believe; they shall lay hands on the sick, and they shall recover."

. . . by Ignatius of Loyola

Ignatius of Loyola lived in the first half of the sixteenth century and was the founder of the Society of Jesus (the Jesuits). He makes this interesting observation about the work of the Spirit:

> The Spirit of God breathes where He will; He does not ask our permission; He meets us on His own terms and distributes His charisms as He pleases. Therefore, we must always be awake and ready; we must be pliable so that He can use us in new enterprises. We cannot lay down the law to the Spirit of God! He is only present with His gifts where He knows that they are joined with the multiplicity of charisms in the one church. All the gifts of this church stem from one source, God. What Paul says in the twelfth chapter of his First Epistle to the Corinthians is still true today! . . . He can lead to Himself in different ways, and he wants to direct the church through a multiplicity of functions, offices and gifts. The church is not supposed to be a military academy in which everything is uniform, but she is supposed to be the Body of Christ in which He, the one Spirit, exerts His power in all the members.

. . . by John Wesley

Ordained as an Anglican priest (1703–91), Wesley is renowned for riding on horseback all round England and preaching in a variety of places, mostly in the open air. Eventually, with his brother Charles, he founded the Methodist Church. There are numerous references in his Journal to miraculous happenings; his own understanding of them is expressed in this letter:

> Yet I do not know that God hath anyway precluded Himself from thus exerting His sovereign power from working miracles in any kind or degree in any age to the end of the world. I do not

recollect any scripture wherein we are taught that miracles were to be confined within the limits either of the apostolic or the Cyprianic age, or of any period of time, longer or shorter, even till the restitution of all things. I have not observed, either in the Old Testament, or the New, any intimation at all of this kind. St Paul says, indeed, once, concerning two of the miraculous gifts of the Spirit (so, I think, that test is usually understood), "Whether there be prophecies, they shall fail; whether there be tongues, they shall cease." But he does not say, either that these or any other miracles shall cease till faith and hope shall cease also, till they all be swallowed up in the vision of God, and love be all in all.

... in the last two centuries

The last two centuries have seen God at work by his Spirit in many different places and in a variety of ways. For example, in the early 1900s there was a powerful moving of the Spirit of God in the United States, a movement in which the gift of speaking in tongues and other spiritual gifts were prominent. This proved to be the birth of the Pentecostal Church, which has become the fastest-growing church in the world today.

There was the Revival in Wales which began in 1904: crowds would gather in the chapels of Wales, often when no meeting had been announced; many were convicted and converted, often when there was no preacher present. It was a sovereign work of God by his Spirit.

There was the Revival in the western islands of Scotland in the 1950s, in which similar things were experienced: unplanned meetings, uninvited speakers, overcrowded chapels, and people overwhelmed by the presence and power of God out in the fields.

Then in Indonesia in the 1960s, God moved so powerfully that, so it was reported, every miracle mentioned in the New Testament was experienced, including the raising of the dead—powerful action of God indeed!

And there have been many other movements of God, large and small, some much publicized, others scarcely heard about. But in all of them, God moved, things happened, and people were saved and brought into the life of the church. And that's effective mission.

A powerful testimony

It is fascinating to find this thread of the miraculous activity of God among his people right through church history. Of course, it is perfectly possible to make a different selection from the pages of history containing no reference to signs and wonders, even including opposition to the whole idea; there is plenty to choose from. Maybe this serves to emphasize the underlying principle that we have already identified: that God is busy doing miraculous things wherever and whenever his people believe and expect. John Wimber sums up his historical survey with these words:

> The main thesis stands: God has never ceased to work signs and wonders in his church, where he can find open, willing people, through whom he could be God. He is still looking for people today who are open to his Holy Spirit, and through whom he can continue to act.[3]

God in action today

If God is unchanging and still wanting to continue his miraculous activity among his people, why is it that we don't see very much "action" today? The problem is that we don't believe, and therefore don't expect.

Ironically, often it is actually the church traditions with which we have grown up that have caused this unbelief. Some of us have been nurtured in a "liberal" view of scripture, which has removed all miraculous elements. And if miracles didn't happen then, we are unlikely to look for them now. Others have been brought up with a more "conservative" view of scripture, encouraged to believe that everything actually happened just as the Bible says, including the miraculous parts. But we have also been told that such things no longer happen, and we should therefore not expect them. Either way our faith has been undermined and there is little expectation of God doing miraculous things.

---

[3] From John Wimber's lecture notes "Signs and Wonders and Church Growth" (Section 6).

Add to that our western worldview (we looked at this in Chapter 4): we tend to see our world in a very scientific, logical, materialistic way which leaves very little room for God to break in and do something unscientific, illogical and non-materialistic—something, that is, which cannot be explained in the normal way. So, both our view of scripture and our view of the world might actually be against us as we get involved in mission!

We need to catch fresh vision of God and his greatness, the God of whom the angel said to Mary: "For there is nothing that God cannot do" (Luke 1:37, GNB). We need to remove our western-culture blinkers and our theologically conditioned spectacles to see what God can do, given half a chance!

Does it really help?

But why do we need God's action? What does it achieve? Remember, the miracle is supposed to draw people's attention to God: the aim is not that they simply see a miracle, but that they look to the God behind the miracle, believe in him and worship him. And that is the aim of mission too.

There is a sense in which we need God's action even more today than in previous generations. We live in a word-resistant society, that is, a society which is not very good at listening to words, at least, not too many of them. Educationalists know that what people see usually makes a bigger impression on them than what they hear—and advertisers are very well aware of that principle.

If we had to rely simply on words to communicate the gospel, how well would we get on? If, just occasionally, people saw some action and were able to say: "Wow! Did you see that!", and then were told that it was God, they might begin to get the message. It would certainly help, wouldn't it? These words of Paul have often challenged me: "For the kingdom of God is not a matter of talk but of power" (1 Corinthians 4:20). A little less talk and a little more power in our mission would not go amiss!

A word of warning, though: success is not guaranteed just because we are involved in miraculous activity. Clearly, it didn't always work for Jesus, so it certainly won't for us. Even after Jesus had been publicly preaching and teaching for some time, many would not or could not believe, although there had been plenty of "action" accompanying his teaching. John records: "Even after Jesus had performed so many signs in their presence, they still would not believe in him" (John 12:37).

The towns of Chorazin and Bethsaida also remind us that miracles don't guarantee success. Jesus had apparently worked many miracles in those towns and yet they did not believe; as a result, Jesus spoke some of his sternest words of judgement to them:

> Woe to you, Chorazin! Woe to you, Bethsaida! For if the miracles that were performed in you had been performed in Tyre and Sidon, they would have repented long ago, sitting in sackcloth and ashes. But it will be more bearable for Tyre and Sidon at the judgment than for you (Luke 10:13–14).

The early Christians certainly found this to be true: Paul and Barnabas, for example, experienced it in Iconium. Luke records:

> So Paul and Barnabas spent considerable time there, speaking boldly for the Lord, who confirmed the message of his grace by enabling them to perform signs and wonders. The people of the city were divided; some sided with the Jews, others with the apostles (Acts 14:3–4).

And I know the truth of it, too. Do you remember the young man at the beginning of this chapter who saw God deliver his friend? Just before I left Cambridge, I went to visit him: "Of all the people I know," I said to him, "you are the one with least excuse for not being Christian!" Despite seeing God in action, and acknowledging it, he had not become a Christian on the strength of it.

Sometimes people say: "If I see a miracle, then I'll believe!" That is not necessarily true; the evidence of scripture and experience suggest otherwise. But having said that, I do believe there are those who, while remaining unconvinced by our words, will believe when they see God in action. Isn't that precisely what Jesus said? "Believe me when I say that I am in the Father and the Father is in me; or at least believe on the evidence of the works themselves" (John 14:11).

Of course, we cannot make miracles happen: only God can do that. Nor can we demand miracles of God: it is entirely up to him if and when he acts. What we can do is to expect that he might want to do something, and to give him space to do so—it would be appropriate to do that in our church services and meetings. What that means in practice is that we try to build into our services and meetings (and into our counselling, too), times of silence, saying nothing, doing nothing. Most of us don't find that easy, but it is one way of giving God some "elbow room". I sometimes wonder if God doesn't get terribly frustrated with us. Does he feel like saying: "Shut up a minute and let me say something!" or "Stop your activity for a moment and let me do something!"? Over the years we have tried to learn that, if we would only give God space, he does come, he speaks, he acts.

The bottom line for Jesus in experiencing the action of God in his mission was staying close to his Father. The miracles Jesus did were not really supernatural at all, but rather very natural: the natural outcome of staying close to God, knowing exactly what God wanted and doing it. In other words, it's all a matter of being at the right place at the right time—God's place, God's time. That's when things happen.

If, with the help of the Holy Spirit, we will learn to "stay close", then we shall see God confirming his word by the signs that accompany it (Mark 16:20)—it will happen very naturally. This is central to the call to discipleship; it's all part of the package: "As the Father has sent me, I am sending you."

8

Sent . . . To Establish a Kingdom

"God rules—OK!" No, not just a bit of graffiti aerosoled on a wall somewhere, though I have seen it. It is, I believe, a serious contender for "the best slogan award" for communicating the heart of the message of Jesus' mission. Even a fairly cursory read of the Gospels (particularly Matthew, Mark and Luke) will reveal how prominent is talk of the kingdom of God in Jesus' teaching. For example, in conversation with Nicodemus in John 3 (we looked at it in Chapter 1), Jesus wanted to help Nicodemus understand how to enter the kingdom of God. So many of Jesus' parables, including some of the well-known ones (such as the parables of the weeds, the mustard seed, the treasure in the field, or the workers in the vineyard), are actually stories about the kingdom of God, which Jesus told to teach us what God's kingdom is like.

Clearly, the kingdom of God was central in his thinking and therefore in his teaching. We are told: "He welcomed [the crowds] and spoke to them about the kingdom of God" (Luke 9:11); and when he felt constrained to move on to other places, he announced: "I must proclaim the good news of the kingdom of God to the other towns also, because that is why I was sent" (Luke 4:43). Matthew, in a passage in which he summarizes Jesus' ministry, wrote: "Jesus went through all the towns and villages, teaching in their synagogues, proclaiming the good news of the kingdom and healing every disease and illness" (Matthew 9:35). Again, Jesus, speaking about some of the things that will happen before the end of the world, and referring to the message he has been preaching, said: "And this gospel of the kingdom will be preached in the whole world . . . " (Matthew 24:14).

When he sent others out in mission, they were instructed to preach the same message: the Twelve were sent out "to proclaim the kingdom of God and to heal those who were ill" (Luke 9:2); the Seventy-two were told that in each town they visited, they were to "heal those there who are ill and tell them, 'the kingdom of God has come near to you'" (Luke 10:9). Even during the period between Jesus' resurrection and his return to heaven, we are told that "he appeared to [the apostles] over a period of forty days and spoke about the kingdom of God" (Acts 1:3). I wonder what he told them—I would love to have been there!

The first Christian preachers took up the same emphasis. Of Philip's ministry, for example, we are told: "But when they believed Philip as he proclaimed the good news of the kingdom of God and the name of Jesus Christ, they were baptized, both men and women" (Acts 8:12). When Paul was in Ephesus, he "entered the synagogue and spoke boldly there for three months, arguing persuasively about the kingdom of God" (Acts 19:8); and when he was under house arrest in Rome "he proclaimed the kingdom of God and taught about the Lord Jesus Christ—with all boldness and without hindrance!" (Acts 28:31).

Clearly, the kingdom of God is high on the agenda both for Jesus and his followers.

It's here!

Mark records the beginning of Jesus' public ministry like this: "Jesus went into Galilee, proclaiming the good news of God. 'The time has come,' he said. 'The kingdom of God has come near. Repent and believe the good news!'" (Mark 1:14–15). That sounds like a pretty important statement, but what does it mean? What "time" has come? What is this "kingdom"?

It may seem strange to us that, although Jesus spoke about the kingdom so much, nowhere did he explain what he meant by it. But then, those who heard him, who were mostly from a Jewish background, would have understood perfectly what he was getting at. Many of them, like Jesus, knew their scriptures (our Old Testament) very well.

So, what *did* Jesus mean?

Understanding the kingdom

In the Old Testament, God is frequently spoken of in kingly terms: for instance, "The LORD sits enthroned over the flood; the LORD is enthroned as King for ever" (Psalm 29:10), and "For the LORD Most High is awesome, the great King over all the earth" (Psalm 47:2). He is king over all. But in a special kind of way, he is meant to be the king of his special people, Israel: "I am the LORD, your Holy One, Israel's Creator, your King" (Isaiah 43:15). In fact, according to one tradition in the Old Testament, at the same time when Israel asked the prophet Samuel to appoint a king for them, God told Samuel: "Listen to all that the people are saying to you; it is not you they have rejected, but they have rejected me as their king" (1 Samuel 8:7).

Although God was meant to be their king, it never really worked out that way. But they looked forward to a future, a better time, when God's reign as king would be fully acknowledged, not only by Israel but by all the world. He will come in a "big way" and nothing will be quite the same again after that. It will be the coming of the king for real!

An earthly kingdom . . . ?

But what exactly did God's people expect when the king came? When the Jews reflected on their history, they saw the period when David was king as the high point, the "golden age". Following the death of Solomon, David's son and successor, the kingdom had been divided into two, the north (usually referred to as Israel) and the south (usually called Judah). From then on, things gradually deteriorated.

Eventually, in the eighth century BC, the northern kingdom was overrun by Assyria. Then the southern kingdom was attacked by the Babylonians, the people taken into exile, and Jerusalem destroyed (in 587 BC). It was a bad time for the Jews, reflected poignantly in the words of Psalm 137:

> By the rivers of Babylon we sat and wept when we remembered Zion. There on the poplars we hung our harps, for there our captors asked us for songs, our tormentors demanded songs of

joy; they said, "Sing us one of the songs of Zion!" How can we sing the songs of the LORD while in a foreign land? (vv. 1–4).

After about 70 years in exile, some Jews returned to Jerusalem and began to rebuild the city. During this time, Jewish hopes began to rise again. Psalm 126 captures that note of optimism well:

> When the LORD restored the fortunes of Zion, we were like those who dreamed. Our mouths were filled with laughter, our tongues with songs of joy. Then it was said among the nations, 'The LORD has done great things for them.' The LORD has done great things for us, and we are filled with joy (vv. 1–3).

Hope continued to grow; perhaps the nation would once again prosper as in the "good old days" under King David; maybe at any moment a great descendant of David would arrive to restore the nation to its former glory. There was real expectancy around that God was going to do something great.

But all their hopes were shattered again, and expectancy was crushed as no David-type king appeared on the scene, and things deteriorated again. Hope was aroused again briefly in the second century BC when the Jews revolted against their rulers, the Syrians. But it was short-lived and by the time Jesus arrived, the Jews were still hoping for a Davidic, political king to come and restore the kingdom, to set them free. And Jesus looked as though he might well fit the bill: he was certainly a descendant of David, as the genealogies in the Gospels of Matthew and Luke show (Matthew 1:1–17; Luke 3:23–38), and his attitude to the Roman authorities (the occupying power) was promising too—he certainly didn't seem to be intimidated by them. Certainly he was a charismatic leader whose preaching and teaching inspired, and whose actions amazed. Could this be the long-awaited king? When he talked about the kingdom of God, was he actually talking about the re-establishment of a Jewish nation and empire?

Clearly, many in Jesus' day thought this way. That's why they wanted to make him king. "After the people saw the sign Jesus performed, they began to say, 'Surely this is the Prophet who is to come into the world.'

Jesus, knowing that they intended to come and make him king by force, withdrew again to a mountain by himself" (John 6:14–15). Later, as he approached Jerusalem, the historic capital city in which David had reigned, some in the crowd thought this was "it": "[Jesus] went on to tell them a parable, because he was near Jerusalem and the people thought that the kingdom of God was going to appear at once" (Luke 19:11). But it wasn't, at least not in the way they were hoping. Even Jesus' own disciples were not immune from this "political" way of thinking. They had spent three years with Jesus, listening to him and watching him, yet, right up until the time he finally left them, they were still asking: "Lord, are you at this time going to restore the kingdom to Israel?" (Acts 1:6). The gist of Jesus' answer was "No!" But he also began to spell out a very different kind of agenda, the carrying out of which would take his followers to the ends of the earth (vv. 7–8). Was he actually talking about the establishing of a different kind of kingdom?

. . . or a heavenly kingdom?

Certainly, there was another way of seeing the whole situation, a different understanding of what the coming of the kingdom of God would mean. Political hopes had been dashed; the return of the Jews to Jerusalem from exile in Babylon had not ushered in the kingdom of God as the people expected. Instead, God's people suffered oppression under one nasty ruler after another. It all felt so desperately evil with no sign of any let-up; all that many felt was despair rather than hope. But if there was no hope of an earthly, political kingdom appearing, what about a different kind of kingdom? As things became worse, the thinking along these lines developed and strengthened: this present age, dominated by evil, would be replaced with a new age in which God would rule. The experience of the Jews during the last few hundred years BC was so awful, like hell on earth, that they reckoned it had to be the result of some kind of heavenly battle, where the "baddies" were winning and the "goodies" were losing.

Certainly, in the writings of the period (mostly found in the collection called the Apocrypha), there is much talk of Satan ruling over a kingdom of evil, of him leading angels astray and using them for his purposes, and of evil spirits affecting life on earth in all kinds of ways.

So they looked forward to a new age, the "age to come": God would break in and establish it. The coming of this new age (or kingdom) would have far-reaching effects: Satan's activity would be destroyed, good would triumph over evil, healing would be experienced, and demons would be cast out. But how would this kingdom be inaugurated?

There is a hint in one of Daniel's visions:

> In my vision at night I looked, and there before me was one like a son of man, coming with the clouds of heaven. He approached the Ancient of Days, and was led into his presence. He was given authority, glory and sovereign power; all nations and peoples of every language worshipped him. His dominion is an everlasting dominion that will not pass away, and his kingdom is one that will never be destroyed (Daniel 7:13–14).

We are never told who this strange "son of man" is but, apparently, he has a strategic role given him by God (the "Ancient of Days") to establish a kingdom which will last for ever.

As time went on, all the hopes of God's people became focused on the coming of a special individual, the "Messiah". Based on a Hebrew word, it means "God's anointed one"; the Greek equivalent is *Christos*, or Christ. All this throws light on the Gospels. For example, the words of the angel that first Christmas night: "Today in the town of David a Saviour has been born to you; he is the Messiah, the Lord" (Luke 2:11). Later, when Peter was beginning to understand who Jesus was, in response to Jesus' question, "Who do you say I am?", he answered: "You are the Messiah, the Son of the living God" (Matthew 16:15–16). Then there was Jesus' own name for himself: time and time again he referred to himself as "the Son of Man". Was he referring back to Daniel's vision? Could this be his way of saying who he was? Was it a sort of secret code? And Jesus' words at his trial are significant too: Pilate talked to Jesus about whether or not he was a king. Jesus admitted to being a king (John 18:37), but he also made it clear: "My kingdom is not of this world" (John 18:36). How ironic that when Jesus was crucified just hours later, the official notice fixed to the cross read: "Jesus of Nazareth, the King of the Jews"! That is exactly what Jesus was—and more!

Whatever . . . it's coming!

One way or another, there was great expectation. Whether they thought in political (i.e. earthly) terms or spiritual (i.e. heavenly) terms, the Jews of Jesus' day were certainly looking for the coming of a great king, God's Messiah, who was even greater than David. This king would usher in a new age in which God would come and reign as he was supposed to have been doing all along. All this is the background to the life and ministry of Jesus, and the context of his mission. Unless we understand a little of this background, we risk misunderstanding Jesus' mission and thus our own. (That's why I have explained it as fully as I have—I hope you have stayed with me!)

Can you imagine, now, what it must have felt like to have been a Jew in the crowd when John the Baptist turned up and announced: "Repent, for the kingdom of heaven has come near" (Matthew 3:2)? Could it really be true that what they had looked forward to for so long was at last about to happen? Imagine the mixed emotions: excitement, fear, apprehension, anxiety, joy, hope, scepticism! Or what must it have been like to have been there not long after that when Jesus himself came on the scene, proclaiming "The time has come. The kingdom of God has come near. Repent and believe the good news!" (Mark 1:15)? Something great was beginning, and whatever else it was, it had something to do with God and his kingdom! And this "something" is still going on today. We get involved in it when we get involved in mission.

What's it all about?

So Jesus was born in David's town, Bethlehem, a descendant of David, Israel's greatest king. His birth was heralded as the arrival of one who was "the Messiah, the Lord"; he came calling himself the Son of Man, and talking a lot about the kingdom of God.

But how are we supposed to understand Jesus' talk of the kingdom of God? If we are not careful, we begin with a wrong impression because we tend to think of a kingdom as something geographical, an area which you can mark on a map and colour red (or whatever colour you fancy!).

After all, I live in a kingdom, the United Kingdom, and even I could mark that on a map of Europe.

However, the word for "kingdom" in both Hebrew and Greek really means "kingship", "royal rule", "dominion", or "reign" rather than "realm" or "kingdom": it refers to what the king does rather than to where he does it. So the kingdom of God is really "the rule of God", and to be in the kingdom of God is to be under the rulership of God.

To rule or not to rule

Take the example of the United Kingdom. Officially it consists of England, Wales, Scotland and Northern Ireland; but there are a few tiny pockets (mostly in Northern Ireland) where the kingdom is resisted. The people refuse to be subject to the king, fail to recognize the king's laws and courts, and violently oppose the presence of the king's police officers and armed forces. So, in effect, the king is not allowed to reign where he is entitled to reign, because the people refuse to have him. Something very similar is true of the kingdom of God: he can only reign effectively where his rulership is accepted. "God's rule de Jure [rightfully] exists universally over the heavens and earth; but de facto [actually] it exists in this age only when men and women submit themselves to the divine rule."[1] In other words, God's kingdom comes where God's will is done. That's why, in the Lord's Prayer, we pray: "Your kingdom come, your will be done . . ."—the two things really amount to the same thing. Whenever anyone brings their life into line with what God wants, for example, when a person repents and believes in Jesus, or they are healed, or they are set free in some way, there God begins to rule, his kingdom comes. Thus, when we are involved in mission, we are involved in establishing God's kingdom.

Here and now . . . ?

There is an aspect of Jesus' teaching about the kingdom which is, at first sight, puzzling. With the coming of Jesus, had God's kingdom come or was it still to come?

At times, Jesus clearly implied that the kingdom was available here and now. For example, he urged Nicodemus to be born again so that

---

[1]   George Eldon Ladd, *Jesus and the Kingdom* (London: SPCK, 1966), p. 140.

he might see and enter the kingdom of God (John 3:3,5); he told the crowd listening to the Sermon on the Mount (Matthew 5–7) that the most important thing for anyone to do is to "seek first [God's) kingdom and his righteousness" (6:33); and parables such as the hidden treasure and the fine pearl (Matthew 13:44–6) suggest that the kingdom is already available to be found and purchased right now. In addition, when Jesus was challenged about his handling of demons, he replied: "If it is by the Spirit of God that I drive out demons, then the kingdom of God has come upon you" (Matthew 12:28). (More about that in a moment.) So the kingdom is here and now.

. . . or not yet?

In other places, however, Jesus seemed to say something different. For example, that occasion when Jesus approached Jerusalem for the last time and people thought that the kingdom of God was imminent: he told them a parable which clearly implies that that was not so (Luke 19:11–27). The story is about a man "of noble birth" who called his servants, gave them each some money to use profitably, and then went off "to a distant country to have himself appointed king and then to return" (v. 12). When he returned, he asked the servants to report on their activities and to account for the money they had been given. Clearly, this story is about Jesus himself: he is the man who was made king. So the implication is that the final coming (or return) of the king is still in the future.

Later, he spoke in some detail about the future, referring to signs of the end of the age and to the coming of the Son of Man in glory unexpectedly:

> Then will appear the sign of the Son of Man in heaven. And then all the peoples of the earth will mourn when they see the Son of Man coming on the clouds of heaven, with power and great glory . . . But about that day or hour no one knows, not even the angels in heaven, nor the Son, but only the Father (Matthew 24:30,36).

He also told a series of parables illustrating the same theme, highlighting the need to keep watch for the coming of the king and warning that his coming will involve judgement and separation (Matthew 25).

Again, with his disciples at the Last Supper, Jesus said to them: "And I confer on you a kingdom, just as my Father conferred one on me, so that you may eat and drink at my table in my kingdom and sit on thrones, judging the twelve tribes of Israel" (Luke 22:29–30). Whatever precisely Jesus had in mind, he was clearly speaking of the future again. So the kingdom is "not yet".

Here and now and not yet

"Here and now" and "not yet". How do we make sense of that? With the coming of Jesus, the kingdom (or rule) of God has been inaugurated: he has begun to reign, to bring in the good things of the "new age". In that sense, the kingdom has already come. But it is equally clear that the reign of God is not complete; he doesn't yet reign everywhere.

One day God will reign supreme over all: there is plenty in the New Testament about that, particularly in Revelation. But for that final day of triumph, we have to wait: in that sense, the kingdom has not yet come.

In between the inauguration of the kingdom (the first coming of Jesus) and its completion or consummation (which will be marked by the Second Coming of Jesus), the kingdom of God is in the process of coming. It is that ongoing process begun by Jesus and continued by the first Christians which is the task of the church today, and it will continue to be so until Jesus comes again. This is the mission to which we are called. "As the Father has sent me, I am sending you."

The battle of the kingdoms

But establishing the kingdom of God is not entirely straightforward, at least, not as Jesus saw it. We have already seen how the Jews, in the years just before the arrival of Jesus, experienced such persecution and suffering that they believed it was the effects of a kingdom ruled over by Satan and therefore evil. They longed for God to come and overthrow the rule of Satan.

This appeared to be Jesus' perspective as he came on the scene. His task was not to establish a kingdom where no kingdom had been, nor to put a king on a throne where there had been none before; but rather, it was to overthrow one kingdom in order to establish another, and to put a king on the throne where one already reigned. Jesus came as king to establish a kingdom: to achieve that, he had to invade the kingdom already established, throw the king off the throne and reign in his place, and then set about undoing all the evil things that the previous king had done.

This is how the New Testament understands it: a battle between two kingdoms, or ages, the age to come (Ephesians 1:21) versus "the present evil age" (Galatians 1:4). The ruler of this present age is the devil: Paul calls him "the ruler of the kingdom of the air, the spirit who is now at work in those who are disobedient" (Ephesians 2:2), while John tells us that "the whole world is under the control of the evil one" (1 John 5:19). The coming of Jesus was the future age invading the present age, the rule of God challenging the rule of Satan. Thus, in Jesus, the devil is defeated. That, at least, is how Jesus himself saw it; referring to his forthcoming death, he said: "Now is the time for judgment on this world; now the prince of this world will be driven out" (John 12:31). Paul explained it like this: "And having disarmed the powers and authorities, he made a public spectacle of them, triumphing over them by the cross" (Colossians 2:15). Not only is "King Satan" defeated by "King Jesus", but all the evil work that Satan has been doing is undone by Jesus. John states it simply: "The reason the Son of God appeared was to destroy the devil's work" (1 John 3:8). More than that, because of the coming of Jesus, men and women can be rescued from the clutches of Satan, from out of his rule, and transferred to the rule of another: "For he has rescued us from the dominion of darkness and brought us into the kingdom of the Son he loves, in whom we have redemption, the forgiveness of sins" (Colossians 1:13–14).

This rescue work is still going on today; and we are involved in it.

Life in the overlap

But if the enemy is defeated in Jesus, how is that he still fights on? Most of us are only too aware of it! One way to understand it, which I find helpful, is to compare it with the latter part of the Second World War. (This analogy was first put forward in 1946 by a German theologian, Oscar Cullmann, in a book called *Christ and Time*.) There were two significant days in the final year of the war: D-Day and VE Day. D-Day was on 6 June 1944, when a decisive battle was fought and won. The Allied troops were the victors, the enemy's back was broken, and, to all intents and purposes, the eventual outcome of the war was decided that day. However, that was not the end of the war: there were many more battles and more lives were lost—in fact, apparently more lives were lost during this period than at any other time during the war. The war eventually ended some eleven months later on VE Day, 8 May 1945.

So it is with the kingdom of God. The crucial battle has been fought and won: the enemy has been defeated as a result of the birth, life, death and resurrection of Jesus. The coming of Jesus dealt a fatal blow to Satan and his kingdom, but it was only D-Day. VE Day is still to come, that last, victorious battle when the enemy is finally routed and the war is over. Revelation speaks of that final battle, its visionary language offering a vivid picture of the final defeat of Satan: "And the devil, who deceived [God's people], was thrown into the lake of burning sulphur, where the beast and the false prophet had been thrown. They will be tormented day and night for ever and ever" (Revelation 20:10).

So we are between two crucial battles, and the time for mission is the period between those two battles—now! We live in the "overlap", we engage in mission just at that point where God's kingdom has begun to invade Satan's kingdom. Diagrammatically it looks like this:

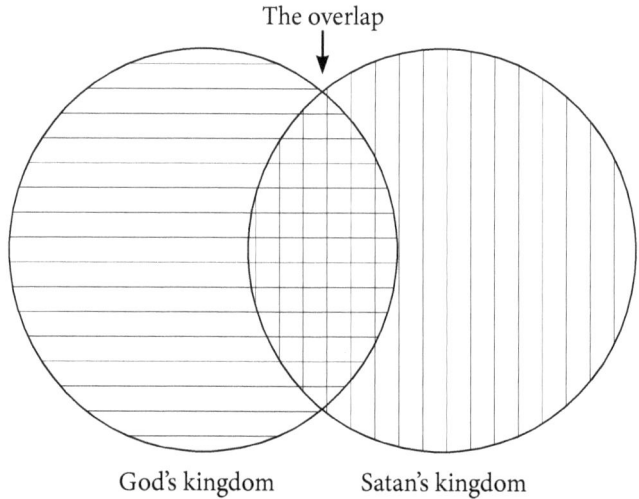

The overlap

God's kingdom   Satan's kingdom

I believe this is why Christian mission is so often a struggle; this is why Christians sometimes get hurt when they get involved in mission, just as Jesus did. We are involved in a battle, the object of which is to invade territory occupied by an enemy. And this is why success in mission is never guaranteed; the enemy sees to that. That's why healing doesn't always happen when we pray; that's why people don't always get "saved" when we try to witness to them; that's why there are still many "nasties" evident in the world, and Christians are not immune from them! We are living where Satan still tries to rule and the hallmarks of his rule are evil, darkness, destruction, death, everything that's negative and evil.

No wonder Paul, after years of experience in mission, writes: "For our struggle is not against flesh and blood, but against the rulers, against the authorities, against the powers of this dark world and against the spiritual forces of evil in the heavenly realms" (Ephesians 6:12)—he was speaking from considerable first-hand experience.

Of course, there are those today who dismiss this kind of talk as primitive and out of date: we have grown up and matured, we see the world rather differently now, we have a different worldview. It would be nice to believe that; it might make our task easier. But my experience in mission, albeit limited, tells me that very little has changed, and unless we recognize this spiritual dimension, we shall be defeated before we have started.

In fact, in the 35 years since this book was first written, things have deteriorated in all sorts of ways: intellectually, the philosophical challenge has become more sophisticated and multifaceted; physically, the opposition to Christians and the Christian church is now fiercer and more ruthless (as we saw in Chapter 4); and spiritually, there is so much more competition, from other faith groups, as well as a veritable smorgasbord of spiritual and pseudo-spiritual activities that offer a response to people's spiritual needs, and which are sometimes deeply critical of Christianity.

Face to face with the enemy . . .

Understanding Jesus' mission in this way, that is, as a battle between two kingdoms, gives new significance to much of what he said and did.

Often, for example, we read statements like this in the Gospels: " . . . the crowds were amazed at [Jesus'] teaching, because he taught as one who had authority . . . " (Matthew 7:28–9). Or this: "The people were all so amazed that they asked each other, 'What is this? A new teaching—and with authority! He even gives orders to evil spirits and they obey him'" (Mark 1:27). Here is the authority of a king engaged in battle, clear about his strategy, precise about his objectives, advancing into enemy territory: in word and action he was claiming his ground, establishing his kingdom.

This confrontational, almost aggressive, note is sounded right at the outset of his ministry when Jesus went to the synagogue in Nazareth and read from the book of Isaiah. It has been called "Jesus' manifesto":

> The Spirit of the Lord is on me, because he has anointed me to proclaim good news to the poor. He has sent me to proclaim freedom for the prisoners and recovery of sight for the blind, to set the oppressed free, to proclaim the year of the Lord's favour (Luke 4:18–19).

When Jesus had finished reading, he said, in effect, "This is it! I'm here! The battle is on!"

One writer has said: "A war is going on! Cosmic war! Jesus is the divine invader sent by God to shatter the strengths of Satan. In that light, the whole ministry of Jesus unrolls. Jesus has one purpose—to defeat Satan."[2] Is this what Jesus meant when he said: "From the days of John the Baptist until now, the kingdom of heaven has been subjected to violence, and violent people have been raiding it" (Matthew 11:12)?

---

[2]   James Kallas, *Jesus and the Power of Satan* (Philadelphia, PA: The Westminster Press, 1968), p. 60. (Quoted by John Wimber.)

. . . in the man from the tombs

This battle is seen most clearly when Jesus was face to face with evil, ministering to a person who had been infected by evil (or demons). Probably the best known of these incidents is the man who lived among the tombs in the region of the Gerasenes (or Gadarenes) (Mark 5:1–20). Here is a tragic demonstration of what damage Satan can do in a man's life, given the opportunity, of the suffering and destruction he can bring, the havoc he can cause. Every area of this man's life had been affected: socially he had become ostracized; physically he was suffering, mostly from self-inflicted wounds; mentally and emotionally he was in torment, crying out day and night; no doubt he was in a mess spiritually, too— who wouldn't be, in that state? Jesus, having discovered there were many demons involved, ordered them out of the man and into a convenient nearby herd of pigs, which promptly rushed off down the bank into the lake and were drowned. The outcome of Jesus' confrontation with the demons was total restoration for that man; he was left "sitting there, dressed and in his right mind" (v. 15)—his sanity, his dignity, his humanity were all restored. In a word, he was made whole, although it was all somewhat frightening for those who witnessed it.

. . . in the epileptic boy

Jesus was introduced to a boy who displayed symptoms very similar to severe epileptic seizures (Mark 9:14–29). However, the cause was spiritual, at least, that seems to be the way everybody who was there understood it. This boy had been infected by evil, by a spirit (v. 17). As a result, he was severely damaged, every area of his life spoiled. His father described his condition like this: " . . . a spirit . . . has robbed him of speech. Whenever it seizes him, it throws him to the ground. He foams at the mouth, gnashes his teeth and becomes rigid" (vv. 17–18). Jesus confronted the spirit in the boy and ordered it out; it left with a final shriek and violent convulsion (vv. 25–6). Then Jesus was able to return the boy to his father, fully restored. It was dramatic stuff! But it was all part of Jesus' mission.

. . . in the synagogue

Jesus was visiting the local synagogue and taught the people there. Since it was the Sabbath, it was presumably part of the normal Sabbath service, which "consisted of praisings and blessings, with prayers, and the reading of the Law and the Prophets, accompanied by an exposition or sermon".[3] Jesus was invited to preach that morning (Mark 1:21–8).

It was in that context of worship and teaching that there was a disturbance: a man cried out in the middle of the sermon. Judging by what he cried out, no doubt accompanied by some unusual behaviour, it was clear that he was suffering from the effect of an evil spirit. Once again, Jesus confronted the spirit and ordered it out; it went with a shriek. The congregation that morning was amazed: they'd never seen anything like it! Such authority; it was the authority of the king come to establish his kingdom.

The kingdom has come

And that was just the way Jesus himself talked about it. The Pharisees, always keen to find fault with him, challenged him about this aspect of his ministry (Matthew 12:22–32). "It is only by Beelzebub, the prince of demons, that this fellow drives out demons" (v. 24). Jesus' reply showed up just how silly their accusation was; but it is also a clear statement from Jesus about his mission:

> Every kingdom divided against itself will be ruined, and every city or household divided against itself will not stand. If Satan drives out Satan, he is divided against himself. How then can his kingdom stand? And if I drive out demons by Beelzebub, by whom do your people drive them out? So then, they will be your judges. But if it is by the Spirit of God that I drive out demons, then the kingdom of God has come upon you (vv. 25–8).

As far as Jesus was concerned, the mission in which he was engaged involved head-on conflict with an enemy, Satan. Dealing with demons was simply one way, albeit rather dramatic, in which that conflict was

---

3   Hugh Anderson, *The Gospel of Mark* (London: Oliphants, 1976), p. 89.

manifested. It was all part of the battle of the kingdoms: Jesus was invading the kingdom of Satan and destroying all his evil activity wherever he found it.

The battle continues

So Jesus' mission was to establish his kingdom, and he did it chiefly in three ways: preaching the gospel, healing the sick, casting out demons. When he sent others out in mission, those were the things they found themselves involved in: both the Twelve and the Seventy-two preached the gospel, healed the sick and cast out demons (Luke 9:1–2; 10:9,17). We have already seen that in his final commission to his followers (Matthew 28:18–20). Jesus told them to go and teach others to obey everything that he had commanded them to do. In brief, that was to preach the gospel, to heal the sick, and to cast out demons—and Acts tells how they went about the task.

The continuing mission of establishing the kingdom is now ours, and the methods are still the same: preach the gospel, heal the sick and cast out demons.

Demons today?

But wait a minute: are we really likely to encounter demons today? Before we answer that question, let's clear away a couple of misunderstandings.

There are two words which are often used in connection with this area of mission which are unhelpful and not really biblical. The first is "demon-possessed". That is the way the first English translations of the Bible translated the Greek word *daimonizomai*, and it has, unfortunately, stuck. The word really only means "demonized" or "influenced by demons", and that can happen in various ways and to varying degrees—in other words, a person can be demonized or influenced by demons without being "possessed", which implies a complete takeover of the person. That condition, in reality, is probably extremely rare. It is possible that the man in the tombs is the only "possessed" person in the whole of the Gospels.

And then there is the word "exorcism". This word usually conjures up thoughts of candles, incantations and holy water, encouraged by the way these things have been portrayed in films. This is not a biblical idea, nor is it the way Jesus dealt with the matter. In fact, what amazed people in Jesus' day was that "he drove out the spirits with a word" (Matthew 8:16). That is a much better model for us.

Evil—how do we get it?

If it is true, as I believe it is, that Satan is still at his destructive work today, and that demons still exist and are active, in what circumstances are we likely to find them? How do people get infected with evil? Remember, we have suggested that most of the demonized people Jesus met were not actually "possessed"; they were afflicted to some degree in an area of their life, like the man who was dumb in Matthew 9:32–3. The same is true today: rarely, if ever, will we meet a person totally taken over by evil, or "possessed", but we will come across those who have been afflicted (or infected) by evil.

There are a variety of ways in which we can become infected, in which Satan gets a foothold in our lives. First, there is direct access. It is a greater possibility today with the rise in occult activity of various kinds, sometimes subtly disguised. These things are clearly "enemy territory", and a person exposed to them risks being infected by evil.

Second, there is indirect access. Sometimes relatives or close friends are involved in some occult activity and put some other person under a "curse". (I know this kind of talk sounds fanciful and straight from the world of fiction, but it happens, it's real, and we would be foolish to dismiss it out of hand.)

Then there are a number of more subtle points of access. Participating in some forms of meditation, or getting involved in the "hard drug scene" can both provide footholds for the enemy. Fixed mental attitudes, into which we slip frequently almost without noticing, particularly negative ones such as anxiety, fear, pessimism, etc., can provide access for the enemy. Sin of various kinds (such as anger, hatred, unforgiveness, sexual perversion, and the like), particularly if they become habitual, can be the door through which we are influenced by evil. Certain traumatic experiences can also be the starting place for enemy activity.

However, having highlighted these things, it is important to stress that while all of them may give access to the enemy, none of these activities (except probably direct involvement in the occult) will always and inevitably result in demonic influence. And if we are minded to dismiss this kind of talk as fanciful, then we should note this: the hallmark of the enemy's activity is always to spoil us and bind us; the hallmark of Jesus' activity is always to free us and make us whole. Two kingdoms at war! The important thing is that, as we get involved in mission, we know these things are possible and have some idea how of how to handle them.

Evil—how do we get rid of it?

So what do we do in such circumstances? This is not a textbook about ministry to those infected with evil, but because it is part of our God-given mission, some guidelines might be helpful.

In no way do we need to go looking for demons. If we are doing what we are supposed to do: worshipping the Lord, teaching about the kingdom of God, and ministering in the power of the Spirit, demons will sooner or later show up—if there are any!

In this connection, I find the incident in the synagogue helpful (Mark 1:21–8). During the course of an ordinary Sabbath morning worship service at which Jesus was the preacher, a demon manifested itself in a member of the congregation. Just a couple of times over the years I have experienced something like that: during a service of worship and teaching, an evil influence in a person's life has been revealed, either through strange physical behaviour or by causing the afflicted person to cry out. It's unnerving and frightening when it happens, but if we are involved in the mission of establishing the kingdom, then I think it is inevitable. But we don't go looking for it.

When we are involved in ministry, unless the person has already shown signs of evil affliction, then we do not begin counselling by "digging for demons". If the problem is sin, repentance and absolution is probably appropriate; if there is no change, or there is a return of the problem after a while, then it may be right gently to investigate whether some evil influence is holding the person. Similarly with healing: if there is no improvement after prayer, or there is a recurrence of the problem after a while, then demonic influence may be the cause. Again, whatever the problem, we don't go looking for demons—if there are any, they will probably show up anyway.

Often, if demonic influence exists, there will be tell-tale signs. For example, sometimes the person will react physically, even violently, to the presence of a cross, or to the mention of the name of Jesus. I have also known people to jerk their heads back involuntarily when we have tried to lay hands on them for prayer. We need to get used to recognizing these signs if we want to minister effectively.

This kind of ministry should not be attempted alone but with others, preferably with those who know what they are doing and have some authority from their church for it. It should be carried out privately rather than publicly whenever possible, both for the sake of the person concerned and others who may be present. It should also be done calmly and in a peaceful atmosphere, never in one that is highly charged.

In this ministry, we need to remember that Jesus has given us authority over all evil powers. When he sent the Twelve out, for example, "he gave them power and authority to drive out all demons and to cure diseases" (Luke 9:1). As John Wimber has helpfully said: "Christians ought to be much more aware of what they can do to demons than of what demons can do to them." Thus, we minister in the name of Jesus, speaking with the authority of Jesus, commanding every evil power to "shut up and go!". And that does not necessitate shouting; demons are not deaf!

It is crucial, having commanded all evil to go, that we pray that the person be filled with the Holy Spirit, so that every place that may have been infected with evil will be not just cleaned out but filled with the light and life of God, otherwise, the person could be prone to further attack. Jesus emphasized the danger with this story:

> When an impure spirit comes out of a person, it goes through arid places seeking rest and does not find it. Then it says, 'I will return to the house I left.' When it arrives, it finds the house swept clean and put in order. Then it goes and takes seven other spirits more wicked than itself, and they go in and live there. And the final condition of that man is worse than the first (Luke 11:24–6).

This story is not intended to frighten us or put us off, but it does highlight the danger of not doing the job thoroughly. By way of further precaution, the person should be encouraged to become, if they are not already, a part of a praying Christian fellowship where they will receive ongoing help and support.

This ministry can be messy and tiring; certainly, it's not exactly fun! But it is part of the mission to which Jesus has called us; it's all part of establishing his kingdom. We have no option but to agree to be involved when necessary—it is part of being a disciple. "As the Father has sent me, I am sending you."

Life in the kingdom

There is another important aspect to our consideration of the kingdom of God. We have seen that establishing the kingdom is a battle in which we get caught up when we become involved in mission. Earlier, in Chapter 1, we saw through Jesus' conversation with Nicodemus that the way into the kingdom is by being born again by the Spirit of God—that's the way we get "signed up" for the battle.

But we have also noted that being in the kingdom really means being under the rule of the king, being subject to him. Like any king, God has rules for life in his kingdom and he expects those of us who claim to be his subjects to live by them. They cover every area of life, not just the spiritual—that's what you would expect from one who is committed to our "wholeness".

The rules were first outlined after the Exodus, when God made a covenant with his people and, through Moses, spelled out the conditions of that agreement: the Ten Commandments (Exodus 20:1–17). Here was the basis upon which those who were God's people should order their lives. Even then God made it clear that he was looking for more than the right religious observance. That was important, as Commandments 1–4 spell out, but so was family life and relationships (Commandment 5), the sanctity of human life (Commandment 6), sexual morality and fidelity (Commandment 7), honesty in action and word (Commandments 8 and 9), and right attitudes and motives (Commandment 10).

Living by the rules

God's people struggled to live by these rules. Time and again God had to remind them. Just before Moses died, for example, God reminded them as they were about to enter the Promised Land: "For I command you today to love the LORD your God, to walk in obedience to him, and to keep his commands, decrees and laws; then you will live and increase, and the LORD your God will bless you in the land you are entering to possess" (Deuteronomy 30:16).

As time went on, the reminders became reprimands: the people kept breaking the rules. In particular, God censured them for their hypocrisy: they kept up the religious observance—well, mostly!—but conveniently forgot the rest. Through Isaiah, God told them in no uncertain terms:

> New Moons, Sabbaths and convocations—I cannot bear your worthless assemblies . . . When you spread out your hands in prayer, I will hide my eyes from you; even when you offer many prayers, I am not listening. Your hands are full of blood! Wash and make yourselves clean. Take your evil deeds out of my sight; stop doing wrong. Learn to do right; seek justice. Defend the oppressed. Take up the cause of the fatherless; plead the case of the widow (Isaiah 1:13,15–17).

Amos had a similar message for them:

> Away with the noise of your songs! I will not listen to the music of your harps. But let justice roll on like a river, righteousness like a never-failing stream! . . . Hear this, you who trample the needy and do away with the poor of the land, saying, "When will the New Moon be over that we may sell grain, and the Sabbath ended that we may market wheat?"—skimping on the measure, boosting the price and cheating with dishonest scales, buying the poor with silver and the needy for a pair of sandals, selling even the sweepings with the wheat (Amos 5:23–4; 8:4–6).

Living God's way was all about not short-changing in the marketplace, as well as right worship in the meeting place. God's people were proud of their religious activities. Yet God didn't always respond with showers of blessing. Why not? Because God had different priorities:

> Yet on the day of your fasting, you do as you please and exploit all your workers. Your fasting ends in quarrelling and strife, and in striking each other with wicked fists . . . Is not this the kind of fasting I have chosen: to loose the chains of injustice and untie the cords of the yoke, to set the oppressed free and break every yoke? Is it not to share your food with the hungry and to provide the poor wanderer with shelter—when you see the naked, to clothe them, and not to turn away from your own flesh and blood? (Isaiah 58:3–4,6–7).

God made no secret of what he expected from his people, he pulled no punches! He looked for more than simply doing the right religious things; he was more concerned with justice, equality, right living, good relationships, honest activities and respect for all people.

The king shocks the people!
These are the concerns of the king and his kingdom. No wonder, then, that Jesus, the king, when he came on the scene, worked hard trying to explain what the implications of living in the kingdom of God were. He took over where the prophets left off, unafraid, like them, to be ruthlessly honest, criticizing inconsistency and hypocrisy whenever he saw them.

He was particularly hard on the religious leaders of his day—they ought to have known better:

> Woe to you, teachers of the law and Pharisees, you hypocrites! You give a tenth of your spices—mint, dill and cumin. But you have neglected the more important matters of the law—justice, mercy and faithfulness. You should have practised the latter, without neglecting the former. You blind guides! You strain out a gnat but swallow a camel (Matthew 23:23–4).

That's telling them!

Over the years, generation after generation of religious leaders had taken up the mantle of interpreting God's law for his people. But in the process, the original intent and spirit of God's law had been forgotten and replaced by hundreds of petty rules and regulations, imposed with a heavy hand and without mercy. "And you experts in the law, woe to you," Jesus said to them, "because you load people down with burdens they can hardly carry, and you yourselves will not lift one finger to help them . . . You have let go of the commands of God and are holding on to human traditions" (Luke 11:46; Mark 7:8).

Jesus' task was a hard one: to change what people believed about God and his laws. And that's why he was so bitterly opposed by other religious leaders: he challenged their traditions, upsetting the status quo. This kingdom he talked about sounded weird to their ears—an upside-down kingdom with upside-down values!

Stories with stings in their tails!
Take some of the parables, for example. Jesus loved to tell stories and the people loved to hear them, but some of them had totally unexpected endings, stings in their tails. (These stories are so familiar to us that we often don't appreciate the real shock to the system they were to the original hearers.)

What about the Good Samaritan, for example (Luke 10:25–37)? To the Jew, even to put those two words together ("good" and "Samaritan") was unheard of. For a Samaritan to be a hero was unbelievable, that a Samaritan might actually help a Jew inconceivable—the whole idea was inexplicable. Jesus' message that Jews and Samaritans should be neighbours was outrageous—they were sworn enemies. But they cannot remain so in the kingdom of God: all the barriers that people have erected between person and person have to go. In God's kingdom all are equal, all are important, all are neighbours.

As for the Prodigal Son (Luke 15:11–32), those who listened to Jesus would, again, have expected a very different ending. If Jesus' story had ended with the father refusing to receive his returning, penitent son, kicking him out with words such as "And don't you dare show your face around here again!", no one in the crowd would have batted an eyelid—that would have been the reasonable, even the proper thing to do with such a good-for-nothing son. Their sympathies would definitely have been with the elder brother. But Jesus' ending was very different, outrageously different. Instead of kicking him out, the father rushed to welcome his son home, embracing him and kissing him. To add insult to injury, he threw a party to celebrate his homecoming and gave him gifts. And not any old gifts either: there was a robe, which indicated honour (after his dishonourable conduct!), a ring, which spoke of authority (when he deserved nothing!), and shoes, which demonstrated his status as a son (when he deserved to be nothing more than a slave!). No wonder the elder son complained—none of it was fair.

But that's how things are in the kingdom of God. The father not only welcomed his son back but forgave him all his wrongdoing and restored to him all that he had lost. And that is just how God behaves towards anyone who comes home and says "Sorry." Jesus put it like this at the end of his story about a lost sheep which was found: "I tell you that in the same way there will be more rejoicing in heaven over one sinner who repents than over ninety-nine righteous people who do not need to repent" (Luke 15:7).

The implication is clear: if the king behaves like that, then those who belong in his kingdom need to do the same. In the kingdom of God forgiveness and restoration are writ large—it's all part of the good news.

Then there was Jesus' story about the Pharisee and the tax collector (Luke 18:9–14): they both went to pray in the Temple. Everyone who heard Jesus would take it as read that the Pharisee would automatically be heard and accepted by God, while the tax collector would have no chance of being heard at all—well, he was a sinner and an outcast, everyone knew that.

Everyone, that is, except God! For, in Jesus' story, to the amazement of all, after they had finished praying, Jesus said that the tax collector went home accepted by God ("justified") and not the Pharisee. That's an upside-down kind of outcome! And Jesus added this explanation: "For all those who exalt themselves will be humbled, and those who humble themselves will be exalted" (v. 14). In God's kingdom pride and hypocrisy are "out", honesty and humility are "in".

How those religious people of Jesus' day struggled with these upside-down values: Samaritans as neighbours, no-gooders forgiven, sinners accepted rather than upright Pharisees! Whatever next? But these are the values of the kingdom of God. And they remain unchanged today.

Jesus explains the rules

If the people struggled to make sense of Jesus' stories, they also struggled with his interpretation of the Law. He made it sound like a whole new set of rules, though he claimed he was simply explaining the old ones. "Do not think that I have come to abolish the Law or the Prophets," he said; "I have not come to abolish them but to fulfil them" (Matthew 5:17). That may be so, but he certainly turned a few of them on their heads in the process!

The Law said: "Do not murder." Jesus said that as far as he was concerned, being angry was just as bad (Matthew 5:21–2). The Law said: "Do not commit adultery." That's fine, except that Jesus said that merely to look at a woman lustfully was as bad as committing adultery—you'd done it in your heart (Matthew 5:27–8). For years the principle, "Eye for eye, and tooth for tooth" had been accepted as a fair basis for punishment. But not for Jesus: "Do not resist an evil person. If anyone slaps you on the right cheek, turn to them the other cheek also" (Matthew 5:38–9). And in the area of social relationships, most people operated on the principle, "Love your neighbour and hate your enemy." Even that Jesus turned on its head: "Love your enemies and pray for those who persecute you," he said (Matthew 5:43–4).

But why such radical principles? Jesus explained: " . . . that you may be children of your Father in heaven" (Matthew 5:45). And if that is not a high enough aim, what about this one? "Be perfect, therefore, as your heavenly Father is perfect" (Matthew 5:48). The standards are high, the guidelines are radical, but only because they reflect the character of God himself: the Father wants his children to reflect him, the king wants his subjects to live as he lives. It's a tall order, but it's all part of the process of establishing the kingdom of God here on earth: it's part of our mission, it's how disciples should live and call others to live.

The hallmarks of the kingdom are . . .

Jesus the king offers not just salvation "for the soul" but a whole new way of life, a new way of living, an alternative lifestyle, alternative to what existed in his day; alternative, too, to the lifestyles of today.

The challenge of the kingdom for us is this: God expects a kingdom lifestyle from those engaged in kingdom mission. Or, as somebody has helpfully put it: "The church must be good news before it preaches good news!" We are going to look more fully at the role of the church in mission in Chapter 10. For now, by way of summarizing what we have been saying, let's ask the question: "What are the hallmarks of the kingdom?"—well, some of them at least.

. . . love

At the heart of the kingdom is love, for its king is a God of love. But as we have already discovered in Chapter 3, kingdom love, unlike much human love, is neither selective nor exclusive. All are equally welcomed in the kingdom, whoever they are, whatever they are, even the unlovely and unlovable.

Jesus has shown us the way. He loved those whom others despised, like Zacchaeus, the cheating tax collector; he loved those whom others discarded, like the blind beggar; he loved those whom others considered nobodies, like lepers. That's kingdom love: and it needs to be visible in our mission.

. . . forgiveness

Forgiveness is central to the gospel of the kingdom too. Jesus accepted people whom others rejected because he was willing to forgive when others weren't. Some wanted to condemn the woman caught in adultery: Jesus forgave her; some wrote off men like Zacchaeus: Jesus offered forgiveness and the chance to start again. Even with his dying breath, Jesus offered forgiveness to the penitent thief dying on a cross alongside him and prayed that those who crucified him might be forgiven.

Paul highlights the challenge of this when he writes: "Forgive as the Lord forgave you" (Colossians 3:13). And yet it's not easy, is it? Unforgiveness, or bearing grudges, is so common, even within the church. How often do we hear: "I can't forgive him!" or "I'll never forgive her as long as I live!"? Actually, this kind of talk usually hurts the unforgiving more than the unforgiven. But there is no room for such attitudes in the kingdom. The king invites us to be forgiven so that we might be forgiving; he urges us to pray: "Forgive us our sins, as we forgive those who sin against us."

. . . justice

Justice rules in the kingdom, for the king is just in all he does. We have already seen him criticizing, through prophets, the injustices among his people. He is angry when he sees those with influence taking priority over those with none; he grieves when those who have power ride roughshod over those with none; he cries out when those who have money use their wealth to put down those who have none.

As far as I know, the king has not changed! He is concerned today (if not angry!) that one quarter of the world's people manage to use three-quarters of the world's resources, leaving three-quarters of the world's people to survive on one quarter of the world's resources—and many fail to survive. We should share his concern. He is concerned when powerful nations, groups or individuals abuse their power and cause others to suffer. We should share his concern. As I rework this book, this agenda has been made so much worse because of the phenomenon of climate change, which results in radically changing weather patterns, destroyed crops and communities under threat of extinction. And so often it is the people who can least cope with these traumatic changes that bear the brunt of them. All their difficulties are compounded by the extravagant lifestyle of the rich which is threatening the shaky lifestyles of the poor even more. Justice is a concern of the king and therefore of the kingdom—and it needs to be our concern too.

. . . equality

"All people are equal, some more equal than others"—words based on a quote from *Animal Farm* by George Orwell. In theory, we may think that all people are equal, but in practice some are very definitely more equal than others. It is true today, and it was even more true in Jesus' day.

We have already noted the deeply entrenched hatred of Jew for non-Jew: Jews really were more equal than others, or so they believed. Jesus tried to show them that with God all are equal, whatever race or culture or colour—even the hated Samaritans! How they struggled with that. And how we struggle still with that principle, too: it was sharply focused in the apartheid struggle in South Africa, and too-often seen in parts of the United States and elsewhere too. But if we are honest, it also rears its head much nearer home, perhaps at work, or even down our street. There is no room for racial discrimination in the kingdom.

All people really are equal in the kingdom—and that includes women. Women were very definitely second-class citizens in Jesus' day. But women were among Jesus' closer friends, supporting Jesus' ministry and his disciples "out of their own means" (Luke 8:2–3). They were there at his death and at his burial, and women were the first to be told about his resurrection. The kingdom of God as demonstrated in Jesus was, in effect, a women's liberation movement.

Children in those days had no rights either. Imagine the struggle people had, therefore, when Jesus took a child, stood him in front of a crowd, and said:

> Truly I tell you, unless you change and become like little children, you will never enter the kingdom of heaven. Therefore, whoever takes the lowly position of this child is the greatest in the kingdom of heaven. And whoever welcomes one such child in my name welcomes me. If anyone causes one of these little ones—those who believe in me—to stumble, it would be better for him to have a large millstone hung round their neck and to be drowned in the depths of the sea (Matthew 18:3–6).

Children are no less valuable than adults; women are as important as men. In the kingdom, all the distinctions go, all the barriers are down: all men (and women, and children) really are equal.

James, in his letter, challenges us not to have favourites: how easy it would be to give the best seat to a wealthy, well-dressed person while telling a poor, shabbily dressed person to sit on the floor (James 2:1–4). That's not the kingdom way.

Paul had to learn this. As a devout Jew, he would have prayed every morning, thanking God that "thou hast not made me a Gentile, a slave or a woman". For Paul the Christian, all the distinctions have gone, and he can write: "There is neither Jew nor Gentile, neither slave nor free, nor is there male and female, for you are all one in Christ Jesus" (Galatians 3:28).

Today the barriers may be different, the categories may have changed, but the message of equality is still relevant. In the kingdom, all really are equal: we must proclaim it and demonstrate it in our mission.

. . . holinesss

The holiness of God is a prominent theme in the Bible, and if the king is holy, then those who are his subjects will also be called to holy living: "But just as he who called you is holy, so be holy in all you do; for it is written: 'Be holy, because I am holy'" (1 Peter 1:15)—the call to discipleship is a call to holiness.

It is also a call to be honest and sincere in all we think, say and do; it is a call to be self-controlled in our personal lives and selfless in our attitude to others. The call to holiness is uncompromising; Paul spells it out like this: " . . . sexual immorality, impurity and debauchery; idolatry and witchcraft; hatred, discord, jealousy, fits of rage, selfish ambition, dissensions, factions and envy; drunkenness, orgies, and the like. I warn you, as I did before, that those who live like this will not inherit the kingdom of God" (Galatians 5:19–21). So there will be times when those who belong to the kingdom of God have to say "No"; at times it will be costly too, particularly when it results in the loss of a friend or of a job. But it is part of our commitment to the kingdom.

But holiness is not just negative, saying "No" to things; at its best it is positive and attractive—the Psalmist speaks of "the beauty (or "splendour") of holiness" (Psalm 96:9). That's why Paul goes on: "But the fruit of the Spirit is love, joy, peace, forbearance, kindness, goodness, faithfulness, gentleness and self-control. Against such things there is no law" (Galatians 5:22–3). Our privilege and responsibility in mission is not simply to frown upon sin whenever we see it (although there is a place for that), but to proclaim and to demonstrate the joy, the wholeness, the beauty of life lived as God intended, kingdom life, holiness.

. . . concern for the poor

Jesus' mission was " . . . to proclaim good news to the poor . . . to proclaim freedom for the prisoners and recovery of sight for the blind, to set the oppressed free . . . " (Luke 4:18). Jesus fulfilled this by spending time with the poor, the vulnerable, the weak, the "underdogs", those dismissed by others as unimportant, of no value, even good-for-nothing sinners. He did it so much that in the end he was dubbed "Friend of Sinners"—it was meant as a term of abuse, but I suspect he welcomed it more than any other name.

We need to have a similar emphasis if we would be faithful to our call to mission. Our "poor" may well be the unemployed, the one-parent families, the chronically sick, people with disabilities, the elderly; whoever they are, whatever their need, for the sake of the king and his kingdom we need to be there for them.

At one of the churches where I was vicar, I sometimes wondered, if Jesus were to visit our church but only had time to look in on one thing, what would he choose? I had a sneaking suspicion that he wouldn't have come to one of the Sunday services, or to one of the house fellowships, but would have turned up at seven o'clock on a Tuesday evening in the parish centre. There he would have found "Centrepoint", a club for people with various disabilities, run by members of the church family: they used to have a marvellous time together, the atmosphere was great, and I think Jesus would have felt at home: a taste of the kingdom here and now on earth.

Dabbling in politics?

Should the church (or Christians) be involved in politics? The fact that this question is asked at all (and it is asked both inside and outside the church) reveals a lack of understanding of the church's mission. If our mission were simply to win individuals to Jesus, we would have little cause to dabble in politics. If our mission were chiefly to build the church, we might avoid getting caught up in it. But our mission is to establish the kingdom of God here and now on earth; that will inevitably and unavoidably involve us in political issues.

Although he didn't set out to do so, it was inevitable that Jesus got caught up in the politics of his day: his activities so often brought him into conflict with the authorities. The early Christians also clashed frequently with political leaders—and at times they were disobedient, deciding that it was more important to obey God rather than people (Acts 4:19). If we are committed to establishing God's kingdom, we too need to be ready for conflict at times.

Often, in recent years, Christians have challenged new legislation where it seemed to be unfair, particularly where the rich appeared to gain at the expense of the poor. Naturally, that sort of issue could easily be seen as party political, the church opposing government policies. But much more important are the kingdom principles of justice and concern for the poor, the powerless and the weak.

The more the church seeks to follow the principles of God's kingdom the more we shall find ourselves in opposition to secular authorities of all shades of political opinion, and the more we shall be accused of "dabbling in politics". But those who complain about the church's involvement in politics have never read the New Testament: if they had they would know that Jesus always challenged, and argued with, the political leaders of his day. It is inevitable today, too, whenever the church takes seriously the establishment of God's kingdom—it is an important aspect of our mission.

Your kingdom come

The task to which we have been called is a big one: bigger than winning individuals for Christ, bigger than filling the churches with people. Since I first wrote this book conferences have been held and resources produced to encourage church growth, which is much needed in the UK. Since 2007, I have been involved in the Leading Your Church into Growth initiative, helping to teach simple principles to churches to encourage their growth. Important though this is, we must not lose sight of the fact that, according to the New Testament, growing healthy churches should not be seen as an end in itself but rather a crucial means to an end, establishing God's kingdom here on earth—the church is an agent of the kingdom.

The call to discipleship is a call to be involved in establishing God's kingdom here on earth. We shall find ourselves involved in spiritual battles and, at times, in conflict with secular authorities. But this is the inevitable result of taking seriously Jesus' call to mission; this is the cost of being part of the answer to our prayer: "Your kingdom come, your will be done." This is part of Jesus' call to make disciples. "As the Father has sent me, I am sending you."

9

Sent . . . To Serve

If you've ever had the opportunity to meet a significant person in the flesh whom, till that moment, you had only ever seen on television, you may well have been surprised. They were rather different from your impression of them—they were not quite what you expected.

Not quite what they expected!

That was the experience, too, of Jesus' contemporaries: he was not quite what they expected. We saw some of the expectations of Jesus' day in the previous chapter. The people were waiting for a great descendant of David: Jesus was certainly descended from David, but he did not fulfil the political role for which people had hoped. When they tried to make him king, he wasn't interested (John 6:15). When he rode into Jerusalem, the city of the king, he didn't ride a horse as a conquering military hero, but a donkey, as one coming in love and peace—"See, your king comes to you, gentle and riding on a donkey" (Matthew 21:5). He seemed to enjoy considerable power and authority, but when he most needed it, on trial for his life and dying on the cross, he chose not to call for reinforcements (Matthew 26:52–3; 27:41–3).

Probably most bewildering of all for his closest friends was the time when Jesus asked them: "Who do you say I am?" Peter answered correctly and was commended by Jesus for it: "You are the Messiah, the Son of the living God" (Matthew 16:15–16). But immediately afterwards, Jesus began to say the strangest things: "From that time on Jesus began to explain to his disciples that he must go to Jerusalem and suffer many things at the hands of the elders, the chief priests and the teachers of the law, and that he must be killed and on the third day be raised to life"

(Matthew 16:21). What could he mean? The Messiah suffer? The Son of God killed? It couldn't be so, could it? No doubt Peter spoke for the rest of them when he blurted out: "Never, Lord! This shall never happen to you!" (Matthew 16:22). Far from thanking Peter for his concern, Jesus actually put him in his place—and in no uncertain terms! "Get behind me, Satan! You are a stumbling-block to me; you do not have in mind the concerns of God, but merely human concerns" (Matthew 16:23).

It's all in the Book!
The disciples were alarmed, confused and fearful. But they shouldn't have been. If they really knew the Old Testament scriptures, then they should have recognized what Jesus was saying; for alongside the theme of God's Messiah, the Saviour, the coming king in the Old Testament, there was another theme. The scriptures also speak of "God's servant".

This "servant" appears in the second part of Isaiah (Chapters 40—55), probably written during the time God's people were in exile in Babylon. It was a message of hope that God would bring them home from exile. In particular, there are certain key passages in which the servant is prominent, usually referred to as the "Servant Songs" (42:1–9; 49:1–13; 50:4–11; 52:13—53:12). The fourth one is the best known, containing familiar words such as "he was despised and rejected by mankind" (53:3) and "we all, like sheep, have gone astray" (53:6).

Scholars have often discussed who the servant is supposed to be. It could be the nation Israel, God's specially chosen people: "But you, Israel, my servant, Jacob, whom I have chosen, you descendants of Abraham my friend, I took you from the ends of the earth . . . But now listen, Jacob, my servant, Israel, whom I have chosen. This is what the LORD says . . . " (41:8–9; 44:1–2). But if the people of Israel were supposed to be God's servant, they were not very successful at it.

Alternatively, the servant could be the prophet himself: "Before I was born the LORD called me; from my mother's womb he has spoken my name . . . And now the LORD says—he who formed me in the womb to be his servant . . . " (49:1,5). But it is surely beyond the scope of one human being, however great a prophet, to fulfil all that is spoken about God's servant in these passages, especially things such as this, "But he

was pierced for our transgressions, he was crushed for our iniquities . . .",
and this, " . . . the Lord has laid on him the iniquity of us all" (53:5,6).

For Christians, there is only one person who has fulfilled completely
all that is expected of God's servant in Isaiah: that is Jesus. Jesus is the
one who "took up our pain and bore our suffering" (53:4); it is Jesus
whose punishment has brought us peace and by whose wounds we are
healed (53:5).

Jesus the Servant

It is clear from the Gospels that the role of the servant was central in
Jesus' understanding of his mission. If his contemporaries were puzzled
by some of the things he said and did, it was because they had overlooked
this important part of Old Testament prophecy. They expected a king, a
deliverer, a Messiah, but they were not looking for a servant, certainly not
a suffering one. That's why Peter struggled so much when Jesus started
talking about his death (Matthew 16:21–2).

But Jesus knew different: he was the expected Messiah, the hoped-for
deliverer, the eagerly awaited king, but he was also God's servant. Right
at the start of his public ministry, at his baptism, God had spoken to
him: "You are my Son, whom I love; with you I am well pleased" (Luke
3:22). The second part of that is a quote from Isaiah 42:1, part of one of
the Servant Songs, which speaks about "my servant".

Later, Jesus summed up the purpose of his mission in these words:
"For even the Son of Man did not come to be served, but to serve, and to
give his life as a ransom for many" (Mark 10:45). Here, Jesus describes
his ministry in terms of serving, using words reminiscent of part of the
fourth Servant Song: " . . . the Lord makes his life an offering for sin . . .
by his knowledge my righteous servant will justify many, and he will bear
their iniquities" (Isaiah 53:10–11).

Again, during his conversation with his disciples at the Last Supper,
just before he went out into the Garden of Gethsemane and was arrested,
Jesus explained to them what was about to happen, quoting from Isaiah
53:12: "It is written: 'And he was numbered with the transgressors'; and

I tell you that this must be fulfilled in me. Yes, what is written about me is reaching its fulfilment" (Luke 22:37).

It is clear, then, that Jesus saw his mission not just as the anointed Messiah, but also as the suffering servant. If we would understand mission, we need to grasp the significance of this too; for God's servant says: "As the Father has sent me, I am sending you"—the call to discipleship is a call to service.

The privilege and responsibility of God's Servant

The Servant Songs provide a clear picture of both the privilege and the responsibility of being God's servant. To begin with, he is specially called and chosen by God for the task (42:1,6; 49:1); he is loved by God (42:1), and he is taken by the hand and kept by God (42:6). He is given the Spirit of God (42:1), he is protected and strengthened by God (49:2,5), and he is taught by God (50:4).

His God-given mission is to bring justice to the world (42:1,6), to be a light for all nations (42:6; 49:6), to bring "salvation to the ends of the earth" (49:6). This will involve opening blind eyes, freeing prisoners and releasing those in darkness (42:7). In fulfilling this ministry, the servant will be quiet and gentle, not shouting and making a scene (42:2), not breaking bruised reeds or snuffing out smouldering wicks (42:3), which is wonderful imagery of a gentle, pastoral, serving ministry.

But God's servant is not promised an easy time: he will not be considered beautiful, attractive or desirable, but rather people will be appalled at him, despising and rejecting him, hiding their faces from him (52:14; 53:3). He will suffer much (50:6; 53:3,10), almost to the point of despair (49:4); but through all this suffering, he will remain confident that the one who called him is faithful and will stand by him (42:6; 50:10); so he will trust him (50:7–9), obey him (50:4–5) and persevere despite everything (50:7). In the end, he will succeed in the mission to which he has been called, he will win through and complete the task (42:4), and he will be rewarded: "Therefore I will give him a portion among the great, and he will divide the spoils with the strong, because he poured out his life unto death, and was numbered with the transgressors" (53:12).

To be God's servant is a great privilege, a great calling; but with the privilege comes great responsibility, great pain and great cost. Jesus alone has totally fulfilled this high calling.

Serving all the way

So it was as God's servant that Jesus came, and his whole mission was shaped by that awareness. When he came to the synagogue in Nazareth early in his ministry and read from Isaiah, the passage we know as the beginning of Chapter 61, "The Spirit of the Lord is on me, because he has anointed me . . . " (Luke 4:18–19), he was declaring that he knew himself to be called by God, with a mission from God, for which he was equipped by God—he was God's servant. Whenever anyone tried to deflect him from that mission, or tempted him to go about it some other way, he put them in their place in no uncertain terms, whether the attack came directly from his enemy, the devil (Luke 4:1–13), or more subtly through one of his close friends, Peter (Matthew 16:22–3). When he was criticized for the company he kept, the damaged, broken, sinful people he befriended, he took no notice; these were the "bruised reeds" the servant would not break, the "smouldering wicks" he would not snuff out, which the Servant Songs had talked about (Isaiah 42:3). His gentleness, his sensitivity, his compassion, his selfless love: these were all the hallmarks of God's servant.

He was totally committed to the task, too, although it meant giving everything and being prepared to suffer: "I offered my back to those who beat me, my cheeks to those who pulled out my beard; I did not hide my face from mocking and spitting" (Isaiah 50:6). He never complained, even when people did their worst to him; he knew that it was all part of his call to serve, that it was God's will for him:

> He was oppressed and afflicted, yet he did not open his mouth;
> he was led like a lamb to the slaughter, and as a sheep before
> her shearers is silent, so he did not open his mouth . . . He was
> assigned a grave with the wicked, and with the rich in his death,
> though he had done no violence, nor was any deceit in his mouth.
> Yet it was the Lord's will to crush him and cause him to suffer . . .
> (Isaiah 53:7,9–10).

In Paul's words, he became "obedient to death—even death on a cross!" (Philippians 2:8).

It is because Jesus so fully understood the role of God's servant and so completely embraced it that he was able to speak with such certainty about what would happen to him: "The Son of Man must suffer many things and be rejected by the elders, the chief priests and the teachers of the law, and he must be killed and on the third day be raised to life" (Luke 9:22). This is why, in the Garden of Gethsemane, though he hesitated momentarily, he knew he had to go through with it: "Father, if you are willing, take this cup from me; yet not my will, but yours be done" (Luke 22:42). And this is why, when passers-by at his crucifixion challenged him, "Come down from the cross, if you are the Son of God!" (Matthew 27:40), he knew that was the one thing he could not do. Not because he didn't have the power to do so, but because he didn't have permission to do so—he was only a servant, and it was God's will for him to stay where he was.

The king—washing feet!

So Jesus was a king, but a king with a difference! This king came not to rule, but to serve. In so doing, he was declaring yet again the upside-down values of the kingdom of God which we saw in the previous chapter. Whoever heard of a king serving? But that is exactly what Jesus did: he is the servant-king.

He demonstrated this most clearly and poignantly in the Upper Room where he ate his last meal with his disciples (John 13:1–17). They had been travelling together, and such was the state of the roads in those days that travellers' feet got very dusty. So it was considered common courtesy to offer to wash the feet of guests whenever they arrived at a house, a task normally performed by a servant. Apparently, on this particular occasion, although there was water available, together with a bowl and towel, there was no servant. Who was going to wash their feet? They couldn't possibly eat a meal without that being done.

Luke tells us that while they were having this meal together, a dispute arose among the disciples as to which of them was the greatest (Luke 22:24)—and that wasn't the first time they had argued about it (Luke 9:46). Is it possible that even while they were travelling they argued?

And when they found no servant to wash their feet, did they complain? "I'm not doing it!" "It's not my job!" "It's beneath me!" "Where's the servant?" This is only my conjecture. But we do know they were prone to argue about who was the greatest, and that adds poignancy to what happened next. Jesus took off his outer clothing, poured water into the bowl, wrapped a towel round his waist (presumably like an apron), and began to wash the dusty feet of his disciples (John 13:4–5)—the servant's task! Peter was the first to complain, vociferously: "Never, Lord" (v. 8). No doubt his indignation at having Jesus wash his feet was coupled with his embarrassment at having argued about greatness and not offering to do the foot-washing himself. Jesus insisted on washing his feet, and Peter reluctantly let him do it.

When he had finished, Jesus explained to them the significance of what he had done:

> You call me "Teacher" and "Lord", and rightly so, for that is what I am. Now that I, your Lord and Teacher, have washed your feet, you also should wash one another's feet. I have set you an example that you should do as I have done for you. I tell you the truth, no servant is greater than his master, nor is a messenger greater than the one who sent him. Now that you know these things, you will be blessed if you do them (John 13:13–17).

This would have sounded just as radical to the disciples as things like "Love your enemies" or "Turn the other cheek". The prospect of washing one another's feet would have appalled them, not just physically (it was a dirty job), but socially, too (it was the servant's job). Yet, Jesus, their Lord and teacher, did it for them: maybe they should swallow their pride and follow his example. And so should we!

Serving, not ruling!

The problem is that this is radically different from the way the world operates. There people seek to rule, to have power, to exercise authority, and others are expected to serve them. Jesus, as Paul explains, had real power and authority, and was in the position legitimately to rule the world, yet he gave it all up to serve. Paul writes:

> In your relationships with one another, have the same mindset as
> Christ: who, being in very nature God, did not consider equality
> with God something to be used to his own advantage; rather,
> he made himself nothing by taking the very nature of a servant,
> being made in human likeness. And being found in appearance
> as a man, he humbled himself by becoming obedient to death—
> even death on a cross! (Philippians 2:5–8).

(The word Paul actually uses in the Greek to describe Jesus' nature is *doulos*, meaning "slave".)

Some progress report! It begins with God and ends at a criminal's cross; it begins with having everything and ends with having nothing, like a slave. That's upside down! The world says, "Getting on is moving up"; Jesus says: "Getting on is moving down." The world says: "To succeed, grasp for more"; Jesus says: "To succeed, give up what you have." The world says: "You've arrived when you rule"; Jesus says: "You've arrived when you serve."

This is what he tried to explain to his disciples:

> You know that the rulers of the Gentiles lord it over them, and
> their high officials exercise authority over them. Not so with you.
> Instead, whoever wants to become great among you must be your
> servant, and whoever wants to be first must be your slave—just
> as the Son of Man did not come to be served, but to serve, and
> to give his life as a ransom for many . . . I am among you as one
> who serves (Matthew 20:5–28; Luke 22:27).

What a contrast between the way of the world and the way of Jesus! In the world, the aim is to rule "over"; for the servant the aim is to be "among". The world jostles for position and rank so that one person can be above another, better than another, different from another; the servant needs no position or rank but is happy to be alongside others. In the world, rulers love to lord it over others, they enjoy exercising authority, they love to give commands. But whoever heard of a servant doing such things? "Not so with you," Jesus told his disciples. And his directive is strong, even passionate—"This must not be so among you!" In the world, rulers know only how to tell others what to do; the servant shows others how to do it. Thus, Jesus the servant is able to say, for example: "As I have loved you, so you must love one another" (John 13:34). This may be his "new commandment", but he has already shown them how to do it.

Jesus was sent to serve, and he has modelled for us perfectly what serving really means: totally surrendered, totally submissive, totally available—to God. In God's kingdom, this is how all mission should be attempted: with a servant's heart. And Jesus invites us to follow in his footsteps: "As the Father has sent me, I am sending you"—discipleship with a servant heart.

Following in the Servant's footsteps

Jesus makes it quite clear where we start: "Whoever wants to be my disciple must deny themselves and take up their cross daily and follow me. For whoever wants to save their life will lose it, but whoever loses their life for me will save it" (Luke 9:23–4). The terms are demanding, and they are non-negotiable.

The cross is a powerful picture of what is involved, even more powerful for those who lived in Jesus' day. It was part of everyday life to see criminals carrying crosses; if you saw a man carrying a cross out of the city gate, you knew he wouldn't be coming back—he would be crucified on it. To follow in the footsteps of Jesus, the servant, is to give up my life, at least as far as living for myself is concerned—and to do so every day. Paul knew what Jesus meant: "I have been crucified with Christ and I no longer live, but Christ lives in me. The life I now live in the body, I live by faith in the Son of God, who loved me and gave himself for me" (Galatians 2:20).

Jesus also speaks of denying self. Some people opt for self-denial during Lent: giving up alcohol, or chocolate, or something else they enjoy. But Jesus is talking about much more radical action, not me giving up something, but me giving up me! He is calling us to reorientate ourselves totally, giving up focusing on ourselves—what we like, what we want, what we need—and focusing instead on God and what he wants. And that will mean putting others before ourselves too—Jesus showed us that.

Jesus also speaks in upside-down terms about this: that if I hang on selfishly to my own life, I shall in the end lose it; but if I am willing to give it up for Jesus, then I shall save it. And he knows what he is talking about; he gave up equality with God in order to become a human being and serve others. He is asking us to do no more than he has already done. But that is challenging enough!

Servants of the Servant
It is significant that most of the writers of the New Testament describe themselves as servants—in fact, they actually use the word "slave". Paul introduces himself like this: "Paul, a servant (slave) of Christ Jesus, called to be an apostle . . ." (Romans 1:1), and again: "Paul and Timothy, servants (slaves) of Christ Jesus . . . " (Philippians 1:1). James describes himself similarly: "James, a servant (slave) of God and of the Lord Jesus Christ . . . " (James 1:1); so does Peter: "Simon Peter, a servant (slave) and apostle of Jesus Christ . . . " (2 Peter 1:1); and so does Jude: "Jude, a servant (slave) of Jesus Christ and a brother of James . . . " (Jude 1). Clearly, they had grasped the truth that to follow Jesus meant being a servant.

Paul certainly understood it. Writing to the Christians in Rome, for example, he spelt out the effects of the salvation of Jesus like this: "But now that you have been set free from sin and have become slaves to God . . . " (Romans 6:22)—set free to be slaves! And to the Christians in Corinth he explains: "For what we preach is not ourselves, but Jesus Christ as Lord, and ourselves as your servants for Jesus' sake" (2 Corinthians 4:5). Not only do we become servants of Jesus, which is hard enough, but we also become servants of others, which is harder still.

Presumably, it was because Paul had so clearly grasped this that he was prepared to take so much punishment in his missionary work: his catalogue of hardship includes imprisonment, flogging, stoning, shipwreck and dangers of various kinds (2 Corinthians 11:23–8). It's all part of being a servant: Isaiah saw it, Jesus knew it, Paul experienced it—and we must be prepared for it too, if we are going to be "slaves of Christ".

Servant attitude

But what does all this mean for us? How does it affect our mission?

First, we need to have a servant attitude. We have seen how Jesus' disciples argued about greatness and vied for the best positions, and that this is the way of the world so often, too—striving for greatness, eager to get on, wanting to be "top dog". But the upside-down values of Jesus say that it is the "top dog" who serves.

When I was at theological college, there was a story told about the previous principal. The man who cleaned the toilets was off sick and the job was not being done. After a while the toilets began to smell and students began to complain. But, early one morning, the principal got up and cleaned them. That's a servant attitude.

It's not always apparent in the life of the church, however: the structures don't encourage it. At least, the Anglican ones don't: we often talk about "preferment" when a minister moves from one church to another; we give some ministers extra titles, and some ministry roles are deemed more significant than others. From Jesus' perspective, every task is important, every ministry special and all are servants. But we struggle to see it that way, don't we?

Many years ago, when I was on the staff of York Minster, I remember Bishop Morris Maddocks preaching soon after he had been appointed Bishop of Selby. He stood in the pulpit and told us he counted it a privilege to be a bishop. What on earth was he going to say next? He continued: "If Christians are the servants of God, and the clergy are the servants of the servants of God, then a bishop is the servant of the servants of the servants of God." That's a servant attitude—and those of us who knew Bishop Morris knew that he meant it and practised it.

This servant attitude challenges the competitive spirit that is sadly evident in the church and among church leaders—I haven't been immune myself! Even in mission, one Christian group often seems to be competing with another, one church criticizing another. Mission is so important we cannot afford to compete with each other; in the end, we are all servants of Jesus and we are called to serve, not to compete.

As servants, there is no room for ambition either—I have struggled with that one, too, at times. We are called to serve Jesus where we are and not to look for reward, for position, for recognition—that's the servant attitude.

And how often do we miss God's opportunity for service because we consider something is beneath us and we are too proud, rather like the disciples about washing feet? Being at the front in a church service, I often see things which others miss; I've seen exciting and moving things. One little incident during an evening service sticks in my mind: one of the church members, then churchwarden (an important job!), was sitting with Michael, a disabled young person in a wheelchair, helping him with the service. At one point I saw him take his handkerchief from his pocket and wipe Michael's nose. That moved me and challenged me—because that's serving. As I reflected on it, I thought that Michael learned more about the love and acceptance of God through that simple action than from any sermon of mine, however brilliant! You could say that mission is "wiping another person's nose". That's the servant attitude.

Servant obedience

Jesus told an illuminating little story that highlights the role of the servant:

> Suppose one of you has a servant ploughing or looking after sheep. Will he say to the servant when he comes in from the field, "Come along now and sit down to eat"? Won't he rather say, "Prepare my supper, get yourself ready and wait on me while I eat and drink; after that you may eat and drink"? Will he thank the servant because he did what he was told to do? So you also, when you have done everything you were told to do, should say, "We are unworthy servants; we have only done our duty." (Luke 17:7–10).

A servant is not free to do what he wants, his time is not his own; he is under orders, at the beck and call of his master. A servant has to serve whether he likes it or not, whether he wants to or not, whether it is convenient or not—that is what being a servant is all about.

Jesus often knew this pressure himself, when the demands of others took precedence over his own needs. For example, when the disciples had just come back from trying mission for themselves (Luke 9:1–6,10),

Jesus took them away to Bethsaida, presumably to have a de-briefing session (v. 10). But the crowds found out where they were and followed. How did Jesus respond?

In those circumstances, I would be inclined to tell them I was busy and suggest they come back another time. But Jesus "welcomed them and spoke to them about the kingdom of God, and healed those who needed healing" (v. 11). That's servant obedience.

The pressure was so great on Jesus at times that they didn't even have time to eat. Once, when that happened, Jesus tried to escape with his disciples by boat to a solitary place; but the people saw what he was doing, ran round the lake and were waiting for him when he arrived. Was Jesus cross? Did he send them away? No! He had compassion on them and, presumably forgetting they hadn't eaten, began to teach them (Mark 6:31–4). The disciples wanted to send them away, but Jesus didn't.

That's servant obedience, serving whether it is convenient or not. Jesus' obedience to God, his total commitment to being a servant, challenges me, because if I am honest, I like to minister when I choose, when it happens to be convenient for me. But that's not servant obedience: that's self-gratification.

We had been away for a few days' holiday. As we turned into the drive on our return, I noticed a young man sitting on the step of the shop opposite. Within five minutes of our getting in the house, he was ringing the doorbell. He'd been before: a young man with problems and a police record, who tended to turn up on our doorstep whenever he had cash-flow problems—no money! Outwardly I talked with him reasonably, but inside I was irritated: "Why must he come now? Can't he see we've just come back from holiday? Doesn't he realize it's Sunday evening and I have a service to go to in a few minutes?" "Can you come back tomorrow?" I heard myself say to him. It seemed reasonable in the circumstances, but I knew it was wrong: it wasn't what Jesus would have done. Servant obedience means serving anytime, convenient or not. I checked myself in time and gave him what he needed. I got it right that time—just!

But only a few months later, something similar happened—will I never learn? Again, we had been away for a few days and had been home about half an hour. The doorbell rang and there was a young man on the doorstep, clearly bothered about something. I had officiated at his wedding five months before, and now his wife had left him. He'd come to talk to the one person he thought might be able to help him. What is more, one of the first things he had done when his wife left was to dig out the copy of Luke's Gospel I had given them on their wedding day and begin to read it. What a great opportunity! He wanted help, but I had just come back from holiday: "Could you come back later, at about nine o'clock?" I asked him. But he needed help now: he knew that, and so did I, really. It was very inconvenient, I had other things to do—but I invited him in and spent the next one and a half hours with him. That's serving and I almost blew it, again!

Servant obedience, as I understand it, means I am "on duty" whenever Jesus needs me: I serve when he says, not when I want. That's being a servant.

Servant humility

True serving leaves no room for pride, for the servant is nothing and has nothing in himself. That's why Paul got so upset when he learned that the Christians in Corinth were quarrelling and dividing into factions. He challenged them:

> What, after all, is Apollos? And what is Paul? Only servants, through whom you came to believe—as the Lord has assigned to each his task. I planted the seed, Apollos watered it, but God has been making it grow. So neither the one who plants nor the one who waters is anything, but only God, who makes things grow (1 Corinthians 3:5–8).

That puts things into proper perspective: neither Paul nor Apollos wanted a following, but both wanted people to follow Jesus.

John the Baptist had the same attitude. When the people who had been following John began to transfer their allegiance to Jesus, John's disciples were concerned. But John wasn't; his whole purpose was to prepare the way for Jesus, to serve him. "You yourselves can testify," he reminded them, "that I said, 'I am not the Christ but am sent ahead of him.' The bride belongs to the bridegroom. The friend who attends the bridegroom waits and listens for him, and is full of joy when he hears the bridegroom's voice. That joy is mine, and it is now complete" (John 3:28–9). John's desire was to point people away from himself to Jesus: "He must become greater; I must become less," he said (John 3:30). That's servant humility.

That must be our desire too: our mission is not to gain a following for ourselves, but to help people follow Jesus. When someone comes to me riddled with guilt, for example, I can do nothing for them, but I can introduce them to Jesus who can take away their sin and deal with their guilt. When someone comes to me in need of healing, I can do nothing for them, but I can introduce them to Jesus, who can heal them and make them whole. When someone comes to me infected with evil, I can do nothing for them, but I can introduce them to Jesus, who can set them free. I can convert no one, I can heal no one, I can deliver no one: but Jesus can. It is my responsibility and privilege to serve him—and them.

I now realize that over the years, in my enthusiasm to win people for Jesus, I have sometimes tried to do more than it is my responsibility to do; I have tried to do God's job for him. Paul's words to Timothy highlighted this truth for me and challenged me:

> And the Lord's servant must not be quarrelsome but must be kind to everyone, able to teach, not resentful. Opponents must be gently instructed, in the hope that God will grant them repentance leading them to a knowledge of the truth, and that they will come to their senses . . . (2 Timothy 2:24–6).

Paul implies that there is a demarcation between our part (the servant's) and God's part: the servant "gently instructs", and God, hopefully, "grants repentance leading them to a knowledge of the truth". I find that so helpful and liberating! It will be my responsibility as a servant, at times, to challenge sin and speak of the need for repentance; but only God can bring a person to repentance—I can't do that! It may be my responsibility as a servant, at times, to speak of the need for a new start in life, and point to Jesus who offers new birth; but only God can cause a person to be born again—I can't do that! And that takes the pressure off me: I don't have to "clinch it", I can leave God to do that. And it takes the pressure off the other person, too: there is no need for me to twist their arm—if there is any arm-twisting to be done, it's best done by God.

This principle is true in all kinds of circumstances. For example, a member of the church came to me concerned because she had been given a word from the Lord for another member of the church. She had shared that word with the other person, but there had been no response, hence her concern. "Relax!" I was able to say to her. "You've done your bit. It was your responsibility to hear the word and pass it on; it is God's responsibility to bring about a response to that word. Leave it to him: don't try to do his job for him."

The servant needs to learn to give the master space to do what only he can do; servant humility is knowing our place, recognizing our limitations and doing our job. Let's not try to do God's job for him! There are some words in Jeremiah which could almost be a servant's charter:

> Let not the wise boast of his wisdom or the strong boast of his strength or the rich boast of his riches, but let the one who boasts boast about this: that they have understanding to know me, that I am the LORD, who exercises kindness, justice and righteousness on earth, for in these I delight (Jeremiah 9:23–4).

As a servant of God, I have nothing to be proud of except the God who saved me and called me to serve him. Someone has said: "Evangelism is one beggar telling another beggar where to find bread", which is not a bad definition.

Serving together

So far in this chapter we have concentrated on our individual call to be servants and what that means in practice. But there is a corporate aspect of all this, too: that just as Christians are called to be servants, so the church should also have a servant heart and demonstrate that in all its activities. We are going to consider more fully in the next chapter the role of the church in mission. For now, let's simply outline some of the implications of being a "servant church".

In short, it will affect both what we do and how we do it. Our worship, for example, can no longer simply be doing what we like doing, and hoping others will join us: we need to be willing to serve others. For example, in one church where I was vicar, we decided it was right to include our children in our worship, but it was not fair to expect them to cope with formal, liturgical worship. So we adjusted our worship so that the children could relate to it. One older member of our congregation admitted to me that she struggled with the changes, but added: "But it's great to have the children!" Serving the children in our worship is part of our mission to the children.

It will affect our fellowship, too. House groups can become so comfortable: familiar faces, familiar format. But what about new people who join us? Do we expect them to fit in to our pattern? The servant will bend over backwards to make them feel welcome, making whatever adjustments are necessary to effect that.

As we take serving seriously, the nature of our activities may well change, too. Increasingly, over the years, churches have woken up to the call to serve not just the church community through services, study groups and prayer meetings, but to serve the wider community too, through offering lunch clubs for senior people, activities for disabled people, providing unemployed drop-in centres, food banks, and so on. The church has to be sensitive to the needs of the world, to be aware of the hurts in society, and to recognize its responsibility to serve. As I work on this revision the need is growing significantly, living as we now are after a pandemic and as significant national financial issues affect more and more people. The needs are great and urgent: we cannot afford to spend all our time resourcing ourselves and doing what we like. We have to get involved; we are called to serve—that's mission.

> The church must hear the call today to be the servant of Jesus Christ, to be in the world, not to be served, but to serve. It must be ready to identify with "the wretched of the earth." ...The church must hear and heed the call to servanthood for the sake of the

Kingdom of God. It is the servant church which is free for the Kingdom.[1]

Learning to serve

Jesus came to serve not to be served; that must be our attitude, too. Sometimes it will be hard: we shall be misunderstood and opposed both from inside and outside the church. But that is no more than Jesus the servant experienced: his strongest opposition came from his family and from religious leaders—things haven't changed much, have they?

Jesus the servant-king invites us to follow him and be servants; the call to discipleship is a call to serve. "As the Father has sent me, I am sending you."

---

[1]   Howard A. Snyder, *Liberating the Church: The Ecology of Church and Kingdom* (Basingstoke: Marshalls, 1983), p. 145

1 0

Sent ... Together

My bank balance would be slightly healthier if I could have five pounds for every time someone has said to me: "You can be a good Christian without going to church"—or words to that effect. In response, I try to explain (in my nicest possible Anglican way!) that it isn't true.

But it will take rather more than an explanation to change anything. It is so deeply entrenched in people's thinking that religion is a private affair; you don't do it openly and you definitely don't talk about it—that's the British religious tradition! Even hairdressers in training, so I am told, are advised not to talk to their customers about religion.

You in your small corner

Even those who do go public to the extent of going to church often take this attitude with them: "I go to church to worship my God and to say my prayers." It's a case of "you in your small corner and I in mine". And in some of our oldest churches this attitude is nicely reinforced by those impressive box pews: sit in one of them and you can't see who else is in church with you, even if you wanted to.

Of course, you don't need box pews to keep yourself to yourself in church: there are plenty of other effective ways. I heard of one lady who purposefully arrived at church during the first hymn and left during the last: that way she didn't have to speak to anyone!

Some regular Church of England worshippers who liked things this way were deeply shocked in the mid-twentieth century. The church's liturgy had not been revised for many years when in the mid-1960s a collection of new services, usually referred to as Series 2, appeared as a gentle revision of the Prayer Book services. That may not seem so remarkable except, in the Communion Service, there was a new liturgical feature called "The Peace". At this point in the service, just before the Eucharistic Prayer, after an introductory response, people were invited to turn and greet their neighbours. Fifty-eight years on, this seems so normal, accepted by the majority of worshippers, but back in the 1960s it was revolutionary and was resisted in many places—I remember seeing service books with that paragraph neatly crossed out. You could almost hear the person who did the crossing out saying: "We don't do that sort of thing here!"

It's a team game

Sometimes my response to the "Christian-without-church" comment is: "You can be a good Christian without going to church only to the same extent that you can be a good footballer without ever playing in a team!" You can learn most footballing skills in your own backyard—kicking, dribbling, shooting, heading, and so on—but you only really begin playing football when you join a team and play with others. Football is a team game. And so is being Christian. It is something we are supposed to do together, something which necessitates getting involved with others, in a team—and that's the church!

The trouble is that too many people see the church as simply the building on the corner of the street: presumably, if someone were to run amok one night and demolish the building, that would be the end of the church! But the church is not the building; it doesn't even need a building to survive. Isn't that what some regimes, both political and religious, who are committed to persecuting the Christian Church, have discovered: that you don't destroy the Church by destroying its buildings? The New Testament makes it quite clear: the church is not its buildings but its people.

The word "church" is translated from the Greek word *ekklesia*; it comes from a word meaning "to call out" or "to summon together". In Ancient Greece, the *ekklesia* was the assembly of all the citizens of the city of Athens; in the Old Testament, the equivalent Hebrew word *qahal* was used to describe the gathering together of God's people, the Israelites. So, when the New Testament talks about *ekklesia*, it is talking about people: people called out by God to enjoy a special relationship with him, called together to be a community for God in the world. In other words, Christians are the church. If you are Christian, you are church; that's why it is nonsense to suggest that you can be a good Christian without going to church.

But we have a problem. As the late Geoffrey Paul, sometime Bishop of Bradford, memorably stated: "There is no way of belonging to Christ, except by belonging gladly and irrevocably to that glorious ragbag of saints and fatheads who make up the One, Holy, Catholic and Apostolic Church." And this "ragbag" Church is far from perfect, it doesn't have a good press much of the time and it appears to be largely irrelevant—it is not good news. Many would sympathize with the man who said: "The church doesn't scratch where I itch!" and with the student placard which read: "Jesus—Yes! Church—No!"

The Church (in particular the Anglican branch of it) has often been in the news, all too often "washing its dirty linen in public". For example, the doubts of bishops and other Church leaders, particularly concerning the conception and resurrection of Jesus, have in the past been frontpage news. Interestingly, while some in the Church saw this doubt as reasonable and healthy, "outsiders" are puzzled: the reaction of many of them (including my own late mother-in-law) was: "They ought to believe, or else get out!" More recently, the Church has also received a bad press and serious censure for its poor safeguarding policies, and rightly so.

In the face of all this, perhaps we would be better off in getting involved in mission without being involved in the church, and working to establish God's kingdom apart from the church! But fortunately (or is it unfortunately?), we are not free to cut loose from the church—at least, not if we take the teaching of the New Testament seriously.

God's strategy

It is clear from the New Testament that God's mission strategy includes the church; indeed, the church has a crucial role. That amazes me, because I think God would get on much more effectively without us—he certainly has the spiritual "technology" to do so! Yet, although he can do it without us, and sometimes does, he actually wants to do it with us and through us.

Paul spells out God's mission strategy like this: "[God's] intent was that now, *through the church*, the manifold wisdom of God should be made known to the rulers and authorities in the heavenly realms, according to his eternal purpose which he accomplished in Christ Jesus our Lord" (Ephesians 3:10–11—italics mine).

I haven't begun to grasp the full impact of these words, but I do realize that it is a big statement about mission. Mission is more than winning people for Jesus, more than building the church, more even than establishing God's kingdom: it is making God fully known, literally, making known the "multi-coloured" wisdom of God. And if that is not enough, the arena for this mission is big, too: not just human beings, not just the world, but "the rulers and authorities in the heavenly realms". Whatever exactly those rulers and authorities are, wherever precisely the heavenly realms are, that is a bigger congregation than we usually think about! And this great mission God intends to fulfil "through the church"—and that's the amazing thing. God is not only committed to mission in a big way; he is also committed to the church in a big way—and to mission through the church. We are that church, so we must be committed to mission in and through the church too.

God's people
But how does God plan to achieve this? At the heart of God's mission strategy is his desire for a nation, a people he can call his own in a special way. He first spoke about this in the time of Abraham, when he called him to leave his home and go to a new land. God said to Abraham: "I will make you into a great nation and I will bless you; I will make your name great, and you will be a blessing" (Genesis 12:2).

God reiterated this strategy in the time of Moses. The Israelites were in slavery in Egypt, but God acted through Moses to set them free and to bring them again to the land he had originally promised to Abraham. God explained to Moses what he was doing: "I am the LORD, and I will bring you out from under the yoke of the Egyptians. I will free you from being slaves to them, and I will redeem you with an outstretched arm and with mighty acts of judgment. I will take you as my own people, and I will be your God" (Exodus 6:6–7).

This became a recurring theme in God's dealings with the Israelites: his desire that they should be his people and acknowledge him as their God. What is more, it is a consistent theme throughout the Bible. God does not change his mind; he has not altered his strategy: he wants a people to call his own. Even in the vision of the last days in Revelation, a loud voice from God's throne is heard: "God's dwelling-place is now among the people, and he will dwell with them. They will be his people, and God himself will be with them and be their God" (Revelation 21:3).

However, with the privilege of being God's people came responsibility, a responsibility the Israelites struggled to cope with. God's plan was that through his special relationship with them, he would make himself known specially to them. But they were not supposed to keep that revelation to themselves: rather, they were to share it with others, not least by the way they lived. And that's what they struggled with, often failing miserably.

So when God censured the nations for their evil ways, Israel's sin was made worse because the people ought to have known better. "You only have I chosen of all the families of the earth; therefore I will punish you for all your sins" (Amos 3:2). God felt the rebellion of Israel particularly keenly: he loved them so much, they were special. "When Israel was a child, I loved him, and out of Egypt I called my son. But the more they were called, the more they went away from me" (Hosea 11:1–2).

Much later, Paul, an Israelite by birth and upbringing, also felt Israel's failure very personally:

> For I could wish that I myself were cursed and cut off from Christ
> for the sake of my people, those of my own race, the people of
> Israel. Theirs is the adoption to sonship; theirs the divine glory,
> the covenants, the receiving of the law, the temple worship and

the promises. Theirs are the patriarchs, and from them is traced the human ancestry of the Messiah, who is God over all, for ever praised! Amen (Romans 9:3–5).

They had enjoyed all the benefits of being God's special people but had failed in the responsibility that went with it.

God's new people!

But Israel's failure was not the end of God's mission strategy: he didn't give up that easily! He was still determined to have a special people through whom to work. With the coming of Jesus that nation was reconstituted, only this time it was not restricted to the nation of Israel. Now, all who believed in Jesus, the promised Messiah, became members of God's special nation, whether they were Jews or not. It is now the Church, which is the true Israel, the true people of God.

Peter understood this clearly. He addressed his first letter "to God's elect . . . who have been chosen according to the foreknowledge of God the Father, through the sanctifying work of the Spirit, to be obedient to Jesus Christ and sprinkled with his blood" (1 Peter 1:1–2)—that's a pretty good description of Christians. To those Christians he wrote:

> But you are chosen people, a royal priesthood, a holy nation, God's special possession, that you may declare the praises of him who called you out of darkness into his wonderful light. Once you were not a people, but now you are the people of God; once you had not received mercy, but now you have received mercy (1 Peter 2:9–10).

Paul traced the link right back to Abraham, and explained it to the Christians in Galatia:

> Abraham: 'believed God, and it was credited to him as righteousness.' Understand, then, that those who have faith are children of Abraham. Scripture foresaw that God would justify the Gentiles by faith, and announced the gospel in advance to Abraham: 'All nations will be blessed through you.' So those who

rely on faith are blessed along with Abraham, the man of faith (Galatians 3:6–8).

And he finished his letter to the Galatian Christians with this greeting: "Peace and mercy to all who follow this rule—to the Israel of God" (Galatians 6:16).

Remember, both Peter and Paul were Jews, born and bred; in fact, they both struggled with God's desire to include non-Jews in his "nation". But they got the message in the end: in Jesus, Christians are God's special people, the Church is God's chosen nation.

Called for a purpose

As before, with the privilege of being God's special people comes a responsibility, a special task. What is that task? Peter put it like this: " . . . that you may declare the praises of him who called you out of darkness into his wonderful light" (1 Peter 2:9). Our task is to make God known: in other words, our task is "mission".

And how do we fulfil that task? In a word: together. A nation's strength does not lie in its individuals, however many of them there may be, but rather in its structures and relationships which weld those individuals together and make them effective. So it is with the church: we are called not to be a collection of individuals, each doing our own Christian thing our own way, but a community, a people, effective together for God in the world.

All too often our attitude as Christians has been individualistic, if not selfish. We have behaved as if the teaching of the New Testament were addressed to individual Christians, whereas so much of it is written for Christian communities, local churches. We are not aided in this by our English language in which we have the same word for singular "you" and plural "you", whereas in Greek there is a clear distinction, two different words—and most of the text of the New Testament is you plural, meant to be applied corporately. So we get involved in those activities in the church which help us personally, rather than being concerned with the wellbeing of the church as a whole. Growing mature Christians is not our ultimate aim, important though that is: our ultimate aim is growing the church, creating a people effective for God in mission. Remember, the cry of God's heart is for a people to call his own, a nation through whom he can work. "He has commissioned us to reveal him through our corporate life as his 'own people' to a world that does not know him."[1]

That is God's strategy in mission.

God's building

Elsewhere in the New Testament this strategy is explained in a rather different way: in terms of a building. However, this is not the stone building on the corner of the street: this is something very different, a "spiritual" building, built of "spiritual" materials, living stones—that is, made up of people, Christians.

Peter explains it like this: "As you come to him, the living Stone— rejected by humans but chosen by God and precious to him—you also, like living stones, are being built into a spiritual house to be a holy priesthood, offering spiritual sacrifices acceptable to God through Jesus Christ" (1 Peter 2:4–5). Paul writes in a similar vein:

> . . . you are no longer foreigners and strangers, but fellow citizens with God's people and members of his household, built on the foundation of the apostles and prophets, with Christ Jesus himself as the chief cornerstone. In him the whole building is joined together and rises to become a holy temple in the Lord. And in him you too are being built together to become a dwelling in which God lives by his Spirit (Ephesians 2:19–21).

For both Peter and Paul, behind this imagery of a "building" or "spiritual house" is their awareness of Jewish history and their appreciation of Jewish worship. Early in their history, the Israelites, instructed by God and led by Moses, made a tabernacle, a special tent which became the focal point of their worship. "Then let them make a sanctuary for me, and I will dwell among them," God told Moses (Exodus 25:8). There God met with his people, there God spoke to them; the tabernacle was a reminder of God's presence with them.

---

[1]   David Watson, *I Believe in the Church* (London: Hodder & Stoughton, 1978), p. 81.

Much later, when they had settled down in the time of King Solomon, they built a rather more substantial and elaborate "spiritual house", the Temple in Jerusalem. Again, it became the focal point for their worship, a symbol of the presence of God among them—that's why they were so devastated when it was destroyed. (To this day, the Jews have great reverence for the site of the Temple in Jerusalem—it is still a very special, holy place for them.) With the coming of Jesus, things changed. Worship for the Israelites was a very "physical" affair: special places, special buildings, animal sacrifices, holy days and so on.

With Jesus, real worship is "spiritual". That's what Jesus tried to explain to the Samaritan woman he met at the well (John 4). When she started asking about the right place to worship God, Jesus replied:

> Woman . . . believe me, a time is coming when you will worship the Father neither on this mountain nor in Jerusalem . . . Yet a time is coming and has now come when the true worshippers will worship the Father in the Spirit and in truth, for they are the kind of worshippers the Father seeks (vv. 21,23).

The all-important thing is not places or buildings, but people: people worshipping God "in the Spirit and in the truth" (v. 24). These people are the "living stones" which Peter talks about (1 Peter 2:5), and they are the raw material for God's special building. But it's possible to do two things with stones. You can make a pile of them: but a heap of stones serves no useful purpose. Alternatively, you can take the same stones, fit them together, and make a building which is very useful. That is what God wants to do with us, to build us together into a "building". That way we shall become more effective in mission because that's how God intended it to happen—together.

The purpose of the building

Every building is designed for a purpose and God's building is no exception. Peter describes its special purpose: "You . . . are being built into a spiritual house to be a holy priesthood, offering spiritual sacrifices acceptable to God through Jesus Christ" (1 Peter 2:5). Paul explains it like this: "In him the whole building is joined together and rises to become a holy temple in the Lord. And in him you too are being built together to become a dwelling in which God lives by his Spirit" (Ephesians 2:21-2). "Spiritual house", "holy temple", "dwelling in which God lives by his Spirit"—this building is for worship. Just like the tabernacle and the Temple, it is designed to be the place where God meets with his people, where they listen to him and are made aware of him.

We are going to look more closely at the place of worship in mission in a moment. For now, let's re-emphasize this: that God's strategy for mission is to make himself known in and through the church. That will happen not through reordering our church building (though that might be helpful), nor through lots of social activities which make contact with the community (though they will have their place), but when God's people get together, relate together and worship together "in spirit and in truth". That's the heart of it!

The body of Christ

The most familiar picture of the church in the New Testament is "the body of Christ", and it throws further light for us on how God's mission strategy is to be worked out, in particular how we are supposed to focus our efforts for mission.

Paul explains it like this: "For just as each of us has one body with many members, and these members do not all have the same function, so in Christ we, though many, form one body, and each member belongs to all the others" (Romans 12:4-5). He writes something similar to the Christians in Corinth: "Just as a body, though one, has many parts, but all its many parts form one body, so it is with Christ. For we were all baptized by one Spirit so as to form one body . . . " (1 Corinthians 12:12-13a).

In the body of Christ, just as in a human body, there are many parts and an incredible variety of functions. Some bits are more beautiful than others, some seem to be more important than others, but all have a part to play; the body is only fully fit and healthy when every little part is working properly and relating to all the other parts correctly. If one part is missing or separated, the body is disabled, unable to function to its full capacity. If one part is not working properly, the body will have to carry it, rather like a limb out of control, and if one part starts doing its own independent thing, the body develops problems, such as cancer.

This picture of the church as a body is a powerful one and it underlines the principle we have already identified: that we are not supposed to be a collection of independent Christian individuals, each doing our own "thing". Rather, we need to relate to each other, to be interdependent rather than independent, to be concerned for the life of the whole body, not just our bit of it.

God is calling us together to be the body of Christ. Just as he made himself known to the world in and through the physical body of Jesus, today he wants to make himself known in and through the "spiritual" body of Christ. It is through our corporate life together that we shall reveal God to the world—or fail to. That means the quality of our life together is important. No wonder Paul spent so much space in his letters spelling out how Christians should live together, and criticizing those churches where things were not right, which was most of them!

God's desire for us is this:

> . . . that the body of Christ may be built up until we all reach unity in the faith and in the knowledge of the Son of God and become mature, attaining to the whole measure of the fullness of Christ . . . From him the whole body, joined and held together by every supporting ligament, grows and builds itself up in love, as each part does its work (Ephesians 4:12–13,16).

Note these words: "unity", "mature", "joined", "held together", "whole body". That's the kind of church God wants. Why? Because that's the kind of church through which he can make himself known "to the rulers and authorities in the heavenly realms" (Ephesians 3:10).

That's his mission strategy, and if we get it right it will be very effective!

The earliest successful attempt

I am fascinated and challenged by the way in which the very first Christian church, mentioned at the end of Acts 2, seemed to understand God's strategy for mission. I don't suppose for one moment that people consciously or systematically identified the principles (as we have been doing) and then put them into practice. Certainly, they had no other "successful" church to model themselves on: they were the very first, they were on their own. Of course, some of them would have experienced at first hand the ministry of Jesus, listening to him and watching him, and that was the best possible training for mission. What is clear is that, however they learned it, they did it extraordinarily effectively. Luke gives us this description of that first church:

> They devoted themselves to the apostles' teaching and to the fellowship, to the breaking of bread and to prayer. Everyone was filled with awe at the many wonders and signs performed by the apostles. All the believers were together and had everything in common. They sold property and possessions to give to anyone who had need. Every day they continued to meet together in the temple courts. They broke bread in their homes and ate together with glad and sincere hearts, praising God and enjoying the favour of all the people. And the Lord added to their number daily those who were being saved (Acts 2:42–7).

I think there are 14 different activities mentioned or implied here that this first Christian church was busily involved in—can you find more? There are no particular surprises in the list; most of them still happen in one form or another in churches today. However, there is one surprising omission: there is no specific reference to mission.

I am fully aware of the dangers of arguing from silence, trying to base principles on what the Bible doesn't say, rather than on what it does. However, I am left asking the question: why did Luke choose to mention things like teaching, prayer, fellowship, giving, signs and wonders, eating meals, and so on, but made no reference to mission? It cannot be because they were not interested in mission: the rest of the New Testament indicates that mission was high on the agenda from the start. What is more, they were highly successful in bringing new people into the church; indeed, their success would put the statistics of most evangelistic campaigns to shame—"the Lord added to their number daily those who were being saved" (v. 47).

I believe the answer is that whether or not they organized any specific mission activities (and I suspect they didn't, because they didn't need them), the whole of their life together, all their activities, had an evangelistic effect. People came into contact with them one way or another—at a prayer gathering, in a worship service, over a meal, or wherever—and met with God there. If I am right, then this is a supreme example of God's mission strategy in action: God making himself known through the church. And it is an embarrassing challenge to the church today too.

How did they do it?

How did they achieve this effective evangelism through every activity, even ordinary things like eating meals? And can it work for us? Can we expect the same results today?

We have already seen (in Chapter 7) how "signs and wonders", one of the activities listed in Acts 2, can be an effective God-given aid in mission: how people are made aware of God through signs and wonders and come to believe in him and worship him. Let's take a closer look at some of the other activities in the life of that first Christian church. How did they do it?

Through fellowship

"Fellowship" translates the Greek word *koinonia*, which comes from a word meaning "to share in something with someone". It was commonly used to describe such things as business partnerships, trade guilds, dining clubs, even marriage. So it was a natural choice of word for the Christians to adopt to describe their coming together. But very quickly it became obvious that Christian *koinonia* was very different from other kinds. Ordinary *koinonia* brought together those of common mind and purpose. Christian *koinonia* went further: it managed to bring together those who were naturally poles apart. Ordinary fellowship separated people by class or culture or language or some other category: Christian fellowship united them.

The seeds of this were sown during Jesus' ministry: he was able to bring together among his twelve disciples men with very different temperaments, such as Peter and John, and men with radically different political views, such as Simon the Zealot and Matthew. (Under different circumstances Simon, a fanatical Jew who hated the Romans, would have happily throttled Matthew, who worked for the Romans—and he would have slept at night!)

The first Christians followed Jesus' example in their fellowships:

> Here were societies in which aristocrats and slaves, Roman citizens and provincials, rich and poor, mixed on equal terms and without distinction: societies which possessed a quality of caring and love which was unique. Herein lay its attraction.[2]

Many fellowships were renowned for immorality; Christian fellowship was unique in its respect for all people and in its pure relationships between members. And this difference was noticed and drew people in: " . . . this fellowship was absolutely crucial to the advance of the church. Men had to be attracted in from the existing—if shallow—fellowship of their pagan clubs and taverns by another fellowship which was richer and more rewarding."[3] Presumably, this is what happened even in those first days of Christian *koinonia* in Jerusalem: people were attracted to this "richer and more rewarding" fellowship offered by the Christians, and joined them. So "the Lord added to their number daily those who were being saved" (Acts 2:47). That is mission!

But what about today? Doesn't this find us out? Can we honestly say that the life of our Christian fellowship is so excitingly different that men and women will leave their clubs, pubs and societies to join us, attracted to a "richer and more rewarding fellowship"? Sadly, the opposite is too often true: rather than being attracted to Jesus through the church people are put off Jesus by the church. That is not how God meant it to be.

Through unity

One specific aspect of Christian fellowship which was both unique and attractive was its unity. We have already seen how people were brought

---

2   Michael Green, *Evangelism in the Early Church* (London: Hodder & Stoughton, 1970), p. 182.

3   Green, *Evangelism in the Early Church*, p. 183.

together in *koinonia* who would naturally be divided. Clearly, right from the earliest days of the church, Christians understood and demonstrated the truth that in Christ all the barriers are down, all divisions gone.

Paul explained the potential of this in his letter to the Ephesians. He used the example of the longest-standing, most deeply entrenched division of his times: that between Jew and non-Jew (Gentile). The Jew had a great contempt for the Gentile, a contempt which Paul would have shared originally. But Paul, now a Christian, explains how such prejudice can be broken down: "For (Christ] himself is our peace, who has made the two groups one and has destroyed the barrier, the dividing wall of hostility . . . His purpose was to create in himself one new humanity out of the two, thus making peace . . . " (Ephesians 2:14–15). Here is great potential for unity! And those first Christians, although they hadn't yet worked it out theologically, knew the reality of it in their own lives and fellowship: "It was a church which cared so much about fellowship that Jews and Gentiles converted to the faith broke down centuries-old barriers and ate at the same table."[4] Such unity, such breaking down of barriers would have been amazing, unique, and very attractive. So people joined the Christian fellowship—"the Lord added to their number daily those who were being saved".

And this is precisely what Jesus wanted to happen; it was this kind of unity that was on his heart the night before he died, praying for his disciples both present and future. He prayed:

> I pray also for those who will believe in me through their message, that all of them may be one, Father, just as you are in me and I am in you. May they also be in us so that the world may believe that you have sent me. I have given them the glory that you gave me, that they may be one as we are one—I in them and you in me—so that they may be brought to complete unity. Then the world will know that you sent me and have loved them even as you have loved me (John 17:20-3).

---

4   Green, *Evangelism in the Early* Church, pp. 180-l.

The heart cry of Jesus just before his death was for the unity of his followers, a unity that was as close and complete as his unity with his Father. And this was surely still on his heart when, after his resurrection, he commissioned them: "As the Father has sent me, I am sending you." But why is unity so important? "That the world may believe . . ." (John 17:21). The unity of Jesus' followers is one way of convincing the world about Jesus: unity is mission.

Is it any wonder, therefore, that whenever Paul heard of divisions in one of his churches, he was quick to reprimand them. For example, the Christians in Corinth were polarizing around different leaders. Paul responded: "I appeal to you, brothers and sisters, in the name of our Lord Jesus Christ, that all of you agree with one another in what you say and that there be no divisions among you, but that you be perfectly united in mind and thought" (1 Corinthians 1:10). As far as Paul was concerned, disunity among Christians hindered mission and undermined the preaching of "Jesus Christ and him crucified" (1 Corinthians 2:2). The unity of those first Christians in Jerusalem was so real and obvious that others were attracted by it: it was one aspect of their effective mission, one way through which "the Lord added to them daily".

Again, what a challenge to the Church today! According to the Centre for the Study of Global Christianity there are more than 45,000 Christian denominations in the world today—and they are being added to almost daily! What does that say to those we want to reach with the good news of Jesus? And what about our own local churches: do we display so much more unity than other clubs and groups that people would be attracted and join us? Sadly, no! Through our disunity, we are in danger of undermining our mission. When we speak about reconciliation through Christ, we risk being told to put our own house in order first—and that's a fair challenge. Those first Christians managed it: we must too.

As I work to revise the text of this book, the worldwide Anglican Communion is tearing itself apart over one particular issue: sexuality. Some parts of it have declared themselves out of communion with the Archbishop of Canterbury. Here in the UK, there is a significant difference of opinion on the issue, with some standing firm on what they believe to be the Church's traditional stance on these matters, while others are committed to a more open view and practice, the passions on both sides being particularly strong amongst evangelical Christians. As a result, some are being asked to stand down from ministry in their church, while others feel the need to leave.

All this leaves me asking how this helps our priority task of mission: it undermines our credibility in the world, damages our effectiveness in communicating the good news of Jesus. In contrast, as we have seen, part of the attractiveness of the early church, one factor in their effectiveness, was their unity, and Paul was quick to challenge disunity whenever he became aware of it. Writing to the church in Rome, for example, he urges people to accept and respect one another despite their significant differences, summarizing his concern with these words: "You, then, why do you judge your brother or sister? Or why do you treat them with contempt? For we will all stand before God's judgment seat . . . So then, each of us will give an account of ourselves to God" (Romans 14:10,12). This must surely be a word for the Church today: the mission task is so urgent we cannot afford the luxury of falling out with each other.

Through love

This unity was no formal, intellectual affair; it was real, sincere, from the heart. It was undergirded by love, of a quality such as had never been known before. In fact, their love was so different and distinctive that they had to find a new word to describe it: they came up with *agape*.

Actually, it wasn't totally new, but it wasn't used very much. There were three other words in the Greek language which were much more common, but somehow none of them quite fitted the bill: *philia* is found in strong friendships, *eros* describes romantic relationships, *storge* speaks of family relationships. But none would adequately describe the Christian experience of love, and none came anywhere near expressing the depth of God's love for them which they had discovered through Jesus. "Thus *agape* was adopted and invested with new and striking honour . . . Christians took one of the most insignificant words in the Greek language and made it the most important word of all."[5]

---

5   Michael Harper, *The Love Affair* (London: Hodder & Stoughton, 1982), p. 63.

Love was often evident among those first Christians. Paul, for example, writing to the church in Thessalonica, said: "Now about your love for one another we do not need to write to you, for you yourselves have been taught by God to love each other. And in fact, you do love all of God's family throughout Macedonia" (1 Thessalonians 4:9–10a). Whenever love was lacking Paul was quick to point it out, urging his readers not to destroy each other but rather to serve one another in love (Galatians 5:13). Love is, after all, the most excellent way (1 Corinthians 12:31b); it is the fulfilment of the law, summing up all other commands (Romans 13:10). And it was to a church where there were all kinds of petty squabblings and divisions going on, in Corinth, that Paul wrote his best-known words about love (1 Corinthians 13). There he stressed that we may have all kinds of exciting spiritual abilities, but if we lack love, we have nothing (vv. 1–3).

But whenever the church got it right, it proved to be a powerful evangelistic tool. It was not very long before some of the church's fiercest opponents were having to recognize their love—they didn't like their message, but they were challenged by their lifestyle. "See how those Christians love one another!" (words usually attributed to Tertullian, an early Christian writer and theologian).

We have plenty of critics today, many of whom have no time for our message. If only they could experience a little *agape*-love among us, then maybe . . . ! It is always encouraging when people come to our churches and tell us they have experienced love amongst us which helped them to feel accepted and drawn in. None of our churches are perfect, we are far from perfect, and we don't get it right every time, but whenever we do that is great, because that is just what God wants to happen.

It is also what Jesus wanted to happen. When he gave his disciples a new command to love one another, it was for a purpose: "As I have loved you, so you must love one another. By this everyone will know that you are my disciples, if you love one another" (John 13:34–5). In other words, when we love one another with Jesus-type love, people won't just say, "That's nice!" but they will realize that we are Christians—and maybe they will stay around to find out more. And that's mission! Is this what was happening in that young church in Jerusalem? People were attracted by their love, and thus God was able to add "to their number daily those who were being saved". Mission is easy when you do it God's way!

John realized the full potential of this. In mission, we have a basic communication problem: we are involved in introducing people to God, but no one has ever seen God. So how are we supposed to do it? John offers us two answers. In his Gospel, he writes: "No one has ever seen God, but the one and only Son, who is himself God and is in the closest relationship with the Father, has made him known" (John 1:18). In other words, Jesus has come so that we can see God. Thus, later on, when Philip asked Jesus: "Lord, show us the Father and that will be enough for us," Jesus replied: "Anyone who has seen me has seen the Father" (John 14:8–9). We, too, in our concern to introduce people to God, must point them to Jesus, for it is in him that they will see God and meet God.

But John offers another answer to our communication problem, a more surprising one. In his first epistle, he writes: "No one has ever seen God; but if we love one another, God lives in us and his love is made complete in us" (1 John 4:12). In other words, if we love one another in the right way, God's love will be made tangible among us, and thus the invisible God will be experienced among us—people will meet God among us.

If John is right, then our response to the person who is seeking God should be, "Look at Jesus!" and "Look at us!" I find the first of those answers comfortable, the second uncomfortable. The challenge to us is clear: in our churches and fellowships, if there is no love, if we display unloving attitudes or relationships, then we are undermining our mission, getting in the way of people meeting God. But when we begin to love one another, people will begin to meet God among us, and we shall begin to be effective in mission—just like those first Christians. "As the Father has sent me (in love), I am sending you (in love)."

Through generosity

There is another feature of the life of these first Christians which played an important part in their effective mission but which could easily be overlooked: they were extraordinarily generous. Luke tells us: "All the believers were together and had everything in common. They sold property and possessions to give to anyone who had need" (Acts 2:44–5).

A little later we are told: " . . . there was no needy person among them. For from time to time those who owned land or houses sold them, brought the money from the sales and put it at the apostles' feet, and it was distributed to anyone who had need" (Acts 4:34–5). When famine came, those Christians who were able to help did so readily. "The disciples, as each one was able, decided to provide help for the brothers and sisters living in Judea. This they did, sending their gift to the elders by Barnabas and Saul" (Acts 11:29–30).

It was the Christians in Macedonia (the northern part of Greece today) who were particularly renowned for generosity. Paul writes about them enthusiastically:

> In the midst of a very severe trial, their overflowing joy and their extreme poverty welled up in rich generosity. For I testify that they gave as much as they were able, and even beyond their ability. Entirely on their own, they urgently pleaded with us for the privilege of sharing in this service to the Lord's people (2 Corinthians 8:2–4).

What remarkable Christians they must have been! They were suffering, they were poor, and yet they gave very generously, even sacrificially. More than that, they counted it a privilege to give and asked to be allowed to do so! How many Christians, how many churches do you know for whom giving is considered such a privilege that they ask to be involved in it? Not many, I suspect.

Paul realized how this kind of generosity can have real evangelistic effect:

> This service that you perform is not only supplying the needs of the Lord's people but is also overflowing in many expressions of thanks to God. Because of the service by which you have proved yourselves, others will praise God for the obedience that accompanies your confession of the gospel of Christ, and for your generosity in sharing with them and with everyone else (2 Corinthians 9:12–13).

In other words, people will be amazed by their generosity, they will recognize that it must be inspired by God, and they will give him thanks. Isn't that what Jesus meant when he said: " . . . let your light shine before others, that they may see your good deeds and glorify your Father in heaven" (Mathew 5:16)? Is this what was happening amongst those first Christians: even their generosity attracted "outsiders"? The generosity of these Christians was marked in the selfish society of their day; just like their unity and their *agape*-love, it was both different and attractive. Like them, we live in a selfish, greedy society in which the attitude of both government and individual alike seems to be to get much and give little. In the face of this, the church has a marvellous opportunity to demonstrate a radically different and attractive quality: generosity.

Unfortunately, we have succeeded in communicating the opposite: that is, "the church is always after our money"! Have you ever tried carol singing in the local area, not collecting money but knocking on doors to offer a personal Christmas greeting? How many people, as soon as they realize it is the church, respond: "Hang on a minute, I'll get my purse!" They are amazed to discover that the church is on their doorstep to give them something rather than collecting from them! But why? How often does one of those enormous thermometers appear outside old churches informing passers-by how much is needed to repair the tower or the roof? I realize that old church buildings are major headaches for local congregations and that there are usually no outside funds available to help with repairs, but all we communicate to the local community is: "We want your money!" And how does that help our mission?

We communicate this message in more subtle ways, too. I know one inner-city parish, with a high level of unemployment, where, as part of their service to the community, jumble sales are held from time to time. On the face of it, that seems a relevant and good thing to do. But one local man, who happened to be around when a poster advertising the next sale was put up, was heard to remark: "Vicar's after our b . . . money again!" How ironic that the very activity designed to forward the mission of the church was actually undermining it!

Those first Christians knew how to give: as a result, their mission activity was always fully resourced, and they were able to provide generously for those in need. In this, they were responding to the example of Jesus: "For you know the grace of our Lord Jesus Christ, that though he was rich, yet for your sake he became poor, so that you through his poverty might become rich" (2 Corinthians 8:9). They were doing no more than Jesus had done, no less than he asked his followers to do: "As the Father has sent me, I am sending you." How much we have to learn from them! Is it any wonder that their mission was so effective, that they "enjoyed the favour of all the people", and that God "added to their number daily those who were being saved" (Acts 2:47)? The call to discipleship is costly and challenging.

Through worship

Clearly, worship was an important part of the life of the early church: "Every day they continued to meet together in the temple courts" (Acts 2:46). We have already seen, earlier in this chapter, how God's mission strategy is described in terms of building Christians into a "spiritual house to be a holy priesthood, offering spiritual sacrifices acceptable to God through Jesus Christ" (1 Peter 2:5)—and that is worship! But is worship simply another important Christian activity alongside mission, or is it in some way an integral part of mission?

God's people, in Old and New Testament alike, knew that worship can be very effective in bringing others into contact with the living God: worship is mission! For example, 2 Chronicles 5 records the dedication of the first Temple in Jerusalem, built under the leadership of King Solomon. The building and all its furnishings were complete and thorough preparations had been made for the inaugural service. The beginning of the service is described like this:

> All the Levites who were musicians . . . stood on the east side of the altar, dressed in fine linen and playing cymbals, harps and lyres. They were accompanied by 120 priests sounding trumpets. The trumpeters and musicians joined in unison to give praise and thanks to the LORD. Accompanied by trumpets, cymbals and other instruments, the singers raised their voices in praise to the LORD and sang: "He is good; his love endures for ever." Then the temple of the LORD was filled with the cloud, and the priests

could not perform their service because of the cloud, for the glory
of the LORD filled the temple of God (2 Chronicles 5:12–14).

As God's people began to worship, God "turned up", powerfully,
unmistakably, really—and the planned service ground to a halt! Surely,
everybody who was anywhere near the Temple that day, believers or not,
would have known without doubt that God was there,

When did anything like that happen in your church? Wouldn't this
kind of experience make the words in our Anglican Communion service,
"The Lord is here", much more meaningful? We would know it was true
and could respond with real conviction, "His Spirit is with us."

I have never experienced anything quite as dramatic as that, but there
have been times when God has unmistakably "turned up". I remember,
for example, one lady who was not a committed Christian, coming one
Maundy Thursday to an evening Communion service I was leading. It
was a quiet service, focusing on the cross, with no conscious evangelistic
thrust. But clearly, God had "turned up" and was working in her; by
the time she came to the Communion rail, she was gently shaking. We
prayed for her (not being confirmed she did not receive Communion)
and she returned to her seat. She was now weeping, and two members
of the church family went across to her and spent the remainder of the
service quietly talking and praying with her. When I eventually joined
them, she looked up, smiling through her tears, and said: "I have met God
here tonight." Our worship had been effective mission for that lady—and
that's exciting because that was of God!

Paul, writing to the church in Corinth, also explains how worship,
when we get it right, can be very effective in reaching the "outsider".
Speaking specifically about the gift of prophecy in worship, he says:

> But if an unbeliever or an enquirer comes in while everyone is
> prophesying, they are convicted of sin and are brought under
> judgment by all, as the secrets of their hearts are laid bare. So
> they will fall down and worship God, exclaiming, 'God is really
> among you!' (1 Corinthians 14:24–5).

That's effective mission through worship, but how often does that kind of thing happen in your church—and mine?

If our worship was all it should be, there is no reason why it shouldn't be a regular, even daily happening. "The Lord added to their number daily those who were being saved." The late Canon David Watson discovered the truth of this in his ministry as an evangelist:

> When we are taken up with worship, and when we are unashamed of the fact that we are in love with God and in love with one another, that can be very powerful indeed . . . Comparatively few people are asking serious questions about God, partly because there is little or nothing which they see or hear to awake them to any sense of his reality. But when Christians are to be found really worshipping God, loving him, serving him, excited with him, and their worship makes them into a caring community of love, then questions will certainly be asked, leading to excellent opportunities for sharing the good news of Christ.[6]

Through preaching

Preaching also had a crucial role in the advance of the church in those early days. It was, for example, in response to Peter's challenging sermon on the day of Pentecost that the crowd asked, "What shall we do?", and 3,000 people were baptized as a result: effective preaching indeed! What is particularly significant is the content of their preaching and the boldness of their delivery: these people knew what they believed and pulled no punches in proclaiming it to others.

Peter fearlessly proclaimed to the crowd in Jerusalem on the day of Pentecost: " . . . you, with the help of wicked men, put [Jesus] to death by nailing him to the cross. But God raised him from the dead . . . " (Acts 2:23–4)—that's telling them! After the healing of the lame man at the Temple gate, Peter repeated his message: "You killed the author of life, but God raised him from the dead." This time he added, "Repent, then, and turn to God, so that your sins may be wiped out . . . " (Acts 3:15,19). When arrested for healing a lame man and on trial, Peter was still direct:

---

6   Watson, *I Believe in Evangelism*, p. 66.

> If we are being called to account today for an act of kindness shown to a man who was lame and are being asked how he was healed, then know this, you and all the people of Israel: it is by the name of Jesus Christ of Nazareth, whom you crucified but whom God raised from the dead, that this man stands before you healed (Acts 4:9–10).

And he rounded off his defence with this challenge: "Salvation is found in no one else, for there is no other name under heaven given to mankind by which we must be saved" (Acts 4:12).

Stephen was just as direct when he was on trial: "You stiff-necked people! Your hearts and ears are still uncircumcised. You are just like your ancestors: you always resist the Holy Spirit!" (Acts 7:51). Again, that's telling them! And they didn't like it—it was no wonder that they stoned him.

When Paul began preaching, he was just as uncompromising: "The people of Jerusalem and their rulers did not recognize Jesus . . . Though they found no proper ground for a death sentence, they asked Pilate to have him executed . . . But God raised him from the dead . . . " (Acts 13:27–30). Even among Jews on the Sabbath in the synagogue, he was direct: "This Jesus I am proclaiming to you is the Messiah" (Acts 17:3). And when he came across the people of Athens worshipping "an unknown god", he told them: "So you are ignorant of the very thing you worship—and this is what I am going to proclaim to you" (Acts 17:23).

These Christians were clear in their beliefs and uncompromising in their preaching: what they believed to be true they proclaimed without apology and with great effect—and the church grew fast. Today, in those countries and churches where Christians are equally clear about what they believe and similarly uncompromising in their proclamation of it, people are hearing, understanding, responding and joining the church—in some places, in large numbers! But here in Britain, things are a little different. There are doubtful, questioning voices around in the church—they have been there a long time! There are so many questions. Did Jesus actually say it? Is this bit of the New Testament reliable? Was the tomb really empty on Easter morning? Do we really believe in the Virgin Birth (or conception)? Can we believe in miracles today? Is Jesus unique or just one of many world religious leaders? Is Jesus' death on the cross simply an example to us, or did he actually achieve something for us? And the questions go on and on and on. There is nothing wrong with asking questions or airing doubts, but when those questions and doubts compromise our message and undermine our mission, this is unhelpful.

Paul, writing to the church at Corinth, asked this question: "If the trumpet does not sound a clear call, who will get ready for battle?" (1 Corinthians 14:8). Good question! We have so often given an unclear call in our preaching, so how can we expect people to respond and join us? How many people would sympathize with the German poet, Goethe, a self-confessed agnostic, when he said: "Tell me of your certainties. I've enough doubts of my own"?

The story is told of the eighteenth-century actor David Garrick being asked by a preacher: "How is it that you actors are able, on the stage, to produce so great an effect with fiction, whilst we preachers, in the pulpit, obtain such a small result with the facts?" His reply was: "I suppose it is because we present fiction as though it were fact, whilst you, too often, offer facts as though they were fiction."

The effectiveness of the first Christians' preaching lay in the fact that they really believed the message they preached; so it came across with clarity, conviction and authority—and it sounded like the "truth". We could learn from them, for this was surely another reason for their success in mission.

What a church—what a mission!

What a church that first ever Christian church was! And how effective it was in mission! Their fellowship was so good, people were attracted; their unity was so complete, people were amazed; their love was so genuine, people were drawn in; their generosity was so great, people were impressed; their worship was so real, people met with God; their preaching was so clear, people recognized the truth. Add to that the recurring feature of signs and wonders, through which people experienced the power of the living God, and you have a very effective mission "package". In summary, this embryonic Christian community was so impressive that the wider community recognized it and, in effect, said:" There is something good going on over there. Let's go and find out more!" Wouldn't it be great if our local communities were saying that about our churches?

Every element in that package could and should be a feature of the life of our churches today. That, I believe, is what God wants to do among us, and is beginning to do more in these days—wherever we give him half a chance. Surely, this is the kind of scenario that was on the heart and mind of Jesus as he passed on to his first followers the mission he had begun: this is what he saw his Father doing. This is God's own mission strategy: to make himself known through the Church. To achieve this, committed disciples are needed. "As the Father has sent me, I am sending you."

Sent . . . Fully Equipped

I remember many years ago being on holiday with a group of young people in the Lake District. One afternoon we set out to climb Helvellyn, one of the highest peaks in England. When we reached the top there was a warden moving among the climbers, stopping now and again to speak with some of them. He was checking out what people were wearing, explaining to those who wore unsuitable clothing the importance of being prepared for anything when climbing mountains: warm clothes, protection from rain, strong shoes—there were some there that day in very flimsy footwear. The warden was concerned not to spoil people's fun, but to encourage them to be properly equipped; that way they would enjoy it all the more.

"Be properly equipped" is an important principle in all kinds of situations, including mundane ones like do-it-yourself. I am not the world's greatest DIY expert—far from it! But I have discovered that those "little jobs", which seem so difficult, and therefore hang around for months untouched, are sometimes done easily in a matter of minutes when they are tackled in the right way and with the right tools.

What a task!

The task we have been given as followers of Jesus often seems daunting, enormous, even impossible: to carry on Jesus' mission. Of course, he never pretended that it would be easy, he never underestimated the strength of opposition that we would encounter, and he was fully aware of our weaknesses, fears, and potential for getting it wrong. Yet he commissioned that first group of his followers to continue his mission—and through them, each succeeding generation of Christians has been similarly commissioned, including you and me.

They were sent out to "preach the good news to all creation" and to "make disciples of all nations" (Mark 16:15; Matthew 28:19). They were to be witnesses of his death and resurrection, as a result of which "repentance for the forgiveness of sins will be preached in his name to all nations" (Luke 24:47). There is no escaping it. All four Gospel writers in their different ways make it quite clear: Jesus intended his mission to be taken on by his followers—"As the Father has sent me, I am sending you" (John 20:21).

If that were the end of the story, neither they nor we would ever take up the challenge of mission. But, fortunately, it's not the end of the story: with the commissioning comes the resourcing—there is equipment for the task.

Getting started

The story of the first Christians taking on the mission of Jesus, which is told in Acts, makes exciting reading. It is shot through with activity; here is vibrant life, amazing events, incredible growth. Here are people really excited about Jesus, preaching with conviction and acting with power. "With great power the apostles continued to testify to the resurrection of the Lord Jesus" and "the apostles performed many signs and wonders among the people" (Acts 4:33; 5:12).

And it wasn't just the apostles who did it: they all did! When things became difficult, and persecution increased, the Christians scattered, but "those who had been scattered preached the word wherever they went" (Acts 8:4). Wherever they went, they shared "the good news about the Lord Jesus", and it was effective: "The Lord's hand was with them, and a great number of people believed and turned to the Lord" (Acts 11:21). Thousands, in fact, responded, believed in Jesus and joined the church. In a very short time, it was being said of them: "You have filled Jerusalem with your teaching" (Acts 5:28), and not so long after that, some of them were being accused of "turning the world upside-down" (Acts 17:6, RSV). That's successful mission! They weren't daunted by the task—they just got on with it. Or did they? The first chapter of Acts paints a rather different picture.

Here are the same followers of Jesus, preaching nothing, doing nothing except huddling together in an upstairs room praying constantly (Acts 1:12–14). Jesus had left them, telling them to get on with his mission. However, at first, they didn't do it; for Jesus had also told them to wait. For what? I don't think they were quite sure what they were waiting for, until it happened, ten days later—and it changed their lives.

On that Day of Pentecost, they were filled with the Holy Spirit (Acts 2:1–4), and that fearful bunch of believers became a fearless army of missionaries, taking Jerusalem by storm and moving out to turn the rest of the world upside-down. The Holy Spirit brought them power for mission, equipping them for the task. And therein lies the secret of their success.

Equipped for the task
All the resources that they and we could ever need to be effective in mission are available in the one supreme gift of the Holy Spirit. Previously, Jesus had talked with his disciples about the Spirit, promising that although he was going to leave them, "I will ask the Father, and he will give you another advocate to help you and be with you for ever—the Spirit of truth" (John 14:16–17a). Indeed, it would be to their advantage for him to leave them because "unless I go away, the Advocate will not come to you; but if I go, I will send him to you" (John 16:7). The Holy Spirit will resource them, for he will "teach you all things and will remind you of everything I have said to you ... he will guide you into all the truth" (John 14:26; 16:13).

How significant, therefore, that immediately after Jesus had told them he was sending them out in mission, "he breathed on them and said: 'Receive the Holy Spirit ... '" (John 20:22). In a sense, that is all they needed to make a start—and it's all we need, too!

The Father's gift
This gift of the Spirit is very special because it is the gift of the Father to his children. "I am going to send you what my Father has promised," Jesus told them; "but stay in the city until you have been clothed with power from on high" (Luke 24:49). Again, Jesus gave them this command: "Do not leave Jerusalem, but wait for the gift my Father promised, which you

have heard me speak about. For John baptised with water, but in a few days you will be baptised with the Holy Spirit . . . You will receive power when the Holy Spirit comes on you; and you will be my witnesses . . . " (Acts 1:4–5,8).

This "promise" was first spoken about way back in the Old Testament, particularly in those prophecies looking forward to the "new thing" God was going to do—the New Covenant which we discussed in Chapter 1. For example, in Isaiah we read: "I will pour out my Spirit on your offspring, and my blessing on your descendants" (Isaiah 44:3). In Ezekiel, we find this: "I will give you a new heart and put a new spirit in you . . . I will put my Spirit in you and move you to follow my decrees . . . " (Ezekiel 36:26–7). And the prophet Joel, also looking forward, wrote: "And afterwards, I will pour out my Spirit on all people. Your sons and daughters will prophesy, your old men will dream dreams, your young men will see visions. Even on my servants, both men and women, I will pour out my Spirit in those days" (Joel 2:28–9).

It was these words from Joel that Peter quoted when he preached in Jerusalem on the Day of Pentecost. The Holy Spirit had just fallen on that first group of Christians left behind by Jesus. Luke tells us that there was wind and tongues of fire and that it resulted in them going out on the streets of Jerusalem talking in all kinds of languages—dramatic stuff (Acts 2:1–6). That sort of thing doesn't happen every day and, not surprisingly, the people were both afraid and inquisitive. What was going on?

Peter told them. What was happening in Jerusalem on that particular day was the fulfilment of Joel's prophecy given years before: God was doing what he had long-since promised he would do one day, pour out his Spirit on his people. And Peter explained that the event which sparked it off was the death and resurrection of Jesus: "God has raised this Jesus to life, and we are all witnesses of it. Exalted to the right hand of God, he has received from the Father the promised Holy Spirit and has poured out what you now see and hear" (Acts 2:32–3). What is more, this gift of the Spirit was for everyone. All you had to do was repent and believe in Jesus, and you will receive the gift of the Holy Spirit; for "The promise is for you and your children and for all who are far off—for all whom the Lord our God will call" (Acts 2:39).

Power for all

Ever since that day, the gift and power of the Holy Spirit has been an integral part of the Christian "package", for all who believe in Jesus. The Spirit is not an optional extra, not a "bonus" for a spiritual elite, not a reward for services rendered, but the Father's special gift for all his children. But the Spirit is given for a specific purpose, not just to make us feel good, or simply to provide a bit of spiritual "excitement", but so that we may be witnesses for Jesus (Acts 1:8). The Holy Spirit is power to go, power to serve, power to get involved in mission, power to be effective for God. It is by the Spirit that we are resourced and equipped for continuing Jesus' mission.

Power . . . to know God

But what exactly does the Spirit do? How does he equip us for mission? We have already seen some of his activity in earlier chapters. In Chapter 1, for example, we noted how, for Jesus, intimate relationship with his Father was fundamental, the key to his success in mission. I suggested that for us, too, that the only starting point for effective mission for God is personal relationship with God. We went on to see how this intimacy with God which Jesus enjoyed is something the Spirit longs to make real in our experience, too. God gives us the Spirit of his Son so that we can really know that we are also his children, that he is our Father: "By [the Spirit] we cry, 'Abba, Father.' The Spirit himself testifies with our spirit that we are God's children" (Romans 8:15,16). What is more, "if we are children, then we are heirs—heirs of God and co-heirs with Christ . . . " (Romans 8:17).

It is the Spirit's desire to make this a growing reality for us. It is in knowing God like this that both our security and our resources for mission are found. In my own experience, it is as I have become more secure in my relationship with God, that I have become freer, more relaxed, in mission. That's what the Spirit loves to do.

The gift of the Spirit is power to know God—as Jesus knew him.

Power . . . to understand God

We also saw (in Chapter 2) how Jesus had that amazing ability to know exactly what God wanted him to do and say. That's why his mission was so effective: he was always in the right place at the right time, doing and saying the right thing—God's place, God's time, God's thing. More amazing still, we also saw that we have that same potential, to know exactly what God wants. That's because we have within us the Spirit of God, and that Spirit knows and understands God totally (1 Corinthians 2:9–12). By the Spirit we can know the heart and mind of God—we discussed that amazing privilege and resource in Chapter 2.

But how does this work in practice? In a variety of ways, but, personally, one way I have known something of this is through tears. There have been just a few occasions when, as I have been praying with someone, I have found tears welling up within me, and I have cried over them—literally! (I am not, by nature, one who readily shows feelings outwardly.) The only way I can understand this is that God is letting me in on how he feels about that person: the Spirit is enabling me to experience the heart of God. If I'm right, that's exciting!

It works corporately, too. I remember in one church, at a meeting of the leadership team, we were praying, spending time in quiet before God. Out of that time of prayer discussion arose, focusing chiefly on some young people who were on the fringe of the church; although the services at the time were fairly lively, they did nothing for them. We found ourselves asking the question: what do we need to do to reach those particular young people for Jesus? None of us had come determined to raise this issue; for me, it was fairly low down my list of priorities. But, apparently, it was top of God's agenda that night—and the Spirit showed us that. We needed to keep it on our agenda because God had revealed to us it was his mission priority for us at that time.

The gift of the Spirit is power to understand God, to know the mind and heart of God—just like Jesus did.

Power . . . to be free

Our greatest asset, and our greatest liability, as we embark on mission is our humanness. It's an asset because, as we saw in Chapter 4, our calling is to be human beings living in this world—that's why God became a human being and lived among us. But it's also a liability because, as we are only too well aware, we are far from perfect and our humanness holds us back so often in mission—the spirit is willing, but the flesh is weak!

Fortunately, God doesn't wait till we are perfect before he signs us up for action. And there are many of us who need to hear that loud and clear; we are so good at disqualifying ourselves because of our shortcomings. "I'm not good enough!" "I can't talk to people!" "I have too many problems of my own to sort out!" "I haven't been a Christian long enough!" "Others are better at it than me!"—and so on.

God knows all about us, and I think he can handle us! He doesn't overlook our failings as if they are unimportant, but neither does he allow them to disqualify us. In fact, rather than waiting until we're perfect before letting us get involved, he seems to operate on the principle that if we get involved, he'll make us perfect as we go. I don't think Peter and Paul, those great leaders of the early church, were perfect before they got started in mission, but I suspect they were just a little more perfect by the end!

We have seen that Jesus came to save us, in the fullest sense of that word (Chapter 5), and to make us whole (Chapter 6). Jesus also said he had come to give us life to the full (John 10:10), and that the things he said could set us free—we can be "free indeed" (John 8:32,36). Life, wholeness, freedom: it is as we experience the reality of these things for ourselves that our message becomes all the more pertinent. "Jesus is setting me free—let him set you free too!" "Jesus is making me whole—let him make you whole too!"

This is what the Spirit longs to work in us. Paul, writing to Timothy, urging him to "fan into flame the gift of God, which is in you . . .", reminds him: "For the Spirit God gave us does not make us timid, but gives us power, love and self-discipline" (2 Timothy 1:6–7). As this Spirit gets to work on us, so we shall become more effective for God.

As a pastor, it always thrills me to see this happening for people. I think, for example, of Pam in one of the churches I have served in. When she first joined, she thought she had little to offer, but she proceeded to bring other people into the church, to take on an important behind-the-scenes responsibility, to be involved in praying for others, and even ended up "up front" speaking to the whole church. What happened? Pam got to know God more intimately, she found release from things that bound her, and experienced healing deep inside—she found a greater degree of wholeness in Jesus. As that happened, she became more involved, and as she became more involved, she found more healing and so became more involved—and so the pattern continued. This is the work of God through his Spirit. Pam never claimed to be perfect but she was on the way and she was involved.

The gift of the Spirit is power to be free within myself and so to be effective for God—as Jesus was.

Power . . . for action

In these ways, then, the Spirit starts us in mission. Once we are involved, there are all kinds of specific tasks that we can do. The Spirit is able to equip us for every one of them—we shall never be on our own! God offers to us "gifts of the Spirit". If we fail to see this and don't avail ourselves of them, then getting involved in mission will be like climbing a mountain without the proper gear, or doing a job without the right tools. These gifts are not only available to us, they are crucial for us: the gifts of the Spirit are God's equipment for God's people so that we can fulfil the mission of Christ in the world today. Mission is our task from God: the gifts of the Spirit are God's equipment for that task. The more proficient we are in using the equipment, the more effective we shall be in the task—equipment for disciples. The gift of the Spirit is power for action, Jesus' action.

Examining the equipment

There are a number of places in the New Testament where gifts of the Spirit are mentioned; for example, 1 Corinthians 12:4–11,27–31; Romans 12:3–8; Ephesians 4:7–13; 1 Peter 4:7–11. I am sure these are not intended to provide an exhaustive list of all the gifts. But we are offered examples: these are some of the ways in which the Spirit works, equipping us for mission. Let's take a closer look at some of them and examine some of our equipment.

A word of wisdom

If the gifts of the Spirit are specific equipment for specific tasks, then, I suggest, the gift of "a message of wisdom" (1 Corinthians 12:8) is not simply the gift of being wise—although, of course, all wisdom comes from God (James 1:5). Rather, it is that ability to say the right thing in the right way, just when it is needed.

We see this in the ministry of Jesus: for example, in conversation with the Samaritan woman at the well (John 4). Jesus was getting too close to the truth about her for her liking and she was feeling uncomfortable. So she introduced a marvellous red herring into the conversation—have you noticed how often people do that when they are feeling uncomfortable? This particular red herring concerned where people should worship (v. 20). Jesus replied that it is not where you worship but how you worship that matters, for "God is spirit, and his worshippers must worship in the Spirit and in truth" (v. 24). Brilliant! A word of wisdom.

On another occasion, Jesus was asked an awkward question about whether or not taxes should be paid to Caesar. It was designed specifically to trap him, because whichever answer he gave they would accuse him of disloyalty—it was a Catch-22 situation for him (Matthew 22:15–22). But Jesus took a coin and asked them whose picture was on it. Caesar's! "Then he said to them, 'So give back to Caesar what is Caesar's, and to God what is God's'" (v. 21). Brilliant! They were amazed at his answer and went away. A word of wisdom.

I have at times been aware of something like this—and probably missed many more such moments! For example, in discussion with someone, I might find myself saying something that I've not heard before (it's a strange experience when it first happens, listening to yourself and learning). The response is often significant, too: "That's interesting!" or "I've never seen it that way before" are typical responses. It has often proved to be a breakthrough in the conversation. A word of wisdom, given by the Spirit just when it's needed.

I am reminded, too, of Jenny. She wasn't a member of the church, but phoned me to say that her two children, then aged ten and eleven, wanted to be baptized, and she was so happy about it. Without thinking, I asked her why she was so happy. Was that a word of wisdom? Certainly it challenged her, and set in motion a process which brought both the children and Jenny into active membership of the church.

There is another, slightly more unsettling way in which this works. Jesus spoke about it with his disciples like this: "When you are brought before synagogues, rulers and authorities, do not worry about how you will defend yourselves or what you will say, for the Holy Spirit will teach you at that time what you should say" (Luke 12:11–12). What does that mean for us? Imagine this scenario: it is Monday night and I am due to meet a friend for coffee at 10.30 on Friday morning, when there will be an opportunity to talk to him about Jesus. I could pray tonight asking Jesus to tell me what to say to him, and he might well do that. But, on the basis of the words we have just quoted, he might just as easily respond: "I'll tell you on Friday morning at 10.30!" "The Holy Spirit will teach you at that time what to say"—then, not now! That's a bit unsettling, but it works. And I am always thrilled when a member of the church tells me with excitement: "The words just came!" They are really pleased, and encouraged to have another go, too.

A word of wisdom: a gift of the Spirit, a piece of equipment for disciples to help us in mission.

A word of knowledge

Again, I think this gift ("a message of knowledge"—1 Corinthians 12:8) is more specific than simply having the ability to understand things, though that is God-given. It is the ability to know something that you would have no way of knowing naturally: God tells you.

We see this happening in Jesus' ministry. For example, in his conversation with the woman at the well, just before she introduced that red herring, Jesus had asked her to fetch her husband (John 4:16). She told him she had no husband, whereupon Jesus proceeded to tell her that she had had five husbands, and that the man she was living with then was not her husband (v. 18). No wonder the woman began to feel uncomfortable and introduced a red herring–wouldn't you? But how did Jesus know? Had he known before this? No! God told him—it was a word of knowledge.

There is also a remarkable incident in Acts 5 (vv. 1–11). The Christians were giving to the church. One couple, Ananias and Sapphira, sold some land; they agreed to keep some of the proceeds for themselves, but to pretend to give everything to the church. When Ananias came to bring their gift to Peter, Peter told him exactly what Ananias and his wife had agreed. Ananias was so shocked, he dropped dead on the spot (vv. 5–6)—and his wife died in the same way later (vv. 7–10). No wonder fear seized the church (v. 11)! But how did Peter know? God told him—it was a word of knowledge.

I have had this kind of experience from time to time. For example, a couple came for prayer at the Communion rail one evening. I asked what the problem was, they told me, and I began to pray for them—about something completely different! The wife began to weep, because I was praying for the real problem. But how did I know? God told me—it was a word of knowledge.

This often happens in counselling too. I remember, for example, one particular occasion, while we were waiting quietly in prayer, a clear picture came into my mind of a small boy about to cross a busy road. I shared this picture with the young man we were counselling, and it immediately reminded him of a frightening incident when he was about eight years old. As a result, we were able to make progress in our counselling. But how did I know about that? I didn't, but God did, and he told me—it was a word of knowledge.

I also remember one particular service in our church. The teaching had just finished and we were having a time of ministry. The visiting speaker came back to the microphone: "There is a lady here who has had trouble with her left eye for some time." He paused, then added: "Her name is Jean!" Some minutes later a lady approached me and said that she had problems with her left eye. Then she added: "My name is Jean!" I am always amazed when that kind of thing happens, but how did our speaker know about Jean? God told him—it was a word of knowledge. And we were able to pray for Jean that night, which might not have happened but for that word.

A word of knowledge: a gift of the Spirit, a piece of equipment for disciples to help us in mission. I sometimes wonder whether we might experience more of this Spirit-inspired insight if we were more expectant and more open to the Spirit.

Faith

Faith is much in evidence in the Bible but, as a gift of the Spirit, I believe it is rather like the previous two: it is a specific gift for a specific task, the ability given by God to believe something specific in a given situation. In Jesus' ministry, we see this clearly in his handling of the death of Lazarus (John 11). Even before he left for Bethany, he was able to say to his disciples: "I am going there to wake him up" (v. 11)—there was a quiet confidence in what God was going to do.

Quiet confidence that God is going to do something: for example, that John is going to be healed this morning, or that Susan is going to become a Christian tonight, or that we shall reach our target of £10,000 for our gift day next month. It is unspectacular, but an extraordinarily valuable gift: when one or another of the church family receives this gift from God, the rest of us are encouraged to trust too, and to look for the action of God.

The gift of faith: a gift of the Spirit, a piece of equipment for disciples to help us in mission.

Prophecy

There is a common misconception that prophecy is foretelling. However, the gift of prophecy (1 Corinthians 12:10) is really the ability to know and relate what God thinks about a particular situation. There are plenty of examples of this in scripture, particularly in the Old Testament. Amos, for example, brought a challenging word from God about the people's priorities: "Away with the noise of your songs! I will not listen to the music of your harps. But let justice roll on like a river, righteousness like a never-failing stream!" (Amos 5:23–4). Similarly, when God's people complained that God wasn't taking any notice of their spiritual disciplines, including fasting, he gave them a straight answer through the prophet, Isaiah: "Is not this the kind of fasting I have chosen: to loose the chains of injustice. . . . to share your food with the hungry and to provide the poor wanderer with shelter . . . .?" (Isaiah 58:6–7). These were God's priorities for them, and they heard it through a prophetic word spoken by Isaiah.

The prophetic word will often challenge human attitudes, priorities and actions, because God has a different (and better) perspective. But if God's word is to be enacted, it needs to be heard and communicated by men and women. We desperately need to hear God's word today: we need to know what he thinks, to discover his agenda for his church and his world. So we need those who have time (or will make time) to pray, to be with God, to listen to God; they are the ones most likely to bring God's word into the church.

I am challenged (and found lacking) by God's reprimand of false prophets in Jeremiah's day: "But which of them has stood in the council of the Lord to see or to hear his word? Who has listened and heard his word? . . . But if they had stood in my council, they would have proclaimed my words to my people . . . " (Jeremiah 23:18,22). Thankfully, some *are* learning to stand in God's council and to hear his word, and we are learning to value their ministry among us. In one church, for example, one of the young mums shared with us a "prophecy" which was a word of encouragement and direction from God for us in our mission; it helped us to see what was going on in our church from God's perspective. At the heart of this message were these words: "Get yourselves right, get your own hearts right, and while you're doing that, I'll be working outside preparing hearts, so that when the time is right the two will come together."

We were thrilled with that: it was all about God preparing us for mission. But it also provided us with a point of reference, so that we could check whether what we are planning is in line with what God was doing. Are we able to say, like Jesus, that we are doing only what we see the Father doing?

The gift of prophecy: a gift of the Spirit, a piece of equipment for disciples to help us in mission.

Discernment

The longer I am involved in ministry, the more I think the gift of discernment ("distinguishing between spirits"—1 Corinthians 12:10) is possibly the most necessary piece of equipment of all: it will often keep us from making mistakes. So often we need to know "What is happening here?" or "What is God doing here?" The Spirit is able to help us.

We often see this in Jesus' ministry. For example, when Nicodemus came to him, Jesus seemed to ignore what he said and talked about something different (John 3:1–8). As we suggested in Chapter 1, he discerned Nicodemus' true need. Again, when the rich young ruler came to Jesus asking about eternal life, Jesus seemed to know exactly what his problem was and challenged him about it—he discerned it (Luke 18:18–25). And when Jesus was put on the spot by his opponents and asked awkward questions, he discerned their true intentions and handled it accordingly—for example, when asked about paying taxes to Caesar (Matthew 22:15–22).

Similarly, when Paul and Silas were visiting Philippi, a girl attached herself to them, crying out: "These men are servants of the Most High God, who are telling you the way to be saved" (Acts 16:16–17). That was certainly true and seemed to be good; but Paul became concerned. He realized that she was inspired not by God but by an evil spiritual power—he discerned the truth. Once he saw what was happening, he dealt with it, commanding the evil to leave (v. 18). Those who were using her for money were none too pleased and had Paul thrown into prison.

We need that ability today, not least, perhaps, in our counselling ministry. I think, for example, of a lady who came asking for prayer. She had already decided what was wrong with her: she wanted us to lay hands on her and cast out the evil she was convinced was in her. But as we prayed with her, we saw no evidence of evil, and none of us felt it was appropriate to pray in the way she wanted. We thought that her problem was chiefly medical and suggested she saw her doctor. I believe the Spirit helped us discern what was going on. It's not always as straightforward as that and we don't always get it right, but it's reassuring to know that the Spirit can help us in this way.

The ability to distinguish between spirits: a gift of the Spirit, a piece of equipment for disciples to help us in mission.

Dreams and visions

Joel, in the passage quoted by Peter on the Day of Pentecost, talked about old men dreaming dreams and young men seeing visions (Joel 2:28). There are many instances in the Old and New Testaments, where God speaks through dreams and visions. God often appeared to Abraham, for example, and sometimes that was in a vision: "After this, the word of the Lord came to Abram in a vision ..." (Genesis 15:1). Sometimes he communicated with his prophets the same way, as Amos, for example, explains: "This is what the Sovereign Lord showed me . . . " (Amos 7:1,4,7; 8:1).

Peter was directed by God to go and preach the gospel in the home of Cornelius through a vision (Acts 10:9–22); and Cornelius had a vision too, which meant he was waiting for Peter when he arrived (Acts 10:23–33). When a meeting is so obviously set up by God like that, it is bound to be successful—the whole of Cornelius' household was baptized by the time Peter left (Acts 9:34–48). Saul was dramatically converted to Christianity as a result of a vision of the risen Jesus (Acts 9:1–19); and later, on his travels, he was guided by a vision of a man from Macedonia asking for help (Acts 16:9–10).

We have discovered that God still works in this way today. For example, I remember at a leaders' meeting in one of my churches, while in prayer, one of the team had a vision: it was of a racecourse, and was in three parts. First, he saw horses milling around at the start, although the race had been started; second, he was looking down the course at a series of hurdles which looked formidable; third, he was going over one of the hurdles, which now seemed a rather flimsy affair.

As we reflected on this together, we felt that God was telling us that there were hurdles he wanted us to clear, and action he wanted us to take. Before the evening was over, we had identified three specific areas in which we believed God was looking for action: evangelism, healing and prayer. As a result, during the following weeks, we had an evangelistic Family Service; we arranged a special service based on healing (until then we had simply offered prayer for healing at our ordinary services in a low-key way); and we began to establish prayer cells within the church family to increase the level of prayer in the church. As we did these things it felt good, because they were not just our ideas but rather what God wanted us to do—God's ideas! Through a vision, God had led us on in mission, and that's exciting!

Dreams and visions: gifts of the Spirit, spiritual equipment for disciples to help us in mission.

Ready for anything!

There are, of course, many other gifts; but I hope we have examined enough of them to see how very practical they are, how they equip us to be effective in mission. They are essential equipment; indeed, I sometimes wonder how I ever did anything for God in the days before I was aware of the availability of these gifts.

There is one other gift of the Spirit that I want to comment on: the gift of "speaking in different kinds of tongues" (1 Corinthians 12:10). I suppose this has been the most talked about of the gifts, perhaps the most misunderstood, possibly the most feared—it seems just a little weird! But this gift, like the others we have discussed, is also, I believe, an aid to mission. How does it work?

The gift of tongues is a gift from God whereby I am able to pray in a language other than English, a language I have never learned. Paul tells us: "Anyone who speaks in a tongue does not speak to people but to God" (1 Corinthians 14:2). So this gift helps me communicate with God, and that must help to strengthen my relationship with him—communication fosters relationship. And that must be good, as Paul says: "He who speaks in a tongue edifies himself . . . " (1 Corinthians 14:4). In other words, the gift of tongues helps me to be in a good place spiritually, and thus ready for action, for involvement in mission. More than that, the gift of tongues actually deepens and extends my praying, enabling prayer to continue when I am unable, for whatever reason, to think and pray in English. Isn't this part of what Paul has in mind when he writes: " . . . the Spirit helps us in our weakness. We do not know what we ought to pray for, but the Spirit himself intercedes for us through wordless groans" (Romans 8:26)?

We have already seen how vital a part prayer played in the life of Jesus, that it was through prayer that he discovered his Father's will and knew what his Father wanted him to do (Chapter 2). Through the gift of tongues, the Spirit helps me to do that too; he enables me to experience, in a small way, something of the prayer life of Jesus. His mission flowed out of prayer; so will mine, with the help of the Spirit.

There have been many testimonies of how this spiritual gift has proved to be a real asset in mission. One of the more remarkable testimonies of this comes from Jackie Pullinger. In her book *Chasing the Dragon* (originally published in 1980 and republished in 2006) she describes her amazing work among drug addicts inside the walled city of Hong Kong. She tells how she was challenged to use the gift of tongues regularly in her own prayer life, and how this resulted in greater effectiveness in her work. In turn, she encouraged those coming off drugs to pray in tongues too, and many found the withdrawal experience much more bearable as a result—a striking example of mission advanced with the help of prayer in tongues.

The gift of tongues: a gift of the Spirit, spiritual equipment for disciples to help us in mission.

Equipped together

So far, in examining our mission equipment, we have concentrated on the equipping of individuals for mission. But God wants to go further than that: he wants us to be equipped together for mission.

We have already seen (in Chapter 10) that God's mission strategy involves not a collection of individual Christians, but the church; it is his intent that "now, through the church, the manifold wisdom of God should be made known to the rulers and authorities in the heavenly realms . . . " (Ephesians 3:10). If mission is to be done by the church, Christians together, then the equipping must be for the church, Christians together.

Paul speaks about this in Chapter 4 of Ephesians:

> But to each one of us grace has been given as Christ apportioned it. This is why it says, 'When he ascended on high, he took many captives and gave gifts to his people' . . . So Christ himself gave the apostles, the prophets, the evangelists, the pastors and teachers, to equip his people for works of service, so that the body of Christ may be built up . . . attaining to the whole measure of the fullness of Christ (vv. 7–8,11–13).

Paul highlights here the kind of strategic ministries which will help a church mature and become effective in mission. (These kinds of specialist skills are not often evident in our churches today; we tend to prefer ministers who can do a bit of everything. Maybe this is one reason why we are so ineffective in mission compared to the New Testament church!) The important thing to note, however, is that God gifts these leaders for a specific purpose: "to equip his people for works of service" (v. 12). In other words, the leadership in a church, whatever precise form that takes, is not so much to do with ministry, but to equip God's people (the members) for ministry; not so much to engage in mission, but to enable God's people to be effective in mission.

The implications of this are enormous, and possibly threatening for those of us who are ministers—after all, ministry is what we are trained and paid to do, and, for some of us, that's where our security lies too. And often congregations resist this model of ministry, too, their concern neatly summarized thus: "Ministers minister, congregations congregate!" But Paul would urge us to handle it differently: instead of being "doers" leaders should be "enablers", training the whole church for mission. That is a much more effective and efficient way of working. The leaders' task, then, is to work with the Spirit of God to equip God's people for mission. What a privilege!

Equipping the saints . . .
The Greek word Paul uses in Ephesians 4:12, usually translated "prepare" or "equip", is *katartizo*, a fascinating Greek word with a wealth of meaning. It appears in several places in the New Testament and is translated in a variety of ways, helping us to appreciate its rich meaning.

. . . by uniting them
In 1 Corinthians 1:10, Paul writes: "I appeal to you, brothers and sisters, in the name of our Lord Jesus Christ, that all of you agree with one another in what you say and that there be no divisions among you and that you may be perfectly united in mind and thought." "Perfectly united"—that's the word *katarizo*.

We have already seen (in Chapter 10) how Jesus was deeply concerned for the unity of his followers, praying earnestly for it the night before he died (John 17), and seeing unity as the way in which the world would understand the message: " . . . so that they may be brought to complete unity. Then the world will know that you sent me . . . " (John 17:23). It should not be surprising, therefore, that one aspect of equipping the saints is to encourage and to work with them so that they discover and enjoy a deep unity among themselves. This unity is greatly needed in the church today (2024) which, as we saw in Chapter 10, is sadly divided over the issue of sexuality.

. . . *by training them*

Jesus told his disciples: "The student is not above his teacher, but everyone who is fully trained will be like their teacher" (Luke 6:40). "Fully trained"—that's the word *katartizo*.

Naturally, there is a training element in equipping God's people for mission. Part of that training will be helping them to understand the gospel, to know the scriptures. Paul often stresses the crucial importance of preaching the word and teaching the faith; to Timothy, for example, he writes: "Until I come, devote yourself to the public reading of Scripture, to preaching and to teaching" (1 Timothy 4:13). He also reminded Timothy why this was so important: "All Scripture is God-breathed and is useful for teaching, rebuking, correcting and training in righteousness, so that the people of God may be thoroughly equipped for every good work" (2 Timothy 3:16–17). "Thoroughly equipped" is our aim, too.

But for Jesus, there was much more to training than simply filling people with facts. He spent three years training a group of twelve men; of course, he taught them a lot, but they also saw a lot. It is clear from the Gospels that they were there for most of Jesus' ministry: they saw him heal the sick, cast out evil, raise the dead, still the storm; they watched him handle people sensitively, they listened as he talked with them—this was all valuable training. When he thought that they had learned a little, he sent them out to have a go themselves (Luke 9:1–6)—and that was part of the training, too. And he had a debriefing session with them when they came back (Luke 9:10)—no doubt they learned from that, too.

Jesus was concerned that his followers should be fully trained. He didn't just teach them about mission, he showed them how to do it and he modelled it for them. Those of us who are leaders must learn to do the same. After all, people learn much more by watching than by listening, and even more by trying for themselves. So we need to let people watch us, maybe by taking them with us as we visit (even that will be threatening for some of us!); and we need to let them try—and that's risky, because they might make a mess of it. But it's a risk we must take, I believe, if we are to see our people "fully trained" for mission.

. . . by restoring them

Paul, writing to the Christians in Galatia, urged them: "Brothers and sisters, if someone is caught in a sin, you who live by the Spirit should restore them gently" (Galatians 6:1). Peter, rounding off his first Epistle, wrote: "And the God of all grace, who called you to his eternal glory in Christ, after you have suffered a little while, will himself restore you and make you strong, firm and steadfast" (1 Peter 5:10). "Restore"—that's the word *katartizo*.

None of us is perfect, we all make mistakes and get things wrong. But unless these negative experiences are handled correctly, we shall be in danger of dropping out, doing nothing, and feeling we've failed. We need to be "restored".

I love the incident recorded in John 21:15–22. After the resurrection, Jesus talked with Peter. As if to give him the opportunity to make up for his three denials, he asked him three times: "Do you love me?" Each time Peter confesses his love for Jesus, and Jesus, in turn, invites Peter to look after his sheep—"Feed my lambs", "Take care of my sheep", "Feed my sheep" (vv. 15–17). Then Jesus says to him: "Follow me!" (v. 19). That must have made Peter feel good: those were possibly the first words Jesus ever said to him, when they met by the Sea of Galilee (Mark 1:16–18). Now Jesus repeated them: after all that had happened, his mistakes, his impetuosity, and, worst of all, his denials, he hadn't ruined everything after all! Jesus still wanted him to follow him! He was forgiven; more than that, he was restored. Better still, he had a job to do for Jesus—he'd not been disqualified!

This is an all-important aspect of equipping the saints: they need to know that when they fail they won't be written off, but can be restored—and carry on. In the past, people have joked with me about my leadership style because they can't win: if you do something well, you are asked to do it again; if you do something badly, you get the chance of having another go after a little debriefing! But there is an important principle at work here: forgiving, restoring, where necessary offering help and correction, but giving ongoing encouragement to carry on. Restoration is a crucial aspect of our ministry.

. . . by mending their holes!

Perhaps the most illuminating use of the word *katartizo* occurs when Jesus goes down to the Sea of Galilee and calls four fishermen to follow him. Having called Simon and Andrew, we read: "When [Jesus] had gone a little farther, he saw James son of Zebedee and his brother John in a boat, preparing their nets [or "mending their nets"]" (Mark 1:19). "Preparing"—that's the word *katartizo*.

Some years ago, I was in Brighton and as I walked along the lower promenade, I noticed in an open doorway a man with a large needle and green nylon thread. He was mending nets—and it reminded me of this incident by the Sea of Galilee. Nets are made for catching fish, but if there are large holes in the net, it can no longer be used; it needs to be mended.

Many of the people in our churches have holes in them that need mending: one way or another, they have been damaged and are unable to do the job they are supposed to do—mission. It is the responsibility of the church leaders to look after the people, to make sure they are fit for the task, and to provide "mending" when they are not. Sometimes they will simply need to be loved; sometimes they will need to discover forgiveness; they may need prayer for healing or some in-depth counselling—we ought to be able to provide all these things within our churches. More importantly, they need ongoing fellowship with others, to be part of a small group where they are known, loved, accepted and cared for; where they can be prayed for, helped, encouraged, and picked up when they are down. Fellowship is a vital back-up resource for all of us active in mission, and we neglect it at our peril!

It is all part of equipping the saints, the aim of which is to build up the body towards maturity and effectiveness, so that each part of the body plays its full part (Ephesians 4:11–16). And the saints can only do this if their holes are mended!

Look, no hands!

We have seen how God wants to equip us individually and corporately to be effective in mission. But he has another mission tactic, a particularly effective one: to do the job himself, with little or no human involvement.

I think, for example, of Margaret who lived in the parish where I was vicar some years ago. She came to a service at the church to hear her daughter's marriage banns read. She hated it—she told my colleague, John, in the supermarket the next week! A few months later, I became involved with her again when her mum was ill. During that time, she took me on one side and said: "Look, John, I must tell you something: I don't believe, I don't feel anything, and I've no interest in the church."

I think that was rather like throwing down the gauntlet to God. Not very long after that, one Friday night, she had a dream in which she heard my name (I think that makes it a nightmare!), and the reference Isaiah 6:7. Margaret tells the story:

> I got up and made breakfast, and then the words came back, and I wondered if there was an Isaiah in the Bible. I knew we had a Bible somewhere, so I went to look for it. I couldn't believe it when I couldn't find it; but most of all, I couldn't believe that I was even looking for it. "Don't be stupid," I said to myself, "forget it!"

But she wasn't able to. The words kept returning, time after time. Eventually, she borrowed a Bible:

> I . . . started to flick through the pages, as I had no idea where to look. And then I saw it: Isaiah. I was shocked; I thought surely 6:7 won't make sense. But it did, and I trembled when I read it: "He touched my lips with the burning coal and said, 'this has touched your lips and now your guilt is gone and your sins are forgiven.'"

It was all happening to her, but she wished it wasn't. She struggled with it for the rest of the week and was beginning to feel ill.

> On Friday evening I was thinking things over and I realized I
> believed, and I prayed. I trembled so much I felt drained. My
> exact words were: "OK. Leave me alone now!"

But that was not to be. The next afternoon the trembling came over
her again and she felt she had to go to church to take Communion.
(Remember, the last time she came she hated it!)

> I was ready for church so early the next morning: I couldn't
> wait to get there . . . What a relief it was to be there and to take
> Communion—it was so right. And I've been coming to church
> ever since and now I'm reading the Bible.

God met with her sovereignly—we couldn't have done it better if we'd
tried. Margaret not only started coming to church regularly, but she read
everything that was put into her hands, and happily told people what
had happened to her. That's God—and we were excited! What is more I
have been back to that church recently, 30 years on, and Margaret is still
there—I sat and chatted with her over coffee.

Part of being equipped for mission is simply to have that expectancy
that God can do it himself; but also to be ready to co-operate with him
when that is appropriate too.

The cupboard is bare

God has made full provision for us so that we can get involved in mission
and be effective. But what if we still feel ill-equipped, unable to get
started: what do we do? Ask for help!

Jesus told a story about a man who had a friend visit him unexpectedly
late at night (Luke 11:5–8). He had nothing in the house to give him—do
you know the feeling? So he went and knocked up a neighbour and
asked him to help. The neighbour got up and gave him all he needed to
entertain his guest.

How often are we in that kind of situation spiritually: we have an
opportunity to say or do something for Jesus, but the cupboard is

bare—we cannot find it within us to do anything? What do we do? We "knock up" the one who has resources for us: Father God. " . . . ask and it will be given to you," Jesus went on; "seek and you will find; knock and the door will be opened to you. For everyone who asks receives; the one who seeks finds; and to the one who knocks, the door will be opened" (Luke 11:9–10). But will he respond? Of course he will, Jesus says: "If you then, though you are evil, know how to give good gifts to your children, how much more will your Father in heaven give the Holy Spirit to those who ask him?" (Luke 11:13). And remember, not only is he our Father, but the Holy Spirit is the gift he promised to give us—of course he'll respond!

Jesus said the same thing in different words on another occasion: "Let anyone who is thirsty come to me and drink. Whoever believes in me, as Scripture has said, rivers of living water will flow from within them" (John 7:37–8). In case we misunderstand, the Gospel writer John, explains: "By this he meant the Spirit, whom those who believed in him were later to receive" (v. 39).

Later, the first Christians, threatened by the authorities because they continued Jesus' mission, prayed: "Now, Lord, consider their threats and enable your servants to speak your word with great boldness" (Acts 4:29). That prayer was answered in no uncertain way: "After they prayed, the place where they were meeting was shaken. And they were all filled with the Holy Spirit and spoke the word of God boldly" (v. 31).

Remember two things: first, the power and gifts of the Spirit are equipment for action, not for personal blessing; second, being filled with the Spirit is not a one-off experience, but needs to be an ongoing experience. Paul, writing to the Ephesian Christians, urged them: "Be filled with the Spirit" (Ephesians 5:18)—which is better translated "be being filled" or "go on being filled".

Perhaps a small girl was aware of this when she prayed: "Lord, fill me with your Holy Spirit every day—because I leak!" That's it!

Fully equipped and ready to go

Faced with our God-given task of continuing Jesus' mission, one thing we can't say is "I'm not equipped for it!" All the equipment we will ever need is available to us, fully provided by God, both individually and corporately. Through the power and gifts of the Holy Spirit and, we hope, through the church of which we are part, it's all there for us. We may be effective in mission like Jesus was.

And we need all this equipment if we are to respond to the challenge "Go . . . make disciples". After all, the call is not just to make disciples but to "teach them to obey everything [Jesus] has commanded you" (Matthew 28:20)—disciples are students, apprentices and need training. Hopefully, filled with the Spirit and fully equipped by him, we can all play our part to help others become effective disciples of Jesus, who in their turn, will hopefully go and make disciples. So, what are we waiting for? Let's get on with it! "As the Father has sent me, I am sending you."

.